Langenscheidts Aufbaukurs Englisch

Ein Lehrgang für Fortgeschrittene

von Hans G. Hoffmann

LANGENSCHEIDT
BERLIN · MÜNCHEN · WIEN · ZÜRICH · NEW YORK

Langenscheidts Aufbaukurs Englisch
Ein Lehrgang für Fortgeschrittene
von Hans G. Hoffmann

Materialbeschaffung und Recherchen: Brigitte Hoffmann
Sprachliche Durchsicht und Beratung: Dr. Sonia Brough, Dr. Selwyn Jackson
Phonetische Durchsicht und Beratung: Martin Fellermayer
Redaktion: Dr. Sonia Brough, Helga Krüger, Michael Reiter

Quellennachweis für die Abbildungen (Seitenangaben in Klammern):
BBC London Calling (120); British Airways (11); Sonia Brough (108); Deutsche Lufthansa AG (6); Patrick Doherty / The Image Bank (30); Polyglott-Verlag, München (219); PUNCH (12, 150); Syndication International (1986) Ltd., London (96); United States Travel and Tourism Administration (Umschlagbild und Seite 240); UPI / Bettmann Newsphotos (72, 84); Copyright 1988, USA Today, reprinted with permission (102, 138).

Hinweis: In diesem Buch wird mehrfach die Telefonvorwahl (*the code*) 01 für London erwähnt. Diese Vorwahl wurde inzwischen durch zwei *codes* ersetzt: 071 für *inner London* und 081 für *outer London*. Entsprechend würde zum Beispiel die Nummer 01–327 4065 auf Seite 31 jetzt 071–327 4065 lauten.

Die zu diesem Lehrbuch erschienenen 2 Audiocassetten (Best.-Nr. 26504) enthalten Aufnahmen der 75 englischen Texte mit britischen bzw. amerikanischen Sprecher(inne)n.

Auflage: 5. 4. 3. | Letzte Zahlen
Jahr: 1994 | maßgeblich

Druck: Druckhaus Langenscheidt, Berlin-Schöneberg
Printed in Germany / ISBN 3-468-26500-X

Inhaltsverzeichnis

Hinweise für den Gebrauch dieses Lehrbuchs

Langenscheidts Aufbaukurs Englisch wurde speziell für Lernende mit Vorkenntnissen entwickelt. Solche Vorkenntnisse sind häufig unbestimmter Art, d. h. sie stammen etwa aus dem (mitunter länger zurückliegenden) Schulunterricht, aus der Teilnahme an Anfängerkursen in der Erwachsenenbildung, aus der Durchnahme eines Anfängerlehrbuchs oder aus Kontakten mit Englischsprachigen zu Hause oder im Ausland.

Lernende mit „unbestimmten", vielleicht „unsystematisch" erworbenen Vorkenntnissen machen oft den Fehler, daß sie bei gelegentlicher Wiederaufnahme des Unterrichts immer wieder in einen Anfängerkurs gehen bzw. ein Anfängerlehrbuch im Selbststudium durcharbeiten, weil sie ein „solides Fundament" erwerben und Enttäuschungen durch die Nichterfüllung von höheren Anforderungen vermeiden wollen. Die Folge ist, daß sie viel zu langsam im Spracherwerb fortschreiten. Sie sind besser beraten, wenn sie ein Lehrbuch wie das vorliegende durcharbeiten, das nicht „bei Null" einsetzt, sondern sie unter ständiger Zurückholung und Wiederholung verschütteten Wissens rascher zu einem höheren Kenntnisstand emporführt, als dies ein Anfängerkurs könnte.

Langenscheidts Aufbaukurs Englisch wurde für Selbstlerner geschaffen, eignet sich aber auch gut für die Durchnahme im Gruppenunterricht. Die 25 Lektionen sind so aufgebaut, daß beim Lernen ein schneller Wechsel zwischen verschiedenartigen sprachlichen Aktivitäten stattfindet: hören, still lesen, sprechen, Verständnis sichern, schreiben, Wörter und Phrasen lernen, Gelerntes testen, Sprachgebrauchsregeln erkennen, üben – diese für den Spracherwerb wichtigen Tätigkeiten lösen einander in rascher Folge ab, das Lernen wird nie eintönig und ermüdend, die Motivation wird in kurzen Abständen immer wieder aufs neue belebt. Das „Rückgrat" des Buches bilden die insgesamt 75 kurzen Texte (3 in jeder der 25 Lektionen). Sie sind in der Thematik vielseitig, aktuell und interessant und decken eine große Zahl wichtiger Sprachsituationen ab.

Hinweise für die Durchnahme der jeweils 6 Seiten umfassenden Lektionen:

Seite 1: Hier wird das „Generalthema" genannt, der Inhalt der drei Lektionstexte umrissen und etwas zur Sprechweise in den Tonaufnahmen der Texte gesagt.

Seiten 2–4: Jede dieser drei Seiten enthält in der Regel: Text – Wortschatz – Verständnis- und Wortschatztest.
Gut ist es, wenn Sie den Text zunächst von der Cassette nur hören, ohne mitzulesen. Sie üben dadurch Ihr Hörverstehen. (Lassen Sie sich nicht entmutigen, wenn Sie vieles – mitunter den ganzen Text! – nicht verstehen. Ihre Fähigkeit, nur hörend Aufgenommenes zu verstehen, wird sich durch das Üben bei der Begegnung mit jedem neuen Text allmählich verbessern.)
Nach dem bloßen Hören dann: hören und mitlesen, hören und mitsprechen oder (unter Benutzung der Pausetaste Ihres Recorders) hören und nachsprechen.
Zwischen den einzelnen Hörphasen schauen Sie immer ein paar besonders für das Verständnis wichtige Ausdrücke im Wortschatz unter dem Text nach. Das Textverständnis soll sich allmählich aufbauen!
Sodann systematisches Lernen des Wortschatzes, erst links-rechts, dann rechts-links. Besonders intensiv lernen Sie, wenn Sie eine Spalte abdecken und die jeweiligen Übersetzungen entweder sprechen oder sogar schreiben. Überprüfen Sie Ihre Antwort immer sofort, indem Sie das Abdeckblatt entsprechend herabschieben, so daß die Lösung sichtbar wird. Falls Sie die Aussprache eines Wortes vergessen

haben: Sie können sie entweder in der Tonaufnahme nachhören oder im Wortschatzregister (ab Seite 223) in der Internationalen Lautschrift nachschlagen.
Dann Bearbeitung des Verständnis- und Wortschatztests (den Lösungsschlüssel finden Sie im Anhang ab Seite 156). Falls Sie Schwierigkeiten bei der Beantwortung hatten oder viele Fehler gemacht haben, schauen Sie sich noch einmal die betreffenden Informationen im Text und im Wortschatz an.
Nützliche Schreib-, Wortschatz- und Grammatikübung, bevor Sie zur nächsten Seite gehen: Schreiben Sie den Text ab, und lassen Sie dabei für jedes fünfte Wort eine Lücke. Setzen Sie erst zu einem späteren Zeitpunkt die fehlenden Wörter ein.

Seite 5: Schauen Sie sich intensiv die grammatischen Erklärungen an. Manches wird Ihnen bekannt sein, anderes nicht. In der Englischen Aufbaugrammatik im Anhang (ab Seite 178) können Sie die in der jeweiligen Lektion punktuell gegebenen Informationen in ihrem systematischen Zusammenhang wiederfinden.

Seite 6: Machen Sie als letztes die Übungen (Lösungsschlüssel im Anhang ab Seite 156). Wenn Sie in einer Übung besonders viele Fehler machen, wiederholen Sie die Übung bitte zu einem späteren Zeitpunkt. Fehler sind nützlich, denn sie schaffen für das Lernen wichtige „Aha-Erlebnisse“!

Informationen zum Anhang des Buches (ab Seite 156):

Der Schlüssel zu den Tests und Übungen (ab Seite 156) nennt Ihnen nicht nur die jeweils nächstliegende bzw. durch den Lektionstext nahegelegte Lösung, sondern (nach dem Schrägstrich /) auch noch andere Lösungen, die im Rahmen der Übungsaufgabe möglich sind. Indem Sie diesen alternativen Lösungen Beachtung schenken, können Sie Ihren Sprachschatz weiter (d. h. über den Wortschatz der Lektionen dieses Buches hinaus) ausbauen.

Die Englische Aufbaugrammatik (ab Seite 178) vereinigt die Erklärungsabschnitte der Lektionen zu einem systematischen Ganzen. Es ist nützlich, wenn Sie bei Durchnahme der Erklärungen (jeweils Seite 5 einer Lektion) immer die entsprechenden Abschnitte der Englischen Aufbaugrammatik hinzuziehen. Sie können die gegebenen Informationen dann besser mit anderen Informationen zum gleichen Thema verknüpfen. Das Grammatikregister (ab Seite 220) erleichtert Ihnen das Auffinden der gesuchten Abschnitte. Beachten Sie besonders die „Vorbemerkung zu den grammatischen Fachausdrücken“ in Abschnitt 1 der Englischen Aufbaugrammatik.

Machen Sie den Großen Abschlußtest bitte nach Durchnahme des gesamten Buches. Den Lösungsschlüssel finden Sie nach dem Ende des Tests auf Seite 218.

Das Wortschatzregister (ab Seite 223) sagt Ihnen, in welchen Lektionen die Wörter vorkommen und erklärt sind. Außerdem finden Sie hier zu jedem Wort (auch zu den Namen) die Ausspracheangabe in der Internationalen Lautschrift. Beachten Sie: Anders als in der Tonaufnahme, die zur Übung des Hörverstehens auch von der britischen Standardaussprache abweichende Akzente berücksichtigt, entsprechen die Ausspracheangaben im Wortschatzregister stets der britischen Aussprachenorm, die auch als RP (= Received Pronunciation) bezeichnet wird.

Für den Fall, daß Sie zu diesem Lehrgang ein Wörterbuch benutzen wollen, empfehlen wir Ihnen als „kleinere Lösung“ *Langenscheidts Schulwörterbuch Englisch* und als „größere Lösung“ *Langenscheidts Taschenwörterbuch Englisch*. Beide Wörterbücher bestehen aus zwei Teilen: Englisch-Deutsch und Deutsch-Englisch.

1 Safety in the air

Die Texte der ersten Lektion handeln von Flugreisen und Flugsicherheit. Sie lesen, wie es bei der Landung einer Concorde fast zu einem Unglück kam; Leute unterhalten sich darüber, ob das Fliegen sicherer oder unsicherer geworden ist; Sie erfahren etwas über die Sicherheitshinweise, die zu Anfang eines jeden Fluges gegeben werden.
Beachten Sie beim Hören der Tonaufnahme:
Text 1 wird mit britischem Akzent gesprochen („Nachrichtensprecher-Stimme“).
In Text 2 hören Sie amerikanische Stimmen.
In Text 3 ist die Aussprache wieder britisch.

Demonstrating the emergency equipment before take-off

Concorde lands with five burst tyres

A CONCORDE jet with 93 passengers on board narrowly escaped disaster yesterday. Five of the ten tyres blew as the British Airways flight from London landed at New York's Kennedy Airport.

The pilot managed to bring the supersonic plane to a skidding halt at the end of the runway. No one was injured.

An airline spokesman said: "There was no emergency evacuation and no panic. The passengers disembarked in the usual way." He added: "We don't know why the tyres blew, but the runway is very bumpy there."

A passenger described the landing: "When we hit the runway there were five loud pops. The brakes came on very quickly. We didn't know what to expect. The captain was fantastic. He brought the plane to a halt only a few yards from the end of the runway. We could have all been dead."

Wortschatz

safety	Sicherheit
Concorde	(brit.-französ. Überschall-Verkehrsflugzeug)
burst – burst – burst	platzen – platzte – geplatzt
a burst tyre / *AE* tire	ein geplatzter Reifen
jet	Düsenflugzeug
passenger	Passagier; Fluggast
on board	an Bord
narrowly escape disaster	knapp einer Katastrophe entgehen
blow – blew – blown	platzen – platzte – geplatzt
he managed to bring the supersonic plane to a halt	es gelang ihm, das Überschallflugzeug zum Stehen zu bringen
skid(ding)	rutschen(d)
at the end of the runway	am Ende der Landebahn
no one was injured	niemand wurde verletzt
airline spokesman	Sprecher der Luftverkehrsgesellschaft
emergency evacuation	(„Not-Evakuierung") Noträumung
disembark in the usual way	in der üblichen Weise aussteigen
add	hinzufügen
the runway is very bumpy	die Landebahn ist sehr holprig/uneben
describe the landing	die Landung beschreiben
hit (– hit – hit) the runway	auf der Landebahn aufsetzen
pop	Knall
brake	Bremse
yard	(= 91 cm)
we could have all been dead	wir hätten alle tot sein können

Verständnis- und Wortschatztest

a. Concorde is a ..... jet. ☐ b. Five of the plane's ten ..... blew as it landed at ..... Airport. ☐ c. The pilot managed to ..... the plane to a halt at the end of the..... ☐ d. The jet ..... escaped disaster. ☐ e. A ..... runway may have been the cause of the near disaster. ☐ f. The passengers praised the ..... for landing the plane safely.

Is flying safer today than it used to be?

Brenda: I don't think so. We hear of more crashes than we ever did in the past.

David: That's because far more people fly. In terms of percentages I think the number of accidents has gone down, not up.

Cathy: We never hear about the flights that go well, we always hear about the crashes – all over the world.

Brenda: Still, my gut feeling is that flying is not safe. There are an awful lot of near misses.

David: I feel very safe flying. In fact, I'd rather fly than drive any time.

Cathy: Me too. You have near misses a hundred times a day when you pass other cars on the roads. I know a lot of people who got hurt on the highways; I don't know anyone who got hurt in the air.

Wortschatz

safer than it used to be	sicherer als (es) früher (war)
I don't think so	ich glaube nicht
crash	(Flugzeug-)Unglück, Absturz
in the past	in der Vergangenheit; früher
fly – flew – flown	fliegen – flog – geflogen
in terms of percentages	prozentual (gesehen)
accident	Unfall; Unglück
go – went – gone [gɒn]	gehen – ging – gegangen
the number has gone down/up	die Zahl ist zurückgegangen / hat zugenommen
go well	gut ablaufen; gutgehen
all over the world	in der ganzen Welt
still	trotzdem
my gut feeling is	mein („Eingeweide-Gefühl") Instinkt sagt mir
an awful lot of near misses	schrecklich viele Beinahzusammenstöße
I feel very safe flying	ich fühle mich beim Fliegen sehr sicher
in fact	(*„Verbindungsphrase" ohne klare Bedeutung, etwa:*) tja, sogar, an sich, eigentlich
I'd rather fly than drive	ich fliege lieber, als daß ich (mit dem Auto) fahre
any time	jederzeit; allemal
pass a car	ein Auto überholen
get (– got – got) hurt	zu Schaden kommen
highway	*AE* Hauptverkehrsstraße
I don't know anyone	ich kenne niemand(en)

Verständnis- und Wortschatztest

a. Who thinks flying is safe(r)? Brenda? David? Cathy? □ b. We hear of more crashes than we ever ..... in the past. □ c. If we hear of more crashes, it's possibly because ... □ d. Another expression for *near miss* is ..... □ e. It's easier to get hurt on the highways than in the ..... □ f. A *highway* is a kind of ..... □ g. I don't know ..... who got hurt in the air.

Just in case

Do you pay careful attention when your flight attendant demonstrates how to use the emergency equipment, such as oxygen masks and life jackets, and points out the location of emergency exits in the aircraft?
You don't? Well, you should. Accidents do happen, and when they do, it can make all the difference whether you know exactly what to do, how to use the equipment, where the emergency exits are, and so on.
By the same token, if the FASTEN SEAT BELT signs go on in flight, you should obey them immediately; the aircraft may be about to enter turbulence and unbelted passengers could get some nasty knocks.

Wortschatz

just in case	für alle Fälle
pay careful attention	aufmerksam zuhören
flight attendant	Flugbegleiter(in); Steward(eß)
demonstrate	zeigen; vorführen
emergency equipment	Notausrüstung
such as oxygen masks	wie (etwa) Sauerstoffmasken
life jacket	Schwimmweste
point something out	auf etw. hinweisen; etw. zeigen
the location of the emergency exits	die Lage der Notausgänge
one aircraft – two aircraft	ein Flugzeug – zwei Flugzeuge
it can make all the difference	es kann von entscheidender Bedeutung sein
whether you know what to do	ob Sie wissen, was man tun muß
and so on	und so weiter
by the same token	ebenso; auch; ferner
please fasten your seat belt	schnallen Sie sich bitte an
if the … signs go on	wenn die …-Zeichen angehen (d. h. aufleuchten)
in flight	während des Fluges
obey	gehorchen; (be)folgen
you should obey them immediately	man sollte ihnen umgehend Folge leisten
the aircraft may be about to enter turbulance	vielleicht „ist das Flugzeug im Begriff, eine Turbulenz zu durchfliegen“
unbelted	nicht angeschnallt
get some nasty knocks	sich schlimm/sehr stoßen

Verständnis- und Wortschatztest

a. Another word for *steward(ess)* is ..... ☐ b. Oxygen masks and life jackets are part of a plane's ..... equipment. ☐ c. At the beginning of each flight the stewardess points out the location of the emergency ..... ☐ d. Accidents do ....., and when they do, you should know exactly what ..... do. ☐ e. If the FASTEN SEAT BELT signs go on, you should ..... them immediately. ☐ f. If the plane ..... turbulence, unbelted passengers could ..... some nasty knocks.

1 Erklärungen

1. Adjektiv (ohne *-ly*) oder Adverb (mit *-ly*)?

They had a narrow escape. They narrowly escaped disaster.	*Sie sind noch einmal davongekommen.* *Sie entgingen knapp einer Katastrophe.*
I know their exact location. I know exactly where they are.	*Ich kenne ihren genauen Standort.* *Ich weiß genau, wo sie sind.*
Concorde is a supersonic plane. Concorde flies supersonically.	*Die Concorde ist ein Überschallflugzeug.* *Die C. fliegt mit Überschallgeschwindigkeit.*
The captain was fantastic. The captain reacted fantastically.	*Der Kapitän war phantastisch.* *Der Kapitän hat phantastisch reagiert.*

Die Wortform ohne *-ly* bezieht sich auf Substantive (*the captain was fantastic*) oder Pronomen (*he was fantastic*).
Die *-ly*-Endung wird angehängt, wenn das Wort sich nicht auf ein Substantiv oder Pronomen bezieht, sondern z. B. auf ein Verb (*he reacted fantastically*) oder ein Adjektiv (*the flight time is fantastically short*) oder ein Adverb (*he reacted fantastically fast*).
An Adjektive auf *-ic* wird in der Regel nicht einfach *-ly*, sondern *-ally* angehängt: *supersonic – supersonically, fantastic – fantastically* (Ausnahme z. B. *public – publicly*).

2. Fragewort (*what, who, when, how* etc.) + *to*-Infinitiv

We didn't know what to expect.
Wir wußten nicht, „was wir erwarten sollten" / was auf uns zukam.

She demonstrated how to use the oxygen masks.
Sie zeigte, wie man die Sauerstoffmasken benutzt.

3. *Could* + einfacher Infinitiv und *could* + Infinitiv des Perfekts

Beachten Sie den Unterschied zwischen den beiden Konstruktionen und auch die Stellungsmöglichkeiten für *all*:

We could (all) be dead.	*Wir könnten (alle) tot sein.*
We could (all) have (all) been dead.	*Wir hätten alle tot sein können.*

4. *Rather = lieber/eher*

I'd (= I would) rather fly than drive.
(Wörtlich:) Ich würde lieber fliegen als (mit dem Auto) fahren.

5. Betonendes *do*

Accidents do happen. *Unfälle passieren nun einmal.*

Durch das (besonders betont gesprochene) *do* wird das Verb *happen* stärker betont.
Häufig läßt sich dieses betonende *do* mit *wirklich* oder *tatsächlich* übersetzen:
He does seem to know about it. (= Er scheint wirklich davon zu wissen.)

1. Setzen Sie die fehlenden Wörter ein.

a. A Concorde jet ..... escaped disaster yesterday. Five of the ten tyres blew ..... the plane landed at New York's Kennedy Airport.
b. A passenger said: "When we ..... the runway, there were five loud pops. The brakes ..... on very quickly. The captain ..... the plane to a halt only a few yards from the end of the runway. We could have all ..... dead."
c. In terms of percentages, the number of accidents has ..... down in the last few years. I'd ..... fly than drive any time. I know a lot of people who ..... hurt on the highways.
d. I always ..... careful attention when the flight attendant demonstrates how to use the emergency equipment. When the FASTEN SEAT BELT sign goes on, I always ..... it immediately. I don't want to ..... hurt if the plane enters turbulence.

2. Adjektiv (ohne -*ly*) oder Adverb (mit -*ly*)?
Setzen Sie die richtige Form des eingeklammerten Worts ein.

a. We had a (narrow) escape when our plane landed with five burst tyres.
b. Everything happened (real) (quick).
c. We were (lucky) not to get hurt.
d. (Lucky), nobody got hurt.
e. A passenger said: "We were warned that we might have to use the emergency exits, but in fact we got off quite (normal)."
f. An airline spokesman said: "It was a (normal) flight until the first tyre blew."
g. Concorde is a (fantastic) fast plane.
h. I know some people who got (serious) hurt on the highways, but I don't know anyone who got hurt in the air.
i. The passengers don't (usual) pay much attention when the flight attendant demonstrates how to use the emergency equipment.
j. I (usual) listen very (careful) to what is said on the loudspeaker.
k. When an accident does happen, it's (important) that everyone knows (exact) what to do.
l. Do you know the (exact) location of the emergency exits?

3. Übersetzen Sie.

a. Eine Concorde ist gestern nur knapp ⟨einer⟩ Katastrophe entgangen.
b. Es gelang dem Piloten, das Flugzeug zum Stehen zu bringen.
c. Die Fluggäste sind in der üblichen Weise ausgestiegen.
d. Als wir auf der Landebahn aufkamen, hat es fünfmal laut geknallt.
e. Glücklicherweise ist niemand verletzt worden.
f. Wir hätten alle tot sein können.
g. Prozentual ist die Zahl der Unfälle zurückgegangen.
h. „Ich würde lieber fliegen als ⟨mit dem Auto⟩ fahren." – „Ich auch."
i. Ich weiß nicht genau, wie man die Sauerstoffmaske benutzt.
j. Ich schnalle mich immer an – für alle Fälle!

2 The weather

In der zweiten Lektion ist vom Wetter die Rede. Der erste Text ist eine Wettervorhersage, wie man sie als Telefonansage hören kann; im zweiten Text unterhalten sich zwei Leute übers Wetter und leiten zum dritten Text über, der von einer Dürrekatastrophe in den Vereinigten Staaten berichtet.
Beachten Sie beim Hören der Tonaufnahme:
Text 1 wird mit britischem Akzent im Stil einer Telefonansage gesprochen.
In Text 2 unterhalten sich zwei britische Sprecherinnen.
Text 3 wird von einem amerikanischen Sprecher gelesen. Sprechstil: Fernseh- oder Rundfunkansage.

"So it's a bright, sunny day with perhaps rain, fog, ice and snow, and moderate winds with a chance of reaching hurricane force . . ."

The weather forecast

Here is the British Telecom Weatherline forecast for southeast England until dusk on Sunday, issued by the Met. Office for 6 p.m. on Saturday the 25th of June.

Some showers are likely this evening and overnight, particularly in the west of the region, and where they occur they could be quite heavy. Even in places which escape the showers it will remain rather cloudy, and it will be a mild and humid night everywhere.

It will stay mostly cloudy tomorrow, and again some showers are likely.

Temperatures will be a degree or two down on today's with a mainly light northeasterly wind.

Thank you for calling.

Wortschatz

weather forecast	Wettervorhersage
British Telecom	(*BE* staatseigene Gesellschaft für Telekommunikation, u. a. Telefon)
weatherline	(„Wetterleitung") Wettervorhersage (als Telefonansage)
until dusk	bis zur (Abend-)Dämmerung
issued by the Met(eorological). Office	herausgegeben vom Wetteramt
showers are likely	Schauer sind wahrscheinlich
particularly in the west of the region	besonders im Westen des (Vorhersage-) Gebiets
where the showers occur	wo die Schauer auftreten
escape the showers	den Schauern entgehen
it will remain rather cloudy	es wird ziemlich wolkig bleiben
a mild and humid night	eine milde und feuchte Nacht
it will stay mostly cloudy	es wird überwiegend wolkig bleiben
a degree or two down on today's (temperatures)	ein oder zwei Grad unter den heutigen (Temperaturen)
a mainly light wind	ein überwiegend leichter Wind
northeasterly wind	Nordostwind
thank you for calling	danke für Ihren Anruf

Verständnis- und Wortschatztest

1. Einsetzübung.
a. British Telecom is responsible for the ..... system and other telecommunications services. □ b. London is in ..... England. □ c. The weather forecast is ..... by the Met. Office. □ d. The weather outlook at 6 p.m. on June 25th: There are likely to be ..... this evening and overnight, some of them quite ..... Tomorrow it will be ..... cloudy, and again some showers are ..... Tomorrow's temperatures will be slightly ..... than today's.

2. Austauschübung. Ersetzen Sie die unterstrichenen Satzteile durch solche mit etwa gleicher Bedeutung (Synonyme).
a. The <u>forecast</u> for the next few days isn't very promising. □ b. <u>There'll probably be</u> some showers tonight. □ c. It'll <u>stay</u> rather cloudy over the weekend. □ d. Tomorrow it'll be <u>a little</u> cooler than today.

Talking about the weather

A: A bit close today, isn't it?

B: Yes. I've had a headache since I got up this morning. I wish the weather would clear up.

A: Not much chance of the sun coming out, I suppose.

B: And we're bound to get a couple of showers. I've always got this handy little umbrella with me – just to be on the safe side. Still, it could be worse. My daughter tells me there's a drought where she lives over in the States.

A: Yes, there was something on TV about it. The heat must be terrible. And they haven't had any rain for months in some parts.

B: She says the farmers are having to sell off their cattle, the crops are ruined, there are fires all over the place ...

A: Isn't it dreadful. To think of those poor people, and the animals ...

B: Yes, it's a real tragedy. And we complain about the rain here.

Wortschatz

a bit close (*scharfes* s!)	ein bißchen schwül/drückend
have a headache	Kopfschmerzen haben
get up – got up – got (*AE auch* gotten) up	aufstehen – aufstand – aufgestanden
I wish it would clear up	ich wünschte, es würde sich aufklären/ aufheitern
(there's) not much chance of the sun coming out(, I suppose)	(es besteht wohl) keine große Aussicht auf Sonnenschein
we're bound to get	wir kriegen sicher
a couple of showers	ein paar / einige Schauer
a handy little umbrella	ein handlicher kleiner Schirm
just to be on the safe side	nur um sicherzugehen
bad – worse (*scharfes* s!) – worst	schlimm – schlimmer – schlimmste
a drought	eine Dürre(katastrophe)
in some parts	in einigen Gegenden
sell off cattle (– sold – sold)	(Rind-)Vieh (unter Preis) veräußern / abstoßen
the crops are ruined	die Ernte ist hin
there are fires all over the place	überall sind Brände
dreadful	schrecklich; furchtbar
to think of those poor people	wenn man an die armen Menschen denkt
it's a real tragedy	es ist eine echte Tragödie
we complain about the rain	wir (be)klagen (uns) über den Regen

Verständnis- und Wortschatztest

a. What time did you ..... up this morning? □ b. It was cloudy when we arrived but it has ..... up now. □ c. It gets rather hot when the sun ..... out. □ d. Over in the States the ..... is so bad that farmers are having to ..... off their cattle. □ e. Just ..... of those poor people over there. □ f. We really shouldn't ..... about the weather here.

Drought disaster

MOST OF North Dakota has been proclaimed a disaster area. A mild winter followed by a rainless spring drained the moisture from the soil.

A blazing sun and biting dust storms then devastated the wheat, corn and soybean crops before they had a chance to take root.

Grazing pastures are scorched brown and there is nothing to replenish the rapidly diminishing stocks of hay.

Facing financial ruin and unable to pay for extra animal feed, farmers are selling livestock in the hope that the extra income will help to see them through until the rain comes.

But there is no relief in sight. Hot, dry weather with only scattered rainfall is forecast for the next 30 days. "This is the worst drought I've ever seen," says a farmer. "The only thing left to do is pray."

Wortschatz

North Dakota	Norddakota (US-Bundesstaat)
most of North Dakota	der größte Teil von Norddakota
it has been proclaimed a disaster area	es ist zu einem Katastrophengebiet erklärt worden
drain the moisture from the soil	dem Boden die Feuchtigkeit entziehen
the blazing sun	die brennende Sonne
biting dust storms	beißende/schneidende Staubstürme
devastate the wheat crops	den Weizen vernichten
corn *AE* / *BE* maize	Mais
soybean *AE* / *BE auch* soya bean	Sojabohne
before they had a chance to take root	bevor sie die Möglichkeit hatten, Wurzeln zu schlagen
grazing pastures	Weideland
scorch	versengen/verbrennen/ausdörren
replenish the stocks	die Vorräte/Bestände ergänzen
diminish rapidly	sich schnell verringern
hay	Heu
face financial ruin	vor dem (finanziellen) Ruin stehen
animal feed	Tierfutter
livestock	Vieh(bestand/bestände)
it will see them through	es wird sie über die Runden bringen
there is no relief in sight	es besteht keine Aussicht auf Besserung
scattered rainfall	vereinzelte Niederschläge
forecast – forecast – forecast	vorhersagen – -sagte – -gesagt
the only thing left to do is pray	das einzige, was man noch tun kann, ist beten

Verständnis- und Wortschatztest

a. The state has been ..... a disaster area. □ b. It was the dry spring that ..... the moisture from the soil. □ c. The blazing sun and biting dust storms ..... the crops. □ d. The farmers are unable to ..... their diminishing stocks of hay. □ e. There's no ..... in sight. □ f. Hot weather with hardly any rain is ..... for the next 30 days.

2 Erklärungen

1. Vom Deutschen abweichender Gebrauch der Zeiten

I wish the weather would clear up. *Ich wünschte ...*
Idiomatische Besonderheit: *I wish = ich wünschte.*

I've had a headache since I got up this morning.
Ich habe Kopfschmerzen, seitdem ich heute morgen aufgestanden bin.
Gebrauch des Perfekts (*I've had*) für eine aus der Vergangenheit in die Gegenwart reichende Handlung; Gebrauch der Vergangenheit (*got up*) für eine durch eine Zeitbestimmung der Vergangenheit (*this morning*) „datierte" Vergangenheitshandlung.

2. Verlaufsform oder einfache Form?

The farmers are having to sell off their cattle. *Die Bauern müssen ...*

Die einfache Form *have to sell off* wäre hier ebenfalls möglich, aber die Verlaufsform *are having to sell off* betont, daß diese Notwendigkeit jetzt gerade im Augenblick besteht. Die Verlaufsform verrät auch eine stärkere innere Teilnahme der sprechenden Person.
Dagegen wird mit der einfachen Form *we complain* im folgenden Beispiel ausgedrückt, daß die Leute allgemein über das Wetter klagen, nicht gerade jetzt im Augenblick:

And we complain about the rain here. *Und wir klagen über den Regen hier.*

3. Satzverkürzung durch Partizipialkonstruktionen

Here is the forecast for southeast England until dusk on Sunday, issued by the Met. Office for 6 p.m. on Saturday the 25th of June.
... der vom Wetteramt ... am 25. Juni ausgegeben wurde.

A mild winter followed by a rainless spring drained the moisture from the soil.
Ein milder Winter, auf den ein regenloser Frühling folgte ...

Hier ist durch das *-ed*-Partizip eine Wortgruppe adjektivartig an ein Substantiv (*the forecast, a mild winter*) angehängt worden. Im folgenden Beispiel hat eine durch das *-ing*-Partizip eingeleitete Wortgruppe die Funktion eines Adverbs:

Facing financial ruin, farmers are selling livestock ...
Vor dem Ruin stehend / Dem Ruin nahe, verkaufen die Bauern Vieh ...

4. Besonderheiten im Gebrauch des *to*-Infinitivs

I always take my umbrella – just to be on the safe side.
... um sicherzugehen / um auf Nummer Sicher zu gehen / für alle Fälle
To think of those poor people ... *Wenn man an die armen Menschen denkt ...*

There is nothing to replenish the rapidly diminishing stocks.
Es ist nichts da, womit man die sich rasch vermindernden Vorräte ergänzen könnte.
The only thing left to do is pray. *Das einzige, was man noch tun kann, ist beten.*

1. Setzen Sie die passende Zeitform ein: Präsens, Vergangenheit, Perfekt oder Zukunft – einfache Form oder Verlaufsform.

a. It (remain) rather cloudy overnight and tomorrow.
b. Tomorrow's temperatures (be) a degree or two down on today's.
c. I (have) a headache since I got up this morning. I (wish) the weather would clear up.
d. Oh look, it (stop) raining and the sun (come) out.
e. In some parts of the United States they (not have) any rain since last December.
f. We really shouldn't (complain) about the rain here. Over in the States the farmers (have) to sell off their cattle because of the drought. If they're lucky, the extra income (see) them through till the rain (come).
g. Last year we (have) record crops, but this year most of our wheat and corn crops (be) devastated by the drought.

2. Verkürzen Sie den unterstrichenen Satzteil.

a. This is the weather forecast which has been issued by the Met. Office for 6 p.m. on Saturday the 25th of June.
b. A mild winter which was followed by a rainless spring drained the moisture from the soil.
c. The weather that's being forecast for the next 30 days will make things even worse.
d. All the people who got injured in the accident have now left hospital.
e. The prices that are paid for beef at the moment don't even cover our costs.
f. There is no hay with which they could replenish their rapidly diminishing stocks.
g. This is the worst drought that I've ever seen.

3. Setzen Sie die fehlenden Wörter ein.

a. Where showers ....., they could be quite heavy.
b. It will ..... mostly cloudy tomorrow.
c. We're ..... to get a couple of showers.
d. We shouldn't really ..... about the weather, because there's nothing anyone can do about it.
e. Parts of the state have been ..... a disaster area.
f. Most of the wheat, corn and soybean crops have been ..... by the drought.
g. Many farmers are ..... financial ruin.
h. The weather ..... for the next 30 days offers little hope of relief.

4. Übersetzen Sie.

a. In den Vereinigten Staaten ist eine schreckliche Dürre.
b. In einigen Gegenden haben sie schon monatelang keinen Regen gehabt.
c. Der größte Teil von Norddakota ist zum Katastrophengebiet erklärt worden.
d. Die Heuvorräte verringern sich rasch, und es ist nichts da, womit man sie ergänzen könnte.
e. Die Bauern verkaufen ihr Vieh in der Hoffnung, daß das zusätzliche Einkommen sie über die Runden bringt, bis der Regen kommt.
f. Viele Bauern stehen vor dem Ruin.
g. Für die nächsten 30 Tage wird heißes, trockenes Wetter mit nur vereinzelten Niederschlägen vorhergesagt.

3 On the road

Thema dieser Lektion ist der Straßenverkehr. Sie lesen/hören Verkehrsnachrichten, „erleben" eine Anzeige wegen zu schnellen Fahrens auf einer amerikanischen Autobahn und erfahren einiges über Verkehrsprobleme in den amerikanischen Vorstädten.
Beachten Sie beim Hören der Tonaufnahme:
Text 1 wird im Stil einer britischen Verkehrsfunksendung gesprochen.
In Text 2 sprechen sowohl der Verkehrspolizist als auch die Autofahrerin mit amerikanischem Akzent.
Auch Text 3 wird mit amerikanischer Aussprache gelesen.

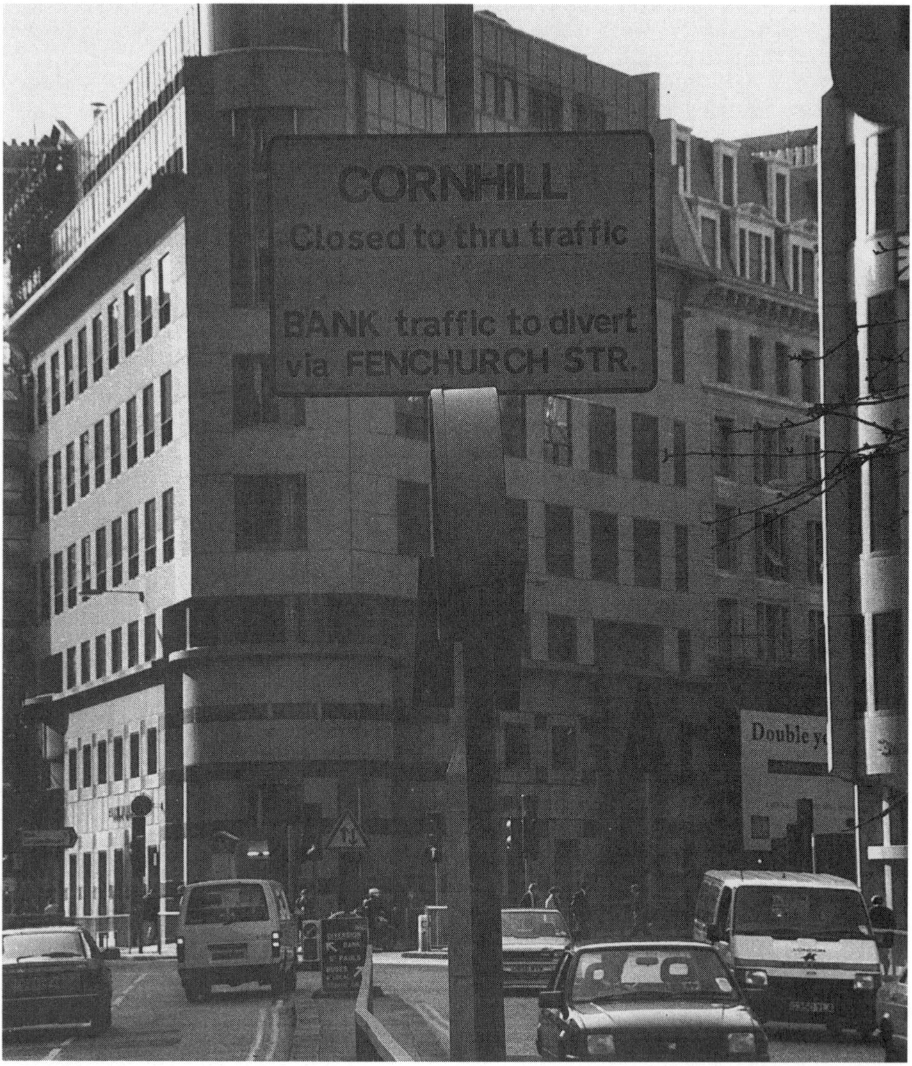

Radio traffic news

Travel news from nine o'clock this morning until four this afternoon.

In southwest London, work on the A309 Kingston Bypass at the Claygate Lane roundabout has been causing long delays for drivers heading into central London, and in the West End Berkeley Square, Berkeley Street and Hay Hill are closed because of a fire.

The Royal Regatta at Henley in Oxfordshire will bring heavy traffic into the Henley and Maidenhead area until Sunday.

In Hampshire, new work is due to begin this morning on the A339 Newbury Road between Headley and Basingstoke, which will involve the use of temporary traffic lights from 9 a.m. until 4 p.m. each day for a week.

And I need hardly remind you that avoiding the Wimbledon area is no bad thing – unless, of course, you're lucky enough to have semifinals tickets.

Wortschatz

traffic news / travel news	Verkehrsmeldungen
bypass	Umgehung(sstraße)
lane	(*eigentlich:*) Gasse, Sträßchen
roundabout	Kreisverkehr
cause long delays	große Verzögerungen/(Verkehrs-)Stockungen verursachen
drivers heading into central London	Autofahrer, die auf dem Weg in die Londoner Innenstadt sind
Berkeley Square	„der Berkeley-Platz“
Royal Regatta	„Königliche Regatta“ (= Ruderbootrennen auf der Themse)
Oxfordshire / Hampshire	(englische Grafschaften [*counties*])
work is due to begin	Arbeiten sind („fällig zu beginnen“) vorgesehen
involve something	etw. mit sich bringen
temporary traffic lights	provisorische Verkehrsampeln
I need hardly remind you	ich brauche Sie kaum (daran) zu erinnern
avoid the Wimbledon area	die Gegend um Wimbledon meiden
be lucky enough to have tickets	das Glück haben, Karten zu besitzen
the semifinals	die Halbfinalspiele

Verständnis- und Wortschatztest

a. Here's the travel news ..... four this afternoon. □ b. Work on the A309 Kingston Bypass has been ..... long delays for the last few days. □ c. Drivers ..... into central London should avoid the Claygate Lane roundabout. □ d. The Royal Regatta will bring ..... traffic into the Henley area. □ e. Work ..... to begin this morning on the A339 will ..... the use of temporary traffic lights. □ f. Avoiding the Wimbledon area is no bad thing – ....., of course, you're lucky enough to have semifinals tickets.

On Interstate 80

A: Good morning, ma'am.

B: Hi, officer.

A: Can I see your driver's license, please?

B: Oh, sure. Just a moment – ah, here you are.

A: You know what the speed limit is on this highway?

B: Yes, 55 miles an hour.

A: You were doing almost 90 back there.

B: Oh, I'm sorry. I sure didn't realize I was going that fast. D'you have to give me a ticket?

A: I'm afraid so, ma'am. If you'll just hold on for a minute ... (*Writes out ticket.*) Will you sign here, please?

B: Hm – what a way to start the day.

A: I'm sorry, ma'am. Have a nice day.

Wortschatz

interstate *AE* / *BE* motorway	(eine Art von US-Bundes-)Autobahn
ma'am *AE* / *BE* madam	(höfliche Anredeform für Frauen)
hi *überwiegend AE* / *BE* hello	(*Begrüßungsformel:*) (guten) Tag
officer	(Anredeform für Polizist[inn]en)
driver's license *AE* / *BE* driving licence	Führerschein
oh, sure	aber sicher
here you are	(*wenn man jem. etw. gibt:*) bitte sehr
speed limit	Geschwindigkeitsbegrenzung
highway	*AE* (Hauptverkehrs-)Straße
55 miles an hour	(ca.) 90 km/h (1 mile = 1,609 km)
you were doing almost 90 back there	Sie sind dahinten fast 145 gefahren
I sure didn't realize I was going that fast	ich habe wirklich nicht gemerkt, daß ich so schnell gefahren bin
ticket	(*hier:*) gebührenpflichtige Verwarnung, „Knöllchen"
I'm afraid so	ich fürchte ja; leider ja
hold on	warten; sich gedulden
sign	unterschreiben

Verständnis- und Wortschatztest

a. In the United States, an interstate is a kind of ..... □ b. In most states you're not allowed to drive a car if you don't have a ..... □ c. There's a .... of 55 miles an hour on this interstate. □ d. If you were doing 90, you were going much too ..... □ e. If you drive too fast, you risk getting a ..... for speeding. □ f. Could you just ..... on while I write out the ticket. □ g. The British word for *driver's license* is .... □ h. The British equivalent of an *interstate highway* is a .....

Suburban "gridlock"

ROADS IN US suburbs are getting more and more congested. "Hurry up and wait. Go 20 feet and stop. What a nightmare," says a commuter who takes an hour to drive the 18 miles from his suburban home to his suburban office, most of it in first gear.

A lot of jobs have moved from the central city areas to the suburbs, there are more women working, more children are being driven to day care – all this has put a lot more cars on suburban highways.

Experts studying the problem of "gridlock" have found that only 6 per cent of commuters use public transit and that there are only 1.2 people in the average rush-hour car.

New roads are being built and existing ones widened despite the protests of "no more growth" citizen groups, which argue that flextime, car-pooling, company buses, and improved mass-transit facilities could solve the problem at less cost and with less damage to the environment.

Wortschatz

suburban gridlock	(*etwa:*) Verkehrsinfarkt in den Vororten
suburb	Vorort
congested	(*Verkehr:*) verstopft
hurry up	sich beeilen
20 feet	(ca.) 6 Meter (1 foot = 0,3048 m)
nightmare	Alptraum
commuter	Pendler(in)
he takes an hour	er braucht eine Stunde
in first gear	im ersten Gang
a lot of jobs have moved	eine Menge Arbeitsplätze haben sich verlagert
day care (centre *BE* / *AE* center)	Kindertagesstätte
public transit *AE* / *BE* transport	öffentliche Verkehrsmittel
rush hour	Hauptverkehrszeit; Stoßzeit
existing roads are being widened	bestehende Straßen werden verbreitert
despite the protests	trotz der Proteste
citizen group	Bürgerinitiative
they argue that	sie vertreten den Standpunkt, daß
flextime (*Warenzeichen*) / *auch* flexitime	gleitende Arbeitszeit
car-pooling	Fahrgemeinschaften
company bus	Firmenbus
mass-transit facilities *AE*	Massenverkehrsmittel
solve a problem	ein Problem lösen
damage to the environment	Umweltschäden

Verständnis- und Wortschatztest

a. The roads in the suburbs are getting more and more ..... ☐ b. It's a nightmare to drive endlessly in first ..... ☐ c. A lot of jobs have ..... from the central city areas to the suburbs. ☐ d. The roads are so congested because so few people use public ..... ☐ e. It isn't good for the ..... if new roads are built all the time.

3 Erklärungen

1. Einfache Form und Verlaufsform des Passivs

(Einfache Form:) New roads are built (every year).
Es werden (jedes Jahr) neue Straßen gebaut.

(Verlaufsform:) New roads are being built (at the moment).
Es werden (zur Zeit) neue Straßen gebaut.

Das Passiv wird im Englischen mit einer Form von *be* gebildet. Beispiele:

is built = wird gebaut	*has been built = ist gebaut worden*
are built = werden gebaut	*have been built = sind gebaut worden*
was built = wurde gebaut	*had been built = war(en) gebaut worden*
were built = wurden gebaut	*can be built = kann/können gebaut werden*

Um auszudrücken, daß es sich um etwas gerade Geschehendes, Vorübergehendes u. dgl. handelt, kann auch im Passiv – hier durch Einschieben von *being* – die Verlaufsform gebildet werden:

A new road is/was being built. *Eine neue Straße wird/wurde gerade gebaut.*

Die Verlaufsform kommt im Passiv vor allem nach *am/is/are* und *was/were* vor. Nach *has/have/had been* und Hilfsverben wie *can* ist sie sehr selten. Dagegen findet man sie durchaus gelegentlich nach dem *to*-Infinitiv:

A new road seems to be being built.
Es scheint gerade eine neue Straße gebaut zu werden.

Gefälliger klingt hier allerdings die Aktivform:
They seem to be building a new road. *Sie scheinen eine neue Straße zu bauen.*

2. Verlaufsform des Perfekts

a. Work on the Kingston Bypass has been causing long delays.

Vergleichen Sie diese Form mit den beiden folgenden:

b. Work on the Kingston Bypass has caused long delays.
c. Work on the Kingston Bypass is causing long delays.

a. Verlaufsform des Perfekts: Die Handlung hat in der Vergangenheit begonnen und dauert noch an. Mögliche Übersetzung:
(Bau-)Arbeiten ... verursachen (seit einiger Zeit) erhebliche Verkehrsstockungen.
b. Einfache Form des Perfekts: Die Handlung ist abgeschlossen. Übersetzung:
(Bau-)Arbeiten ... haben erhebliche Verkehrsstockungen verursacht.
c. Verlaufsform des Präsens: Die Handlung läuft zur Zeit gerade ab. Übersetzung:
(Bau-)Arbeiten ... verursachen (zur Zeit) erhebliche Verkehrsstockungen.

3. *-ing*-Konstruktion als Attribut (also ähnlich einem Relativsatz)

drivers heading into central London
Autofahrer, die auf dem Weg in die Londoner Innenstadt sind
experts studying the problem of "gridlock"
Fachleute, die sich mit dem Problem des „Verkehrsinfarkts" befassen

1. Setzen Sie die richtige Form des Verbs ein.

a. During the past few days, work on the A309 (cause) long delays.
b. Drivers (head) into central London should avoid the Kingston Bypass.
c. Work (begin) on the A339 this morning will cause delays between Headley and Basingstoke.
d. (Avoid) the Wimbledon area is no bad thing.
e. Roads in US suburbs (get) more congested every day.
f. (Drive) the 18 miles from her home to the office takes her an hour.
g. She takes an hour (drive) the 18 miles from home to office.
h. A lot of jobs (move) from the central city areas to the suburbs in the last few years, (put) a lot more cars on suburban highways.
i. New roads (build) all the time, but things aren't getting any better.

2. Ersetzen Sie die unterstrichenen Wörter durch solche mit gleicher oder annähernd gleicher Bedeutung.

a. There was something about the Kingston Bypass in the <u>traffic</u> news this morning.
b. Drivers <u>travelling</u> into central London should avoid the Kingston Bypass.
c. Temporary traffic lights will be in use from 9 a.m. <u>to</u> 4 p.m.
d. Avoiding the Wimbledon area is <u>a good</u> thing.
e. You can't get in <u>if you don't</u> have tickets.
f. <u>May</u> I see your <u>driving licence</u>, please?
g. A lot of people get hurt on the <u>highways</u>.
h. Could you please <u>wait</u> for a moment.
i. <u>I take</u> an hour to drive the 18 miles.
j. Experts have <u>discovered</u> that only 6 per cent of commuters use public <u>transport</u>.
k. <u>Better</u> mass-<u>transit</u> facilities could solve the problem at less cost.

3. Setzen Sie passende Präpositionen ein.

at, because of, by, for, from, into, on, till, to, until, with

a. Drivers heading ..... central London should avoid the A309.
b. Berkeley Square and Berkeley Street are closed ..... a fire.
c. Please hold on ..... a minute.
d. A lot of jobs have moved ..... central city areas ..... the suburbs.
e. Improved mass-transit facilities could solve the problem ..... less cost and ..... less damage ..... the environment.
f. Here is the weather forecast ..... southeast England ..... dusk ..... Sunday, issued ..... the Met. Office ..... 6 p.m. ..... Saturday.
g. Tomorrow's temperatures will be a degree or two down ..... today's.
h. I've always got this handy little umbrella ..... me.

4. Übersetzen Sie.

a. Ich brauche Sie ⟨wohl⟩ kaum ⟨daran zu⟩ erinnern, daß in der Gegend von Wimbledon viel (*heavy*) Verkehr ist.
b. Sie sollten die Gegend von Wimbledon meiden – es sei denn, Sie haben Karten für die Halbfinalspiele.
c. Sie sind da hinten fast 90 gefahren.
d. Ich habe nicht gemerkt, daß ich so schnell gefahren bin.
e. Die Straßen sind immer mehr verstopft.
f. Zur Zeit werden viele neue Straßen gebaut.
g. Ich brauche eine Stunde, um die 18 Meilen ins Büro zu fahren.

4 Careers

In dieser Lektion ist von beruflichen Dingen die Rede. Alle drei Texte handeln von Menschen aus dem britischen Sprachbereich und werden deshalb mit britischem Akzent gesprochen. Der erste Text ist eine Mischung von Erzählstil und direkter Rede, der zweite ein Dialog und der dritte eine kurze Zeitungsstory.

Looking for a job? An employment agency

Double income, no kids

Sandra is a computer programmer, and her husband, Steve, is a steward with a major airline.
"Our lifestyles are very different," says Sandra. "I work nine to five and he's often away for three weeks at a time on long-haul flights. Even when he's at home I still have to go to work."
Steve started work as a steward shortly after he and Sandra got married. He had been made redundant from his previous job. "I enjoy flying," he says. "Of course I miss being at home but I feel that my job gives us a great opportunity to travel to places we couldn't afford otherwise. Sandra gets heavily discounted tickets too. So far we've been to Australia, New Zealand and the Far East."
Both Sandra and Steve feel that flying is not the long-term answer for Steve. They would like a family and Sandra wants to be at home to bring up the children, but she doubts they'll be able to manage on Steve's salary alone, as they're now used to having two incomes

Wortschatz

d(ouble) i(ncome,) n(o) k(ids)	(solche Doppelverdiener ohne Kinder werden umgangssprachl. auch *dinks* genannt)
a steward with a major airline	ein Steward bei einer größeren Luftverkehrsgesellschaft
lifestyle	Lebensstil; Lebensweise
long-haul flights	Langstreckenflüge
even when he's at home	auch wenn er zu Hause ist
get married (– got – got)	heiraten
redundant	überschüssig; überzählig
make someone redundant	jem. (als nicht mehr benötigt) entlassen
his previous job	seine vorherige Arbeitsstelle
I enjoy flying	ich fliege gern
I miss being at home	ich habe Sehnsucht nach Hause
an opportunity to travel	die Gelegenheit/Möglichkeit zu verreisen
places we couldn't afford otherwise	Orte, die wir uns sonst nicht leisten könnten
heavily discounted tickets	stark verbilligte Flugscheine
a long-term answer	eine Lösung auf lange Sicht
they would like a family	sie hätten gern Kinder
bring up children	Kinder großziehen
she doubts they'll be able to manage	sie bezweifelt, daß sie zurechtkommen werden
they're used to having two incomes	sie sind daran gewöhnt, zwei Einkommen zu haben

Verständnis- und Wortschatztest

a. What do Sandra and Steve do for a living? ☐ b. In what way are their lifestyles very different? ☐ c. What "great opportunity" does Steve's job give them? ☐ d. What are Sandra's and Steve's plans over the long term?

What makes a good shop assistant?

A: Debbie Jenkins has just been voted Shop Assistant of the Year. You're one of her regular customers, Mrs Patterson, and it was you who put Debbie's name up for the competition. What's so special about her?

B: Well, you know, Debbie sells cosmetics and, quite frankly, that's a field where you find a lot of salesgirls who are haughty and unsympathetic. But not Debbie. She's so friendly and helpful. She's got such enthusiasm, you've only got to walk past her counter to want to stop, even if you weren't planning to buy anything.

A: And that means handsome sales for her employers, does it?

B: Yes, of course, good service always helps. But Debbie isn't the type of girl who'd sell you something just to make a sale. She knows a lot about the things she sells, and she'll really listen to your problems and try to come up with what's best for you individually. Other salesgirls could certainly learn a thing or two from her.

Wortschatz

shop assistant *BE* / *AE* salesclerk	Verkäufer(in) (in Laden etc.)
she was voted Shop Assistant of the Year	sie wurde zur Verkäuferin des Jahres gewählt
regular customer	Stammkunde; Stammkundin
put someone up for something	jem. für etw. vorschlagen
competition	Wettbewerb; Konkurrenz; Preisausschreiben
she sells cosmetics	sie verkauft Kosmetika
quite frankly	ehrlich gesagt
salesgirl	Verkäuferin
haughty	hochnäsig; überheblich
unsympathetic	wenig mitfühlend; abweisend
enthusiasm	Begeisterung
walk past her counter	an ihrem (Kaufhaus-)Stand vorbeigehen
handsome sales	gute Umsätze
employer	Arbeitgeber(in)
make a sale	einen Abschluß machen; etw. verkaufen
she'll really listen to your problems	sie geht wirklich auf Ihre Probleme ein
come up with something	sich etw. einfallen lassen
what's best for you individually	was für Sie persönlich am besten ist

Verständnis- und Wortschatztest

a. Debbie Jenkins sells ..... ☐ b. A lot of salesgirls working in the cosmetics field are ..... ☐ c. Debbie is so enthusiastic and friendly that it's difficult to walk past her counter without ..... something. ☐ d. But Debbie would never sell you something just to make a ..... ☐ e. She'll really ..... to your problems and try to come up with what's best for you. ☐ f. An American word for *shop assistant* is .....

Keith Rayner quits the BBC

TV NEWSREADER Keith Rayner has shocked the BBC by quitting after almost 25 years.

At 54, the popular newscaster is considering changing his role in life completely – by becoming an actor.

"The stage is something I've been keen on for a long time," he said last night. "It's been one of my big hobbies. Whether or not I'm any good at it is something I'll have to wait and see."

But the newsreader also blamed the increasing pressure of the job for his decision. "There have been so many changes, and the new technology certainly puts so much more pressure on presenters these days. I just felt that it was time for a change and that I should move now while I'm still young enough to adjust to a new life."

Wortschatz

quit – quit(ted) – quit(ted)	(*Job:*) verlassen, kündigen
newsreader *BE* / newscaster *AE&BE*	Nachrichtensprecher(in)
consider doing something	überlegen, ob man etw. tun soll
change his role	seine Rolle ändern; eine andere Rolle übernehmen
stage	Bühne
I've always been keen on the stage	ich habe mich schon immer für das Theater begeistert
whether I'm any good at it	ob ich dafür tauge
blame someone for something	jem. an etw. die Schuld geben
the increasing pressure of the job	der wachsende Druck des Berufes
decision	Entscheidung
there have been so many changes	es hat sich soviel geändert
the new technology	die neue Technik
put pressure on somebody	jem. unter Druck setzen
presenter *BE* / *AE* anchor(wo)man/anchorperson	Moderator(in)
I should move now	ich sollte jetzt den Schritt machen
adjust to a new life	sich auf eine neue Lebensweise einstellen

Verständnis- und Wortschatztest

a. Keith Rayner is a ..... working for the BBC. ☐ b. He has shocked the BBC by ..... after almost 25 years. ☐ c. The ..... has always been one of his big hobbies. ☐ d. He wants to change his role completely by ..... an actor. ☐ e. He feels that he's still young enough to ..... to a new life. ☐ f. Rayner also ..... the increasing pressure of the job for his decision. ☐ g. Another word for *newsreader* is ..... ☐ h. Keith Rayner is *keen* on the *stage*. In other words, he's very ..... in the .....

4 Erklärungen

1. Passiv der Perfektformen

Aktiv: They have voted her Shop Assistant of the Year.
Passiv: She has been voted Shop Assistant of the Year.
Sie ist zur Verkäuferin des Jahres gewählt worden.
Man hat sie zur Verkäuferin des Jahres gewählt.

Aktiv: They had made him redundant.
Passiv: He had been made redundant. *„Er war redundant gemacht worden."*

2. *-ing*-Konstruktion als Subjekt und Objekt

Als Subjekt:
Flying is not the long-term answer for Steve.
Das Fliegen ist für Steve keine langfristige Lösung.
Avoiding the Wimbledon area is no bad thing.
„Ein Vermeiden der Gegend um Wimbledon ist kein Fehler."

Als Objekt:
I enjoy flying. *„Ich genieße das Fliegen."*
I miss being at home. *„Ich vermisse das Zuhausesein."*
He's considering changing his role. *„Er erwägt ein Verändern seiner Rolle."*

3. *-ing*-Form nach Präpositionen

They're used to having two incomes. *Sie sind gewöhnt, zwei Einkommen zu haben.*
He has shocked the BBC by quitting. *„Er hat die BBC durch sein Kündigen geschockt."*
Thank you for calling. *„Danke fürs Anrufen."*

Ein auf eine Präposition folgendes Verb kann nur in der *-ing*-Form (nicht – wie im Deutschen – im Infinitiv) stehen. Vergleichen Sie: *He left without paying. = Er ging, ohne zu zahlen.*

4. Relativsatz ohne Relativpronomen (Kontaktkonstruktion)

She knows a lot about the things (which/that) she sells.
Sie weiß eine Menge über die Dinge, die sie verkauft.
The stage is something (which/that) I've been keen on for a long time.
Die Bühne ist etwas, wofür ich mich schon lange begeistere.

Das Relativpronomen kann wegfallen, wenn es in Objektposition steht. Besser als diese recht abstrakte Regel sagt Ihnen bei hinreichender Spracherfahrung Ihr Gefühl, wann Sie das Relativpronomen weglassen können und wann nicht. Bei den folgenden Relativsätzen zum Beispiel ist die Kontaktkonstruktion nicht möglich:

You find a lot of salesgirls who are haughty and unsympathetic.
Even in places which escape the showers it will remain rather cloudy.
We never hear about the flights that go well.

1. Setzen Sie die Verben in der passenden Form ein.

Steve (start) work as a steward two years ago shortly after he and Sandra (get) married. He (be) made redundant from his previous job. Steve's job (give) them a great opportunity (travel) to places they couldn't (afford) otherwise. So far they (be) to Australia, New Zealand and the Far East. Both Sandra and Steve feel that (fly) is not the long-term answer for Steve. They would like a family and Sandra (want) to be at home to bring up the children, but she doubts they (be) able to manage on Steve's salary alone, as they are now used to (have) two incomes.

2. Setzen Sie die fehlenden Wörter ein.

Debbie Jenkins has just been ..... Shop Assistant of the Year. Mrs Patterson, one of Debbie's regular ....., put her name up for the ..... Debbie, ... sells cosmetics in a large store, is said to be so full of enthusiasm that you can't ..... past her counter without ..... something. But Debbie isn't the ..... of girl who'd ..... you something just to make a sale. She'll really ..... to your problems and try to come ..... with what's best for you.

3. Setzen Sie ins Passiv.
(Lassen Sie die eingeklammerten „Handlungsurheber" im Passiv weg.)

a. (They) have voted her Shop Assistant of the Year.
b. (We) have put your name up for the competition.
c. (They)'ve built a lot of new roads.
d. Why have (they) changed everything?
e. Hasn't (he) taken the children to school?
f. Why haven't (they) proclaimed the state a disaster area?
g. (We) hadn't expected so much rain.
h. The spokesman said that (the passengers) hadn't used the emergency equipment.

4. Ersetzen Sie die unterstrichenen Wörter durch andere mit etwa gleicher Bedeutung.

a. Where are the <u>children</u> – in the garden?
b. 200 workers have <u>lost their jobs</u>.
c. Things are easier if you have two <u>incomes</u>.
d. I <u>didn't want</u> to buy anything.
e. Keith is <u>thinking of</u> becoming an actor.
f. I'm not particularly <u>interested in</u> meeting him.

5. Übersetzen Sie.

a. Reisen ist etwas, was ich sehr genieße.
b. Mein Beruf als Steward gibt uns die Möglichkeit, an Orte zu reisen, die wir uns sonst nicht leisten könnten.
c. Die Verkäuferinnen, die hier arbeiten, sind alle sehr freundlich und hilfsbereit.
d. Wenn ich in der Kosmetikabteilung (*department*) bin, kaufe ich oft Dinge, die ich gar nicht kaufen wollte.
e. Die Dürre, die wir vor fünf Jahren hatten, war viel schlimmer.
f. Die neue Straße, die jetzt gebaut wird, wird das Problem wahrscheinlich lösen.

5 Changing jobs

Text 1: Stellenanzeige in einer englischen Tageszeitung. Gesucht werden clevere Automobilverkäufer für eine besondere Zielgruppe: amerikanische, britische und kanadische Soldaten in Deutschland.
Text 2: Mark Kramer ruft die Firma an und vereinbart einen Termin für ein Vorstellungsgespräch.
Text 3: Tips für das Vorstellungsgespräch – was man tun und was man besser nicht tun sollte.
Alle drei Texte sind „britisch" gesprochen. Text 2 hören Sie realistisch als Telefongespräch, d. h. die Stimme des Angerufenen ist „telefonmäßig verfremdet".

Looking through the job ads

A job advertisement

SALES PEOPLE
(WEST GERMANY)

We are seeking aggressive, career-minded Sales People
to join our expanding sales force in West Germany,
selling personal tax-free motorcars
to American, British and Canadian armed forces personnel.
High commission plus incentive bonuses
make for top earnings potential.
If you have the drive and desire for top earnings
with a highly successful company, then ring:

Mr Terry Johnson on 01–327 4065 today, between 09–1600 hrs,

or write to:

Mr Terry Johnson, Inter Motors Germany GmbH,
Eschersheimer Landstr. 521, D-6000 Frankfurt 50, West Germany

Wortschatz

change jobs	(„Stellen wechseln") sich beruflich verändern
job ad(vertisement)	Stellenanzeige
sales people	Verkäufer(innen)
seek – sought – sought	suchen – suchte – gesucht
aggressive	aggressiv; dynamisch
career-minded	karrierebewußt; ehrgeizig
join a group	sich einer Gruppe anschließen
expanding	expandierend; wachsend
sales force	Verkaufsmannschaft; Außendienst
tax-free	steuerfrei; abgabenfrei
armed forces personnel	Angehörige der Streitkräfte
commission	Provision
incentive bonus	Leistungszulage; Prämie
make for top earnings potential	(*etwa:*) bieten beste Verdienstmöglichkeiten
drive	Schwung; Elan; Tatendrang
desire	Wunsch; Sehnsucht; Verlangen
highly successful	in hohem Maße erfolgreich
company	Gesellschaft; Unternehmen; Firma
ring – rang – rung	anrufen – anrief – angerufen
01 (*gesprochen:* oh one)	Vorwahl (= dialling code) von London
on 327 4065	unter (der Telefonnummer) 327 4065
between 09–1600 h(ou)rs	zwischen 9.00 und 16.00 Uhr

Verständnis- und Wortschatztest

a. What kind of people are Inter Motors Germany looking for? ☐ b. What qualities should these people have? ☐ c. What will their job be? ☐ d. What kind of earnings will they have? ☐ e. Where can Mr Johnson be reached? ☐ f. What's the dialling code for London?

A phone call

A: Inter Motors London. Good morning.

B: Good morning. Could I speak to Mr Johnson, please?

A: One moment, please.

C: Terry Johnson here. Good morning.

B: Good morning, Mr Johnson. This is Mark Kramer. I'm phoning about your advertisement in today's *Daily Mail*.

C: Ah right, Mr Kramer. Have you got sales experience at all?

B: Yes, I have. As a matter of fact, I've been selling cars for the last four years.

C: I see. But you know you'd be based in Frankfurt if you were to work for us.

B: Yes, that's why I'm interested. I've been working here in London for the last couple of years, and I'd like to go back to Germany. I am German, you see.

C: Oh, that sounds interesting. Now, wait a minute – could you come and see me – say – tomorrow morning at ten thirty? I'm here in London only today and tomorrow.

B: Yes, ten thirty tomorrow is all right with me. What's the address?

C: 37 Wells Street, W1.

B: That's off Oxford Street, isn't it?

C: Quite right. Oxford Circus or Tottenham Court Road, if you're coming by Tube.

B: Okay, Mr Johnson. Thank you very much. I'm looking forward to seeing you tomorrow.

C: Yes, till tomorrow then. Thanks for calling, Mr ... Kramer.

Wortschatz

phone about something	wegen etw. / auf etw. hin anrufen
sales experience	Verkaufserfahrung
as a matter of fact	(*überleitende Gesprächsfloskel*)
you'd (= you would) be based in F.	Sie würden in F. „stationiert“ sein
if you were to work for us	falls Sie für uns arbeiten sollten
for the last couple of years	in den letzten (paar) Jahren
I'd (= I would) like to go back to Germany	ich würde gern nach Deutschland zurückgehen/zurückkehren
that sounds interesting	das („klingt“) ist ja interessant
come and see someone	jem. besuchen/aufsuchen
off Oxford Street	in einer Nebenstraße der Oxford Street
Oxford Circus / Tottenham Court Road	(Londoner U-Bahn-Stationen)
the Tube	die (Londoner) U-Bahn
I'm looking forward to seeing you	ich freue mich darauf, Sie zu sehen

Verständnis- und Wortschatztest

a. If you want to change jobs, you should look at the job ..... in the newspapers. ☐ b. The *Daily Mail* is a British national ..... ☐ c. We're looking for a salesperson with a certain amount of ..... ☐ d. If Mr Kramer were to work for Inter Motors, he'd be ..... in Frankfurt. ☐ e. Mr Kramer is interested in the job because he ... ☐ f. Where's Wells Street? – It's ... ☐ g. The nearest Underground stations are ...

The interview: some dos and don'ts

Prepare yourself by trying to find out as much as possible about the company you're applying to.
Make sure you're suitably dressed.
Be punctual.
Bring with you any documents that may be relevant to your application as well as a list of questions you may want to ask the interviewer.
When asked why you're leaving your present job, don't mention any problems you may have had with your previous employer.
Try to give the impression of being confident, enthusiastic and capable, without sounding too aggressive or over-confident.
Don't fiddle with your handkerchief, handbag, pen, etc. while you're being interviewed.
Be pleasant, alert and courteous, try to relax – and smile.

Wortschatz

interview	Vorstellungsgespräch
some dos and don'ts	(*etwa:*) was man tun oder nicht tun / tun oder lassen sollte
prepare yourself	bereiten Sie sich vor
apply to a company	sich bei einer Firma bewerben
make sure you're suitably dressed	achten Sie darauf, daß Sie passend gekleidet sind
be punctual	seien Sie pünktlich
documents relevant to your application	Unterlagen, die für Ihre Bewerbung von Bedeutung sind
questions you may want to ask	Fragen, die Sie vielleicht stellen möchten
don't mention any problems	erwähnen Sie keine Probleme
your previous employer	Ihr bisheriger Arbeitgeber
give the impression of being confident	einen selbstbewußten Eindruck machen
enthusiastic	begeistert
capable	fähig
over-confident	übertrieben selbstsicher/selbstbewußt
don't fiddle with your handkerchief	fummeln Sie nicht an Ihrem Taschentuch herum
be pleasant	seien Sie freundlich/nett
alert	aufmerksam; wach
courteous	höflich
try to relax	versuchen Sie, sich zu entspannen

Verständnis- und Wortschatztest

a. Find out as much as ..... about the company you're applying to. ☐ b. Make sure you're ..... dressed. ☐ c. Bring with you any documents that are ..... to your application. ☐ d. Have you got any questions you'd like to .....? ☐ e. Don't ..... any problems you may have had with your previous boss. ☐ f. Give the impression of ..... confident without ..... too aggressive. ☐ g. You won't make a good impression if you're always ..... with your pen or handkerchief.

5 Erklärungen

1. Die *-self*-Pronomen (rückbezüglich gebraucht)

I	must	prepare	myself	*ich muß mich vorbereiten*
you	must	prepare	yourself	*du mußt dich / Sie müssen sich vorbereiten*
he	must	prepare	himself	*er muß sich vorbereiten*
she	must	prepare	herself	*sie muß sich vorbereiten*
it	must	prepare	itself	*es muß sich vorbereiten*
we	must	prepare	ourselves	*wir müssen uns vorbereiten*
you	must	prepare	yourselves	*ihr müßt euch / Sie müssen sich vorbereiten*
they	must	prepare	themselves	*sie müssen sich vorbereiten*

2. *Can – could – may* in Fragesätzen

Can I see your driver's license, please?	*Kann ich bitte mal Ihren Führerschein sehen?*
Could I speak to Mr Johnson, please?	*Könnte ich bitte mal Herrn Johnson sprechen?*
May I use your phone?	*Darf/Kann ich Ihr Telefon benutzen?*

Could ist höflicher als *can*. *May* ist förmlicher als *can*.

3. *Can* und *may* in Aussagesätzen

It can make all the difference whether you know exactly what to do.
Es kann viel ausmachen, ob Sie wissen, wie Sie sich verhalten müssen.
Bring with you any documents that may be relevant to your application.
Bringen Sie alle Unterlagen mit, die für Ihre Bewerbung von Bedeutung sein könnten.

Can drückt Fähigkeit oder eine durch die Umstände gegebene Möglichkeit aus.
May drückt eine durch ein gewisses Maß an Wahrscheinlichkeit gegebene Möglichkeit aus („vielleicht").
Vergleichen Sie:

There can be problems.
(Durch die Umstände gegebene Möglichkeit:) *Es kann Probleme geben.*

There may be problems.
(Es besteht eine gewisse Wahrscheinlichkeit – „möglicherweise":)
Vielleicht gibt es Probleme. / Es kann sein, daß es Probleme gibt.

4. *May* + Infinitiv des Perfekts

Don't mention any problems you may have had with him.
... *Probleme, die Sie mit ihm gehabt haben mögen / vielleicht mit ihm gehabt haben*

Während *may have had* sich also auf die Vergangenheit bezieht, würde *may be having* die Gegenwart bezeichnen:

Don't mention any problems you may be having with him.
... *Probleme, die Sie mit ihm haben mögen / vielleicht mit ihm haben.*

1. *-ing*-Form, *-ed*-Form oder *to*-Infinitiv?

a. We are seeking aggressive sales people (join) our expanding sales force in West Germany.
b. That was one of the questions (ask) by the interviewer.
c. She's got a job with a company (sell) cars to armed forces personnel.
d. There was nothing (replenish) the rapidly diminishing stocks of hay.
e. When (ask) why he wanted to leave, he said he'd had problems with his employer.
f. Not much chance of the sun (come) out, I suppose.
g. Drivers (head) into central London must be prepared for long delays.
h. It takes him an hour (drive) the 18 miles to his office.
i. I enjoy (fly) but I miss (be) at home.
j. Here is the weather forecast (issue) by the Met. Office for Saturday the 25th of June.
k. He's been considering (change) his job for a long time.

2. Setzen Sie das eingeklammerte Verb in die passende Zeit.

a. We (look) for a man like you for years.
b. She (join) our sales force last year.
c. Another excellent salesman (join) our sales force next month.
d. A car salesman is a salesman who (sell) cars.
e. I (try) to ring her all day – where on earth can she be?
f. Sorry to interrupt, but what on earth (you talk) about?
g. I (sell) cars for the last four years.
h. You'd be based in Frankfurt if you (be) to work for us.
i. Let's talk about it when I (be) in London next week.
j. My husband and I (be) in London next week.
k. I (work) here in London for the last couple of years.
l. He isn't here yet. We're all a bit worried. He may (have) an accident.

3. Ergänzen Sie die Frageanhängsel (*question tags*).

Wells Street – that's off Oxford Street, ...?
Wells Street – that's off Oxford Street, isn't it?

a. A bit close today, ...?
b. He's terribly aggressive, ...?
c. They're expanding their sales force, ...?
d. You sell cars, ...?
e. The ad was in the *Daily Mail*, ...?
f. You've got sales experience, ...?
g. I'd be based in Frankfurt, ...?
h. You're coming by Tube, ...?
i. Sandra's very capable, ...?
j. Sounds interesting, ...?

4. Übersetzen Sie.

a. Könnte ich bitte Herrn Johnson sprechen?
b. Ich freue mich darauf, Sie zu sehen.
c. Ich rufe wegen Ihrer Annonce in der heutigen *Daily Mail* an.
d. Ich arbeite schon seit vier Jahren in London.
e. Sie sollten sich sorgfältig vorbereiten.
f. Sie hatte sich sorgfältig vorbereitet.
g. Sie machte den Eindruck, eine sehr fähige Frau zu sein.

6 Noise

Die Texte dieser Lektion beleuchten das Problem der Lärmbelästigung von verschiedenen Seiten. Der erste – eine Zeitungsstory – erzählt uns, wie Mrs Moore es schafft, ihr Bier im Pub zu trinken, ohne dabei von der Musikbox gestört zu werden. Im zweiten Text äußern sich verschiedene Leute zum Lärmproblem. Der dritte beschreibt in knapper Form Auswirkungen übermäßigen Lärms auf die menschliche Gesundheit. Zur Tonaufnahme: Die ersten beiden Texte sind britisch, der dritte ist amerikanisch gesprochen.

Noise in the street: Pneumatic drills

Woman's fight against noise at the pub

WHEN Mrs Janet Moore goes to the pub, she takes a secret weapon to ensure a quiet, friendly atmosphere.

It is a small notice, which she discreetly places on the jukebox, saying simply: OUT OF ORDER.

"The effect on the place is immediate," she says. "Everyone talks much more."

Mrs Moore, 54, of Bridport, Dorset, is angry that pubs and other businesses bombard their customers with loud, unwanted music.

She believes she is part of a "silent majority" who would prefer to be able to converse without shouting.

Wortschatz

her fight against noise	ihr Kampf gegen (den) Lärm
at the pub	in der Gastwirtschaft/Kneipe
a secret weapon	eine Geheimwaffe
ensure a quiet atmosphere	für eine ruhige Atmosphäre sorgen
a small notice	ein kleines Schild
discreet(ly)	diskret; unauffällig
she places it on the jukebox	sie stellt es auf die Musikbox/Jukebox
out of order	außer Betrieb
the effect on the place	die (Aus-)Wirkung auf das Lokal
immediate(ly)	unmittelbar; direkt; prompt
she is angry that	sie ärgert sich darüber / regt sich darüber auf, daß
bombard someone with music	jem. mit Musik „bombardieren"
unwanted music	ungewünschte/unverlangte Musik
the silent majority	die stille/schweigende Mehrheit
they would prefer to be able to converse	sie würden es vorziehen, sich unterhalten zu können
without shouting	ohne zu schreien/brüllen

Verständnis- und Wortschatztest

a. What's Mrs Moore's Christian name? □ b. How old is she? □ c. Where's she from? □ d. What doesn't she like about pubs? □ e. What's her "secret weapon"? □ f. What's the effect of the OUT OF ORDER sign? □ g. A *friendly* atmosphere – can you think of another word for *friendly*? □ h. She *places* it on the jukebox. – Another word for *places*? □ i. *Converse* without shouting. – Another word or phrase for *converse*?

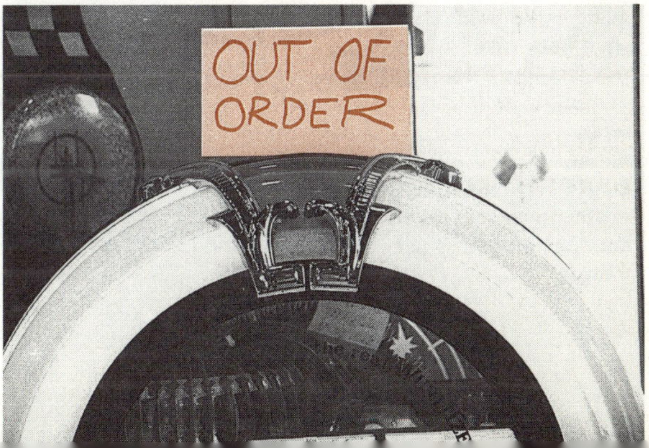

Are we getting noisier?

A government expert: There's been a big increase in complaints about noise from neighbours. Something like two-thirds of all complaints are either about amplified music or about barking dogs.

A noise consultant: Noisy children and noisy neighbours in general are the most common cause of trouble and annoyance in my experience. Social attitudes are changing. We're getting more inconsiderate, more selfish. We're tending to do things for pleasure which cause more annoyance to other people. There's more clay-pigeon shooting, there's more playing of music, there's more riding motorcycles for pleasure ...

A young woman in London's Regent's Park: I don't see why I should have to listen to other people's music just because *they* feel like listening to it.

A man in the street: Pneumatic drills and all the roadworks that are going on – those are the things that annoy me most.

A tenant: When you live in a flat ... the noise from neighbours ... being able to hear practically every move as they walk around, their TV, their radio – you feel you don't have any privacy in your own home.

A villager: The Japanese motorbikes that the youngsters have, and they drive up and down through country villages making this horrible noise – it really gets to me.

Wortschatz

get noisier	lauter werden; mehr Krach machen
complaints about noise	Beschwerden wegen Lärms
amplify – amplifier	verstärken – Verstärker
consultant	Berater(in)
in general	im allgemeinen
the most common cause	die häufigste Ursache
trouble and annoyance	(beides Wörter für „Ärger“)
in my experience	nach meiner Erfahrung
social attitudes	Einstellungen gegenüber den Mitmenschen
inconsiderate	rücksichtslos
selfish	egoistisch; selbstsüchtig
tend to do something	dazu neigen, etw. zu tun
cause annoyance to other people	anderen (Menschen) Ärger bereiten
clay-pigeon shooting	Tontaubenschießen
ride (– rode – ridden) a motorcycle	Motorrad fahren
I don't see why ...	ich sehe nicht ein, warum ...
they feel like listening to music	ihnen ist nach Musikhören zumute
pneumatic drill (*das* p *ist stumm!*)	Preßluftbohrer
annoy	ärgern; belästigen; aufregen
tenant	Mieter(in)
flat *BE* / *AE* apartment	(Etagen-, Miet-)Wohnung
be able to hear every move	jede Bewegung hören können
you don't have any privacy	man hat keine Intimsphäre/Ruhe
villager	Dorfbewohner(in)

motorbike	Motorrad
the youngsters	die Jugendlichen
country village	(kleines) Dorf (auf dem Lande)
make a horrible noise	fürchterlichen Lärm machen
it really gets to me	das nervt mich wirklich

Verständnis- und Wortschatztest (Text 2)

a. What are the main sources of unwanted noise, according to the people speaking in the text? □ b. The "tenant" complains about not having any privacy in her own home. What does she mean by that? □ c. There's been a *big* increase in complaints. Another word for *big*? □ d. Another word for *motorcycle*?

Noise pollution

It has been estimated that more than one in three Americans is affected by noise pollution. Apart from damage to hearing, excessive noise or "unwanted sound" can cause lack of sleep, irritability, heart trouble, indigestion, ulcers, and high blood pressure. Noise-induced stress can create severe tension in daily life and may even contribute to mental illness.

Wortschatz

pollution	(Umwelt-)Verschmutzung
noise pollution	Lärmbelästigung
it has been estimated	man hat geschätzt
be affected by something	von etw. betroffen sein
apart from	abgesehen von
damage to hearing	Schädigung des Gehörs; Gehörschäden
excessive noise	übermäßiger Lärm
unwanted sound	ungewünschte Geräusche
lack of sleep	Mangel an Schlaf; Schlafmangel
irritable – irritability	reizbar – Reizbarkeit
heart trouble	Herzbeschwerden
indigestion	Verdauungsstörung(en)
ulcer	(*z. B.* Magen-)Geschwür
high blood pressure	hoher Blutdruck
noise-induced stress	lärmbedingter Streß
create severe tension	schwere Spannung(szustände) hervorrufen
and may even contribute (to)	und kann sogar beitragen (zu)
mental illness	psychische Erkrankung
may even contribute to mental illness	kann sogar Mitursache einer psychischen Erkrankung sein

Verständnis- und Wortschatztest (Text 3)

a. How many per cent of Americans are affected by noise pollution? □ b. What disorders, according to the text, can be caused by noise? □ c. Stress can *create* severe tension. Another word for *create*? □ d. If you don't get enough sleep, you suffer from ..... of sleep. □ e. What other kinds of pollution can you think of apart from noise pollution?

6 Erklärungen

1. *More*

More than one in three Americans is affected by noise pollution.
Mehr als einer von drei Amerikanern ist von „Lärmverschmutzung" betroffen.

We're getting more inconsiderate. *Wir werden rücksichtsloser.*
We're getting more and more inconsiderate. *Wir werden immer rücksichtsloser.*

2. *Most*

Most of North Dakota has been proclaimed a disaster area.
Der größte Teil von Norddakota ist zum Katastrophengebiet erklärt worden.

Noisy children and noisy neighbours are the most common cause of trouble.
... sind die häufigste Ursache von Ärger.

3. *Would*

I wish the weather would clear up. *Ich wünschte, das Wetter würde sich bessern.*

She'd (= She would) prefer to be able to converse without shouting.
Sie würde es vorziehen, wenn sie sich unterhalten könnte, ohne zu schreien.
I'd (= I would) rather fly than drive any time.
Ich würde allemal lieber fliegen als fahren.

They'd (= They would) like a family. *Sie hätten gern Kinder.*
I'd (= I would) like to go back to Germany.
Ich würde gern nach Deutschland zurückgehen.

4. *Should*

You should pay careful attention. *Sie sollten genau aufpassen.*
I felt that I should move now while I'm still young enough to adjust to a new life.
Ich hatte das Gefühl, daß ich diesen Schritt jetzt tun sollte ...
I don't see why I should have to listen to other people's music.
Ich sehe nicht ein, warum ich gezwungen sein sollte, mir die Musik anderer Leute anzuhören.

5. Wortstellung im Zwischen- oder Nachsatz zu direkter Rede

"The effect on the place is immediate," she says.
"The effect on the place is immediate," says Mrs Moore.

"This is the worst drought I've ever seen," he says.
"This is the worst drought I've ever seen," says a farmer.

Beachten Sie die unterschiedliche Stellung:
Subjekt – Verb, wenn das Subjekt ein Pronomen (hier: *she*, *he*) ist.
Verb – Subjekt, wenn das Subjekt substantivisch (hier: *Mrs Moore*, *a farmer*) ist.

1. Setzen Sie Verben in der passenden Form ein.

When Mrs Moore is at the pub she ensures a quiet atmosphere by ..... a small notice on the jukebox that ..... simply: OUT OF ORDER. The effect is that everyone ..... much more. Mrs Moore ..... she is part of a "silent majority" who would prefer to converse without .....
In the opinion of some experts we're ..... more inconsiderate and selfish. They say we ..... to do things for pleasure which ..... annoyance to other people. We play loud music whenever we ..... like it, even if it disturbs others.
It has been ..... that more than one in three Americans is ..... by noise pollution. Noise-induced stress can ..... severe tension in daily life and may even ..... to mental illness.

2. Adjektiv (ohne -*ly*) oder Adverb (mit -*ly*)?

a. When she goes to the pub, she takes a (secret) weapon with her.
b. When she goes to the pub, she (secret) takes a weapon with her.
c. She (discreet) places the OUT OF ORDER notice on the jukebox.
d. She (discreet) goes to the jukebox and places the notice on it.
e. They made a number of (discreet) moves to solve the problem.
f. The OUT OF ORDER sign has an (immediate) effect.
g. When the jukebox stops playing, everyone (immediate) starts talking.
h. People (angry) protested against the loud music.
i. There were (angry) protests when the jukebox started playing.
j. (Excessive) amplified music can damage people's hearing.
k. (Excessive) noise can cause high blood pressure.

3. Setzen Sie passende Präpositionen ein.

about, at, by, for, from, on, to, with

a. A lot of people complain ..... noise ..... neighbours.
b. We often do things ..... pleasure which cause annoyance ..... others.
c. Doctors have found that noise-induced stress sometimes contributes ..... mental illness.
d. You can reach me ..... 327 4065 from nine to five Monday to Friday.
e. Hello – could I speak ..... Mr Johnson, please?
f. I'm phoning ..... your advertisement in today's *Daily Mail*.
g. Ten thirty tomorrow morning would be all right ..... me.
h. I prepared myself ..... trying to find out as much as possible about them.
i. Will they be able to manage ..... only one salary?
j. I can't see what's so special ..... her.

4. Übersetzen Sie.

a. Ich würde es vorziehen, mich unterhalten zu können, ohne schreien zu müssen.
b. Viele von uns neigen dazu, Dinge zum Vergnügen zu tun, die andere Leute ärgern.
c. Ich hätte Lust, etwas Musik zu hören.
d. In diesen Wohnungen kann man praktisch jede Bewegung hören, die jemand macht.
e. Immer mehr Leute sind von „Lärmverschmutzung" betroffen.
f. Ich sehe nicht ein, warum ich mir anderer Leute Musik anhören sollte.
g. „Übermäßiger Lärm kann zu einer psychischen Erkrankung führen", sagt Professor Harrison.

7 Home

Von Heimat, Wohnung und Obdachlosigkeit handeln die Texte dieser Lektion. Der erste – im Stil einer Zeitungsstory – ist in der Tonaufnahme britisch gesprochen, auch David und Julie im Dialog des zweiten Textes haben einen britischen Akzent, während der dritte Text – über Obdachlosigkeit in New York – amerikanisch gesprochen ist. Der dritte Text enthält eine Reihe von Amerikanismen, denen im Wörterverzeichnis ihre britischen Entsprechungen gegenübergestellt werden.

Cheap homes for locals

SOMERSET FARMER Charles Burstock is selling land worth more than £1 million at half price to help young couples in the village of Wayford.

Mr Burstock, whose family has lived in the village for 170 years, said: "I've been a school governor for over 30 years and seen the youngsters forced to leave the area because of soaring house prices."

Burstock, 69, will sell three acres of his farm to the council at the special knockdown price on condition it is used to build low-priced houses for young couples whose parents live in the village.

Burstock added: "Steps will be taken to ensure the buildings don't fall into yuppie hands."

Wortschatz

the locals / the local people	die Einheimischen
Somerset	(SW-englische Grafschaft [*county*])
land worth more than £1 million	Land, das mehr als 1 Million Pfund wert ist
young couples	junge (Ehe-)Paare
the village of Wayford	das Dorf Wayford
school governor	(*etwa:*) Mitglied des Schulbeirats
they're forced to leave the area	sie sind gezwungen, die Gegend zu verlassen
soaring prices	in die Höhe schießende Preise
acre	(= 4047 qm)
council	(Gemeinde-, Stadt-)Rat
knockdown price	Tiefstpreis; Spottpreis
on condition (that) it is used	unter der Bedingung, daß es gebraucht wird
low-priced houses	billige Häuser
add	hinzufügen
take steps (– took – taken)	Maßnahmen ergreifen
yuppie	(= young urban [*oder* upwardly mobile] professional = junger, karriere- und modebewußter Mensch mit großstädtischem Lebensstil)

Verständnis- und Wortschatztest

a. Where does Charles Burstock live? ☐ b. How old is he? ☐ c. How long has his family lived in the village? ☐ d. Is he still a school governor? ☐ e. What's the problem that's worrying him? ☐ f. What has he decided to do about it? ☐ g. Many youngsters are leaving the area because of ..... house prices. ☐ h. Burstock will sell the land at a ..... price. ☐ i. He wants ..... houses to be built on the land. ☐ j. He wants the houses to be sold to young local ..... ☐ k. He doesn't want the houses to be sold to .....

◁ *Sleeping rough in the middle of London*

Our favourite room

David: Come to think of it, the kitchen's our most important room, isn't it?

Julie: Yes, we do an awful lot of things here, almost everything in fact. But it seems to be a general trend. Just think how many times we've been entertained in other people's kitchens.

David: My parents would never have dreamed of entertaining in the kitchen.

Julie: Mine wouldn't have either, but it was a completely different kind of place then, wasn't it?

David: Yes, it was small and stuffy, the windows were steamed up, and there was always washing hanging from the clothesline.

Julie: Whereas today the kitchen is usually the one room that's properly designed.

David: That's true. I wish we'd given as much thought to the sitting room as we did to planning the kitchen.

Julie: But you don't think we should move the television into the kitchen, do you?

David: No, let's leave it in the bedroom. I need it to get me off to sleep.

Wortschatz

our favourite *BE* / *AE* favorite room	unser Lieblingszimmer
come to think of it	wenn man sich das so überlegt
our most important room	unser wichtigstes Zimmer
we do an awful lot of things here	wir machen hier enorm viel
a general trend	ein allgemeiner Trend
entertain someone	jem. (zum Essen) einladen / bewirten
entertain in the kitchen	Gäste in der Küche empfangen
mine wouldn't have either	meine hätten es auch nicht (gemacht)
small and stuffy	klein und stickig
the windows were steamed up	die Fenster waren beschlagen
there was washing hanging from the clothesline	es hing Wäsche von der Wäscheleine
whereas	während; wohingegen
properly designed	ordentlich/fachmännisch gestaltet
that's true	das stimmt
I wish we'd (= we had) given	ich wünschte, wir hätten gegeben
give thought to something	sich etw. überlegen
sitting room	Wohnzimmer
I need it to get me off to sleep	ich brauche es zum Einschlafen

Verständnis- und Wortschatztest

(Answer *Yes, No* or *I don't know*.) On the basis of what the text says …
a. … do Julie and David do their washing in the kitchen? ☐ b. … do they entertain in the kitchen? ☐ c. … did their parents entertain in the kitchen? ☐ d. … do they consider the kitchen their most important room? ☐ e. … do they listen to the radio in the kitchen? ☐ f. … did they plan their kitchen carefully? ☐ g. … did their parents have a well-designed kitchen? ☐ h. … do they watch television in the kitchen?

Address: Grand Central Terminal

Ray Hensley was panhandling at a subway stop on 42nd Street when he noticed that "nobody was working the door at the bank across the street". He changed over to the other side and has been playing doorman there ever since, wishing people a good day in return for some spare change or the occasional bill. At night he sleeps on the floor or in a telephone booth in Grand Central Terminal.

Hensley, a former trucker, is one of New York's tens of thousands of homeless. A recent survey of 1,000 "typical" homeless people found that more than 80 per cent were male, two-thirds were white, and 87 per cent had once held a job. Their average age was 34. Most had been on the street less than a year. Over a third said they had family they could go to for help, 27 per cent had sought treatment for drinking problems, and 18 per cent had been in a state mental hospital. Asked the main reason for their plight, 21 per cent cited family conflicts, while half named economic factors.

Wortschatz

terminal *AE*	(End-, Kopf-, Haupt-)Bahnhof
Grand Central Terminal/Station	(einer der beiden großen New Yorker Bahnhöfe, an der 42. Straße)
panhandle *umgangssprachl. AE*	betteln
subway stop *AE* / *BE* Underground station	U-Bahnhof
work the door	„die Tür bearbeiten"
doorman	Portier
in return for	(als Gegenleistung) für; gegen
spare change	Kleingeld (das man übrig hat)
the occasional bill *AE* / *BE* (bank)note	gelegentlich ein Geldschein
telephone booth *AE* / *BE* (tele)phone box / call box	Telefonzelle
trucker *AE* / *BE* lorry driver	Lkw-Fahrer(in)
a former trucker	ein früherer Lkw-Fahrer/Fernfahrer
the homeless	die Obdachlosen
a recent survey	eine aktuelle Umfrage/Untersuchung
hold a job (– held – held)	einen Arbeitsplatz haben
average age	Durchschnittsalter
seek treatment (– sought – sought)	sich behandeln lassen
mental hospital	psychiatrische Klinik
the main reason for their plight	der Hauptgrund für ihre Notlage
cite something	etw. angeben
family conflicts	familiäre Auseinandersetzungen
economic factors	wirtschaftliche Faktoren/Umstände

Verständnis- und Wortschatztest

a. Grand Central *Terminal* – another word for *terminal*? □ b. Subway *stop* – another word for *stop*? □ c. The British word for *bill* in ten-mark *bill*? □ d. The British word for *telephone booth*? □ e. In the US they're *truckers*, in Britain they're ..... □ f. People who are *on the street* are ..... □ g. 21 per cent *cited* family conflicts – another word for *cited*?

7 Erklärungen

1. Definierende und nichtdefinierende Relativsätze

a. Mr Burstock's land will be used to build low-priced houses for young couples whose parents live in the village.
... für junge Ehepaare, deren Eltern im Dorf wohnen.

b. Mr Burstock, whose family has lived in the village for 170 years, is sad to see young people being forced to leave the area.
Mr Burstock, dessen Familie seit 170 Jahren in dem Dorf ansässig ist...

In Satz (a) kann auf den Relativsatz nicht verzichtet werden, wenn deutlich werden soll, um was für *young couples* es sich handelt. (Ohne den Relativsatz könnte man z. B. meinen, daß die *low-priced houses* auch ortsfremden Yuppie-Ehepaaren zur Verfügung stehen.) Der Relativsatz hat also eine definierende Funktion, er ist zum Verständnis der von ihm näher bestimmten Substantivphrase *young couples* unentbehrlich.
In Satz (b) wird der Relativsatz nicht zum Definieren von *Mr Burstock* benötigt, er könnte wegfallen, ist entbehrlich. Die in ihm enthaltene Information könnte genausogut in einem separaten Satz gegeben werden.
Der Relativsatz in (a) ist definierend; er wird nicht durch Sprechpause(n) bzw. Komma(s) abgesetzt.
Der Relativsatz in (b) ist nichtdefinierend; er wird beim Sprechen durch Pause(n) und beim Schreiben durch Komma(s) abgetrennt.
Nichtdefinierende Relativsätze (b) sind fast ganz auf die Schriftsprache beschränkt; definierende (a) finden sich außer im geschriebenen auch häufig im gesprochenen Englisch.

2. Negatives oder positives Frageanhängsel (*question tag*)?

It was a completely different kind of place then, wasn't it?
Damals war es eine völlig andere Art von Raum, nicht wahr?
It wasn't the same kind of room then, was it?
Damals war es nicht die gleiche Art von Raum, oder?

You think we should move the TV into the kitchen, don't you?
Du meinst, wir sollten den Fernseher in die Küche stellen, nicht wahr?
You don't think we should move the TV into the kitchen, do you?
Du meinst (doch) nicht, daß wir den Fernseher in die Küche stellen sollten, oder?

Sie erkennen die Regel: Einem positiven Vorderteil folgt ein negatives Anhängsel und umgekehrt.

3. *Would* + Infinitiv des Perfekts

My parents would never have dreamed of entertaining in the kitchen.
Meine Eltern „würden nie davon geträumt haben", in der Küche zu „unterhalten".
Meine Eltern hätten nicht im Traum daran gedacht, Gäste in der Küche zu empfangen.

Die folgende, auf die Gegenwart bezogene Version könnte als Hinführung zu dieser schwierigen Konstruktion hilfreich sein:

My parents would never dream of entertaining in the kitchen.
Meine Eltern würden nicht im Traum daran denken, Gäste in der Küche zu empfangen.

1. Setzen Sie – nur wo notwendig – Relativpronomen ein, d. h. gebrauchen Sie die Kontaktkonstruktion (vgl. S. 28), wo dies möglich ist. Setzen Sie bei nichtdefinierenden Relativsätzen auch die fehlenden Kommas.

a. The kitchen is usually the one room ..... is properly designed.
b. Two-thirds of the homeless don't have a family ..... they could go to for help.
c. Mrs Moore's secret weapon is a small notice ..... she discreetly places on the jukebox, saying simply: OUT OF ORDER.
d. Mrs Moore believes she is part of a "silent majority" ..... would prefer to be able to converse without shouting.
e. We tend to do things for pleasure ..... cause annoyance to other people.
f. Are there any more questions ..... you'd like to ask?
g. New roads are being built despite the protests of "no more growth" citizen groups ..... argue that improved mass-transit facilities could solve the problem at less cost.
h. It may not be a good idea to talk about the problems ..... we've had with her.
i. New work is due to begin this morning ..... will involve the use of temporary traffic lights from 9 a.m. until 4 p.m. each day.

2. Ergänzen Sie die Frageanhängsel (*question tags*).

a. The kitchen's our most important room, ...?
b. Your parents live here too, ...?
c. You don't want the houses to fall into yuppie hands, ...?
d. There isn't anything interesting on TV, ...?
e. Mr Burstock was a school governor too, ...?
f. You didn't give much thought to it, ...?
g. There's a bank across the street, ...?
h. Prices aren't actually soaring, ...?
i. She's got a job, ...?
j. He comes from Somerset, ...?
k. You would have helped him, ...?
l. Our parents wouldn't have dreamed of doing that sort of thing, ...?

3. Setzen Sie ein Verb in der passenden Form ein.

a. Mr Burstock ..... three acres of his farm to the council last year.
b. The council is planning ..... low-priced houses on the land.
c. Steps will ..... to ensure the houses don't fall into yuppie hands.
d. Mr Burstock, who ..... a school governor for over 30 years, is sad to see young couples leave the area because of soaring house prices.
e. "Youngsters from families who ..... here for hundreds of years shouldn't be forced ..... the area," says Mr Burstock.

4. Übersetzen Sie.

a. Meine Eltern hätten „nicht davon geträumt", das Land zu verkaufen.
b. Meine Eltern hätten das Land nicht verkauft.
c. Ich hätte den Fernseher nicht in die Küche gestellt.
d. Sie hätte den Fernseher nie in die Küche gestellt.
e. Ich hätte den Job (nicht) genommen.
f. Ich hätte nicht im Traum daran gedacht, den Job zu nehmen.
g. Seine Familie hätte ihm geholfen.
h. Seine Familie hätte ihm helfen können.
i. Er hätte das Land verkaufen können.
j. Wir hätten den Fernseher in die Küche stellen können.

8 A tourist spot

Leute unterhalten sich über Malta, die Inselrepublik südlich von Sizilien, ein bevorzugtes Ferienziel sonnenhungriger englischer Touristen und anglophiler, d. h. england- und englischbegeisterter Kontinentaleuropäer. Diesmal ist der erste Text ein Dialog; die Texte 2 und 3 mit *background*-Informationen über Malta haben schriftsprachlichen Charakter. In der Tonaufnahme sind alle drei Texte mit britischem Akzent gesprochen.

Malta: Sunshine, water and the stamp of history

A paradise for Anglophiles

A: Malta's always been a favourite among British holidaymakers, hasn't it?
B: Yes, in a way it's seen as an English-type resort. Visitors from other European countries tend to avoid it.
A: Except for Anglophiles.
B: Oh, it's an Anglophile's dream, of course: they speak English, the food's English, and they drive like the English …
A: They drive on the left?
B: Yes, they do.
A: But the weather isn't English, is it?
B: No, far from it. It's the sort of climate you get that far down in the Mediterranean: hot and dry in the summer, and the sea's nice and warm.
A: What about prices?
B: Well, Malta used to have a reputation for being "cheap and cheerful", but that's been changing.
A: It's getting more expensive, is it?
B: Yes. You could say the Maltese tourist industry is moving upmarket. They're improving their hotels and other facilities in order to attract tourists with more money.

Wortschatz

Anglophile	anglophiler Mensch / Englandfreund
Malta is our favourite *BE* / *AE* favorite (country)	Malta ist unser Lieblingsland
holidaymaker *BE* / vacationer *AE*	Urlauber(in)
in a way	in gewisser Weise/Hinsicht
resort	Urlaubsort
visitor	Besucher(in)
except for	abgesehen von; bis auf
the sort of climate	die Art von Klima
that far down	so weit unten
in the Mediterranean	im Mittelmeer
M. used to have a reputation	M. hatte früher einen/den Ruf
cheerful	fröhlich; vergnügt; heiter
the Maltese tourist industry	die maltesische Fremdenindustrie
move upmarket	(*etwa:*) das Niveau anheben
improve something	etwas verbessern
facilities	(*hier* Fremdenverkehrs-)Einrichtungen
in order to attract tourists	um Touristen anzuziehen

Verständnis- und Wortschatztest

a. Malta has always been a ..... among British holidaymakers because it's seen as a kind of English ..... ☐ b. It's an Anglophile's dream for three reasons: ... ☐ c. Fortunately for tourists the climate isn't English – it's ..... ☐ d. Malta used to have a reputation for being "cheap and cheerful" but in recent years things have been ..... ☐ e. The Maltese are ..... their tourist facilities in order to ..... tourists with more money.

Malta: a profile

The Republic of Malta consists of a small group of islands lying about 60 miles south of Sicily and about halfway between Gibraltar and Suez.
Average temperatures are 27 °C in July and 14 °C in January.
Malta has a population of about 350,000, 97 per cent of which are Roman Catholic. The official languages are Maltese and English.
Major industries – apart from tourism – are ship repair, shipbuilding, food and textiles.
For its small population, Malta has an extremely active press, publishing in both Maltese and English. Television is also bilingual, and about half the programmes are produced locally.

Wortschatz

the republic of Malta	die Republik Malta
consist of	bestehen aus
island	Insel
lie – lay – lain	liegen – lag – gelegen
60 miles south of Italy	60 Meilen südlich von Sizilien
halfway between G. and S.	auf halbem Wege / in der Mitte zwischen G. und S.
the average temperature	die Durchschnittstemperatur
14 °C (= 14 degrees Celsius)	14 ° Celsius
population	Bevölkerung(szahl)
official language	Amtssprache
Maltese	Maltesisch; maltesisch
major industries	wichtige Industriezweige
apart from tourism	abgesehen vom Fremdenverkehr
ship repair	Schiffsreparatur
shipbuilding	Schiff(s)bau
food	Nahrungsmittel; Lebensmittel
textiles	Textilien
an extremely active press	eine äußerst aktive Presse
publish	publizieren; veröffentlichen
bilingual	zweisprachig
half the programmes *BE* / *AE* programs are produced locally	die Hälfte der Programme wird im Lande / in Malta produziert

Verständnis- und Wortschatztest

a. The Republic of Malta ..... of a small group of islands. ☐ b. It ..... about 60 miles south of Sicily. ☐ c. ..... temperatures are 27 °C in July and 14 °C in January. ☐ d. 97 ..... of Malta's population are Roman Catholic. ☐ e. The ..... languages are Maltese and English. ☐ f. Malta's extremely active press ..... in both Maltese and English. ☐ g. A republic .... a king or queen. ☐ h. A mile is ..... than a kilometre. ☐ i. A ..... person is someone who is able to speak two languages equally well.

Malta in the past

Because of its strategic importance, Malta was invaded many times and frequently changed rulers in its long and turbulent history. In 1798 it was occupied by the French, and in 1800 it was taken by the British, who ruled until Malta's independence in 1964.

During the Second World War Malta withstood heavy bombing by the Germans and Italians, and in 1942 it was awarded the George Cross for its heroism.

In 1974 Malta became a republic within the Commonwealth.

Since the early 1970s, Malta has followed a policy of strict nonalignment.

Wortschatz

in the past	in der Vergangenheit
because of its strategic importance	wegen seiner strategischen Bedeutung
invade a country	in ein Land einfallen; ein Land überfallen
Malta frequently changed rulers	Malta hat häufig die Herrscher gewechselt
in its turbulent history	in seiner turbulenten/stürmischen Geschichte
occupy a country	ein Land besetzen
take a country	ein Land einnehmen/erobern
rule	herrschen
until Malta's independence	bis zu Maltas Unabhängigkeit
during the Second World War	während des Zweiten Weltkriegs
withstand heavy bombing (– withstood – withstood)	schweren Bombenangriffen standhalten
the Germans and Italians	die Deutschen und Italiener
Malta was awarded the George Cross	Malta wurde das Georgskreuz verliehen (*1940 von George VI. gestifteter Tapferkeitsorden, besonders für Zivilisten*)
heroism	Heldentum
within the Commonwealth	innerhalb des Commonwealth (*lockere Verbindung früher von Großbritannien beherrschter, heute unabhängiger und gleichberechtigter Staaten*)
follow a policy	eine Politik verfolgen
nonalignment	Bündnisfreiheit; Blockfreiheit
policy of nonalignment	(*auch:*) Neutralitätspolitik

Verständnis- und Wortschatztest

a. Malta has a long and turbulent ..... ☐ b. Because of its strategic ....., it was ..... many times. ☐ c. It frequently ..... rulers. ☐ d. The French ..... it in 1798, and in 1800 the British ..... it from the French. ☐ e. During the Second World War Malta ..... heavy bombing. ☐ f. In 1942 it was ..... the George Cross for its heroism. ☐ g. Malta ..... independent in 1964. ☐ h. Since the early 1970s, it has ..... a policy of strict nonalignment.

8 Erklärungen

1. Verlaufsform und einfache Form des Perfekts

a. That has been changing.	*(Etwa:) Das ändert sich in letzter Zeit.*
b. That has changed.	*Das hat sich geändert.*

a. Der „Vorgang des Sichänderns" hat in der Vergangenheit begonnen und dauert zur Zeit noch an.
b. Der „Vorgang des Sichänderns" ist abgeschlossen.

2. Perfekt oder Vergangenheit?

a. Malta was invaded many times.	*Malta ist häufig überfallen worden.*
b. Malta has been invaded many times.	*Malta ist häufig überfallen worden.*

(a) und (b) unterscheiden sich durch den Zeitraum, in dem Invasionen stattfanden oder hätten stattfinden können. In (a) schließt dieser Zeitraum die Gegenwart *nicht* ein, während der Gebrauch des Perfekts in (b) den gedachten Zusatz „bis heute" bedingt.
In den beiden folgenden Beispielen ist der Gebrauch der Vergangenheit (c) durch die Zeitbestimmungen der Vergangenheit (*in 1798, in 1800, until 1964*) und der Gebrauch des Perfekts (d) durch den Bezug zur Gegenwart („bis heute") bedingt.

c. In 1798 it was occupied by the French, and in 1800 it was taken by the British, who ruled until 1964.
d. Since the early 1970s, Malta has followed a policy of strict nonalignment.

3. Positives Frageanhängsel (*question tag*) nach positivem Vorderteil

a. It's getting more expensive, is it?	*Es wird also teurer, was?*
b. It's getting more expensive, isn't it?	*Es wird teurer, nicht wahr?*

Satz (a) „positiv – positiv" entspricht nicht der Regel, daß auf ein positives Vorderteil ein negatives Anhängsel und auf ein negatives Vorderteil ein positives Anhängsel folgt (vgl. S. 46). Diese Variante (a) „positiv – positiv" ist seltener als die Konstruktionen „positiv – negativ" (b) und „negativ – positiv". Sie drückt hier aus, daß der Sprecher das Ausgesagte aus dem vorher Gesagten schließt und eine Bestätigung seiner Aussage erwartet. Die Form „positiv – negativ" (b) dagegen wäre gebraucht worden, wenn der Sprecher das Ausgesagte bereits gewußt, also nicht aus dem vorher Gesagten geschlossen hätte.

4. Nennung des „Handlungsurhebers" im Passivsatz

Passiv: In 1798 Malta was occupied by the French.
Aktiv: In 1798 the French occupied Malta.

Der „Handlungsurheber" wird im Passivsatz mit *by* angeschlossen. Diese Nennung des Urhebers ist die Ausnahme, nicht die Regel, denn die Passivform wird ja gerade dann bevorzugt, wenn der Urheber nicht bekannt oder in dem gegebenen Zusammenhang nicht von Bedeutung ist.

1. Setzen Sie die passende Form der eingeklammerten Verben ein.

a. Why (you drive) on the right? In this country they (drive) on the left.
b. Malta used to have a reputation for (be) "cheap and cheerful".
c. The Maltese tourist industry (move) steadily upmarket in the last few years, and that means that hotel rooms (get) more and more expensive.
d. This hotel (be) improved a lot since our last stay here.
e. Malta (regard) as an English-type resort – tourists from other European countries tend (avoid) it. As a result, Malta (rely) on the British tourists – without them there (probably not be) a tourist industry.
f. "You (come) here every year, don't you?" – "Oh yes, we (make) a lot of Maltese friends over the years that we (come) here, and so we (come) back to see them every year."
g. "How many times (you be) here?" – "Nineteen times, and we hope we (be) back for the twentieth time next year."
h. During the Second World War, Malta (withstand) heavy bombing.
i. Since the early 1970s, Malta (follow) a policy of nonalignment.

2. Setzen Sie ins Passiv wie im Beispiel.

Columbus discovered America. – America was discovered by Columbus.

a. In 870 the Arabs invaded Malta.
b. A. F. Richards designed the new shopping centre.
c. A sunny climate attracts tourists.
d. Tomorrow the Queen will entertain the President.
e. Excessive noise can cause ulcers.
f. The drought has devastated most crops.
g. The council is building a number of low-priced houses.
h. Non-British tourists tend to avoid Malta.

3. Setzen Sie passende Präpositionen ein.

among, apart from, as, because of, for, in, since, until, within

Malta has always been a favourite ..... British holidaymakers. It is often seen ..... an English-type resort. ..... tourism, ship repair and shipbuilding are important industries. ..... its strategic importance, Malta frequently changed rulers ..... its long and turbulent history. The British ruled ..... over 160 years ..... Malta's independence in 1964. ..... 1974 Malta has been a republic ..... the Commonwealth.

4. Übersetzen Sie.

a. Malta ist bei englischen Urlaubern besonders beliebt (*a favourite*).
b. Es hatte früher den Ruf, besonders billig zu sein.
c. In letzter Zeit (*recently*) versucht es Touristen mit mehr Geld anzuziehen.
d. In den letzten Jahren sind neue Hotels gebaut und alte verbessert worden.
e. Malta liegt etwa auf halbem Wege zwischen Gibraltar und Suez.
f. Über 160 Jahre lang war Malta unter britischer Herrschaft (*rule*).
g. Seit 1974 ist es eine Republik innerhalb des Commonwealth.

9 B & B

Wie man in London billig wohnen, sich wie zu Hause und trotzdem wie ein Londoner fühlen kann – der erste Text (eine Originalwerbeanzeige, allerdings mit verändertem Namen) sagt's Ihnen. Text 2 ist ein Dialog, wie er in einer solchen Zimmervermittlung alle Tage vorkommt, und in Text 3 bedankt sich ein zufriedener Gast brieflich für genossene Gastfreundschaft. In der Tonaufnahme sind alle drei Texte mit britischem Akzent gesprochen.

Looking for accommodation

An agency

LONDON BED AND BREAKFAST SERVICES
Stay in London as a guest in a real London home

You can spend your holiday in the unique atmosphere of a real British home, live in the London that only the locals really know and have all the comforts and personal service that would cost a fortune in a hotel.
London Bed and Breakfast Services represent over 500 rooms which have been carefully selected and approved by LBBS staff. They are normally first floor rooms adjacent to bathrooms and you will be given your own key to come and go as you please.
The traditional friendliness and hospitality of Londoners is famous the world over.
Contact us so you can experience the real London from only £10 a night.
London Bed and Breakfast Services
198 Cromwell Road, London SW5 0SW
Telephone 01–373 3536

Wortschatz

B & B (= bed and breakfast)	Zimmer mit Frühstück
agency	Agentur; (*z. B.* Zimmer-)Vermittlung
as a guest	als Gast
spend (– spent – spent) a holiday	einen Urlaub verbringen
the unique atmosphere	die einzigartige Atmosphäre
all the comforts	alle Bequemlichkeiten
cost (– cost – cost) a fortune	ein Vermögen kosten
represent	vertreten; repräsentieren
carefully selected	sorgfältig ausgewählt
the rooms are approved	die Zimmer sind genehmigt/empfohlen
by LBBS staff	durch Mitarbeiter der LBBS
first floor *BE* / *AE* second floor	erster Stock
adjacent to bathrooms	angrenzend an Badezimmer; neben Badezimmern (gelegen)
key	Schlüssel
come and go as you please	kommen und gehen nach Belieben
friendliness	Freundlichkeit
hospitality	Gastfreundlichkeit; Gastfreundschaft
is famous the world over	wird überall in der Welt gerühmt
contact us	setzen Sie sich mit uns in Verbindung
so you can experience the real London	damit Sie das wirkliche/echte London erleben können

Verständnis- und Wortschatztest

a. *B & B* is short for ..... □ b. What does *LBBS* stand for? □ c. Does the agency represent hotels? □ d. What are two advantages of bed-and-breakfast places? □ e. Hotel rooms *cost a fortune* – another way of saying *cost a fortune*? □ f. What does *01* in the telephone number stand for?

Making a booking

A: I'm looking for private accommodation for three nights from today – bed and breakfast.

B: That'd be just for yourself?

A: Yes.

B: And did you have a particular area in mind?

A: Yes, somewhere central, in the West End if possible – Oxford Street, Piccadilly …

B: Belgrave Road in Victoria is the best I can do. There aren't many bed and breakfasts in the Oxford Street area.

A: Belgrave Road sounds okay. It's not far from Victoria Station, is it?

B: A few minutes' walk. Buckingham Palace isn't very far either, and there's a bus stop nearby.

A: That should be all right then. How much is it?

B: Twenty pounds. It's a nice place, well looked after. The landlady's very friendly. She's got a dog – you won't mind the dog, will you?

A: No, I like dogs. There's a bathroom, is there?

B: Oh yes. It's got everything. I'm sure you'll like it. – Now, let me write everything down for you …

Wortschatz

make a booking	eine Buchung/Reservierung vornehmen
look for private accommodation	eine Privatunterkunft suchen
that'd (= that would) be just for yourself?	das wäre nur für Sie / für Sie allein?
did you have a particular area in mind?	hatten Sie an eine bestimmte Gegend gedacht?
in Victoria (= in the Victoria Station area)	in der Gegend der Victoria Station
the best I can do	das Beste, was ich Ihnen anbieten kann
a few minutes' walk	ein paar Minuten zu Fuß
isn't very far either	ist auch nicht weit (entfernt)
there's a bus stop nearby	eine Bushaltestelle ist in der Nähe
how much is it?	was kostet es?
well looked after	sehr gepflegt
landlady	(Zimmer-)Vermieterin, Wirtin
you won't (= will not) mind the dog, will you?	der Hund wird Ihnen doch nichts ausmachen, oder?
it's got everything	(*etwa:*) es ist alles vorhanden
I'm sure you'll like it	es wird Ihnen sicher gefallen

Verständnis- und Wortschatztest

a. I'm looking for private accommodation – just for ….. – for three nights. ☐ b. I'd like it to be somewhere central, if ….. ☐ c. A bed-and-breakfast place in Belgrave Road would ….. okay. ☐ d. It's just a few minutes' ….. from Victoria Station. ☐ e. Twenty pounds …..n't too much for a place that's pleasant and well looked ….. ☐ f. It doesn't worry me if the landlady's got a dog – I don't ….. dogs. ☐ g. Is there a bathroom? – Yes, there's one ….. to the bedroom.

A thank-you letter

Dear Mrs Perkins,

I thoroughly enjoyed my recent stay at your house and would like to thank you once again for looking after me so well and telling me so many interesting things about London.

I enclose the photo I took of you and Bonnie watching TV in the evening. I like that alert, friendly look she has – she's really a lovely dog.

I look forward to my next visit to London and will let you know the date in good time.

With best wishes,

Yours sincerely,

Torsten Hartmann

Wortschatz

thank-you letter	Dankbrief
I thoroughly enjoyed my stay	ich habe meinen Aufenthalt sehr genossen
my recent stay	mein kürzlicher Aufenthalt
I'd (= I would) like to thank you once again	ich möchte Ihnen noch einmal danken
for looking after me so well	dafür, daß Sie sich so nett um mich gekümmert haben
enclose a photo	(dem Brief) ein Foto beilegen
take a photo (– took – taken)	ein Foto / eine Aufnahme machen
watch TV/television	fernsehen
a friendly look	ein freundlicher Blick
a lovely dog	ein reizender Hund
my next visit to London	mein nächster Besuch in London
I'll let you know the date in good time	ich werde Ihnen das Datum rechtzeitig mitteilen
with best wishes	(*als Briefschluß etwa:*) mit (allen) guten Wünschen
yours sincerely	(*etwa:*) (mit freundlichen Grüßen) Ihr

Verständnis- und Wortschatztest

a. Mrs Perkins was Torsten's ..... in London. □ b. Torsten is writing to her to thank her for ..... after him so well. □ c. He thoroughly enjoyed his recent *stay in* London – another expression for *stay in*? □ d. One evening during his stay in London Torsten ..... a photo of Mrs Perkins and her dog ..... TV in the evening. □ e. In the photo, Bonnie doesn't look at all sleepy – she looks very ..... □ f. He's looking ..... to staying with Mrs Perkins again the next time he's in London.

9 Erklärungen

1. Vom Deutschen abweichender Gebrauch des unbestimmten Artikels (*a/an*)

a hundred times a day	*hundertmal am/pro Tag*
the speed limit is 55 miles an hour	*55 Meilen in der / pro Stunde*
only £10 a night	*nur zehn Pfund die/pro Nacht*
Steve is a steward	*Steve ist Steward*
I'm a school governor	*ich bin Mitglied des Schulbeirats*
he's become an actor	*er ist Schauspieler geworden*
stay here as a guest	*wohnen Sie hier als Gast*
I've got a headache	*ich habe Kopfschmerzen*
just a moment	*Moment mal*
he brought the plane to a halt	*er brachte die Maschine zum Stehen*

2. Was *-'s* alles bedeuten kann

-'s = Genitivendung:	The landlady's dog is very friendly.
-'s = *is*:	The landlady's very friendly.
-'s = *has*:	The landlady's got a very friendly dog.
-'s = *us*:	Let's go to Buckingham Palace first.

Beachten Sie auch die Pluralform der Genitivendung:

Singular:	the youngster's friends	*die Freunde des Jugendlichen*
Plural:	the youngsters' friends	*die Freunde der Jugendlichen*
Singular:	our neighbour's house	*das Haus unseres Nachbarn*
Plural:	our neighbours' house	*das Haus unserer Nachbarn*
Singular:	it's a minute's walk	*es ist eine Minute zu Fuß*
Plural:	it's a few minutes' walk	*es ist ein paar Minuten zu Fuß*

3. Positiv: *too/also* – negativ: *either*

Positiv: Sandra gets discounted tickets too.
Sandra bekommt auch/ebenfalls verbilligte Flugscheine.

Negativ: Sandra doesn't get discounted tickets either.
Sandra bekommt auch/ebenfalls keine verbilligten Flugscheine.

Verneintes *auch/ebenfalls* heißt also *either*. Weitere Beispiele:

Positiv:
The newsreader also blamed the increasing pressure of the job for his decision.
… *gab auch dem zunehmenden Arbeitsdruck die Schuld …*
Television is also bilingual. / Television is bilingual too.
Das Fernsehen ist ebenfalls zweisprachig.

Negativ:
Buckingham Palace isn't very far either. *B. P. ist auch nicht weit (entfernt).*
"My parents would never have dreamed of entertaining in the kitchen." – "Mine wouldn't have either." … *„Meine auch nicht."*

1. Mit oder ohne *-ly*? Setzen Sie das eingeklammerte Wort an passender Stelle in der richtigen Form ein.

a. Does it only cost £10? (real)
b. Is he a Londoner? (real)
c. The price is £10. (normal)
d. Our guests stay at least a week. (normal)
e. The rooms have been selected by our staff. (careful)
f. Planning is important. (careful)
g. Please contact us. (immediate)
h. I'm not keen to see the sights. (particular)
i. Is there any area you'd prefer? (particular)
j. It's difficult to find accommodation. (suitable)
k. It sounds very interesting. (certain)

2. Übersetzen Sie.

a. Diese Art von Service würde in einem Hotel ein Vermögen kosten.
b. Sie können kommen und gehen, wie es Ihnen gefällt.
c. Sie spielt oft mit dem Hund unserer Nachbarn.
d. Die Tochter unserer Londoner (Zimmer-)Wirtin ist Stewardeß bei British Airways.
e. Zum Buckingham Palace sind es nur ein paar Minuten zu Fuß.
f. Belgrave Road wäre in Ordnung – Sloane Street wäre auch okay.
g. Wird das Badezimmer neben meinem Zimmer auch von anderen Gästen benutzt?
h. Wir haben keinen Hund, und wir haben auch keine Katze.
i. Ich habe nichts gegen Hunde, und ich habe auch nichts gegen Katzen.
j. Wir freuen uns auf unseren nächsten Londonbesuch.

ANGLOPHILE'S CROSSWORD

ACROSS

1 £12 a night for bed and ..... – that's not expensive.
7 "I'd rather fly than drive." – "..... too."
8 Half ..... TV programmes are produced locally.
9 The sea's ..... and warm, isn't it?
10 A US boxer who was world heavyweight champion three times.
11 She ..... the TV to get her off to sleep.
12 They tell us the number of accidents has ..... down.
13 British Airways.
14 ..... gut feeling is that flying is not safe.
15 You can stay with us ..... a guest.
16 It can make ..... the difference whether you do or don't.

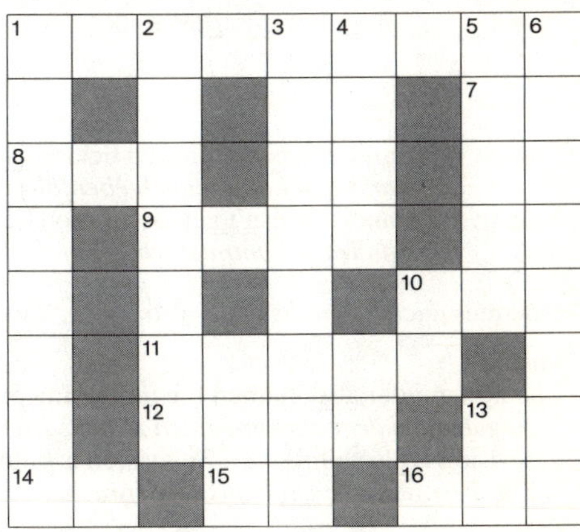

DOWN

1 There's a ..... adjacent to the bedroom.
2 Do you always watch TV in the .....?
3 A lot of people entertain in their .....
4 Armed forces personnel can get them tax-.....
5 It's a ..... and stuffy place.
6 Grand Central .....
10 You can hear practically every move ..... they walk around.

10 Hotels

Text 1 informiert Sie über einen amerikanischen Hoteltyp, der ein besonders günstiges Preis-Leistungs-Verhältnis bietet: *budget hotels*. Text 2 ist eine *key card*, wie man sie beim „Einchecken“ in ein Hotel erhält. Bei Text 3 handelt es sich um einen Dialog am Hotelempfang: ein Gast möchte sein Zimmer erst im Laufe des Nachmittags räumen.
In der Tonaufnahme ist Text 1 amerikanisch, Text 2 und 3 dagegen sind britisch gesprochen.

Budget hotels

As a salesperson who's on the road for something like 45 weeks a year, you know there's one thing you want in the evening: a hotel that offers comfort, cleanliness, an efficient switchboard and a friendly staff – all at a reasonable price.
You can't afford to stay at the Hilton, Sheraton or Holiday Inn, so it's got to be a budget hotel.
Budget hotels used to be sleazy places with smelly rooms, filthy floors and paper-thin walls. But in the United States today there's a new class of "limited-service" hotels that offer excellent value for money: a bright, clean room with comfortable beds, a remote-control colour TV, and a perfectly adequate bathroom.
Of course you won't find the sheets pulled down and a chocolate on your pillow in the evening. And budget hotels don't have restaurants, bars, banquet halls or room service. But there will be a pleasant coffee shop where you can get a decent breakfast with oatmeal or grits, croissants and juice all included in the price.

Wortschatz

budget (hotel/tour/meals etc.)	billig; preisgünstig
salesperson	(Reise-)Vertreter(in); Reisende(r)
cleanliness ['klenlɪnɪs]	Reinlichkeit
efficient	leistungsfähig; gut funktionierend
switchboard	(Telefon-)Zentrale, Vermittlung
a friendly staff	freundliches Personal
a reasonable price	ein vernünftiger/angemessener Preis
a sleazy hotel	ein schäbiges/heruntergekommenes Hotel
smelly	übelriechend; muffig
a filthy floor	ein schmutziger/dreckiger Fußboden
paper-thin walls	hauchdünne Wände
limited-service hotel	Hotel mit begrenztem Service
offer excellent value for money	äußerst preiswert sein
a bright, clean room	ein helles, sauberes Zimmer
comfortable beds	bequeme Betten
a remote-control colour TV (*AE* color)	ein Farbfernseher mit Fernbedienung
perfectly adequate	vollkommen hinreichend/ausreichend
pull down the sheet	die Bettdecke aufschlagen
a chocolate on your pillow	eine Praline auf dem Kopfkissen
banquet hall	Festsaal
room service	Zimmerservice
coffee shop	(kleines) Restaurant (bes. in Hotel)
a decent breakfast	ein anständiges Frühstück
oatmeal *AE* / *BE* porridge	Haferbrei
grits *AE*	(Brei aus grobem Mais-, Weizen- oder Reismehl)
juice	Saft
included in the price	im Preis inbegriffen

Royal Henley Hotel

Coventry Street, London W1
Telephone 01–930 4720

KEY CARD

The Management and the Staff of the Royal Henley Hotel welcome you and hope you will enjoy your stay.

Please keep this card with you at all times. However, would you make sure that your key is always left at the Reception Desk whenever you leave the hotel. The card must be shown if you wish to charge any bill, including meals, to your room account.

Our checkout time is midday. If you wish to retain your room after 12.00 noon, for which an additional charge may be applicable, please notify Reception. If you wish to extend your stay, please give our Reception as much notice as possible.

Please show this card each time you collect your key from Reception.

Verständnis- und Wortschatztest (Text 1)

a. A *salesperson* is someone who travels to visit ..... ☐ b. A *budget* hotel is one that ..... ☐ c. Hilton or Sheraton hotels are not ..... ☐ d. In the past, budget hotels were often ..... ☐ e. Modern budget hotels offer ..... ☐ f. A *filthy* floor is one that's ..... ☐ g. A *smelly* room is a room ..... ☐ h. If the room has paper-thin walls, you can ..... ☐ i. In a budget hotel, you won't be served breakfast in your room, but you can have it in ..... ☐ j. You don't have to pay extra for breakfast – it's .....

Verständnis- und Wortschatztest (Text 2)

a. When must the key card be shown? ☐ b. Does the hotel want you to take your key with you when you go out? ☐ c. By what time are you supposed to have left your room on the day of departure? ☐ d. What can you do if you want to keep your room for longer than the official checkout time?

Wortschatz

key card	(„Schlüsselkarte"); Zimmerausweis
management	Direktion; Geschäftsleitung
welcome someone	jem. begrüßen
keep this card with you	behalten Sie diese Karte bei sich
however	jedoch
would you make sure	achten Sie bitte darauf
leave at the reception desk	an der Rezeption / am Empfang lassen
whenever you leave the hotel	immer wenn Sie das Hotel verlassen
the card must be shown	die Karte muß vorgezeigt werden
charge a bill to an account	eine Rechnung einem Konto belasten (lassen)
including meals	einschließlich Mahlzeiten
checkout	Abreise (aus dem Hotel)
midday / noon	Mittag
if you wish to retain your room	wenn Sie Ihr Zimmer behalten möchten
an additional charge	eine zusätzliche Gebühr
applicable	anwendbar; zutreffend; fällig
for which an additional charge may be applicable	(*etwa:*) was zusätzlich berechnet werden kann
notify someone	jem. Bescheid sagen
extend one's stay	seinen Aufenthalt verlängern
give as much notice as possible	so frühzeitig wie möglich Bescheid sagen
each time you collect your key	jedesmal, wenn Sie Ihren Schlüssel abholen

Staying on

A: Can I help you, madam?

B: Yes, please. I'm in room 409 and I'm due to check out today. But I was wondering ... could I keep the room till about four o'clock this afternoon?

A: Just a moment, please, madam. I'll see if it can be arranged. (*Makes a phone call.*) I'm afraid we're rather heavily booked at the moment, but I could arrange for you to stay on till three o'clock free of charge. Would that help?

B: Oh yes, definitely. Thank you very much indeed.

A: But could you please make sure that you've checked out by three at the latest so the room can be made up in time for the next guests.

B: Yes, of course. Thanks very much.

Wortschatz

I'm due to check out today	ich soll heute abreisen (*d. h., das ist so vereinbart, vorgesehen*)
I was wondering ...	ich wollte mal fragen
could I keep the room?	könnte ich das Zimmer behalten?
I'll see if it can be arranged	ich schau mal, ob sich das machen läßt
make a phone call	einen Anruf machen; telefonieren
I'm afraid	ich fürchte; leider
we're rather heavily booked	wir sind ziemlich ausgebucht
stay on till three o'clock	noch bis drei Uhr bleiben
free of charge	kostenlos
yes, definitely	ja, auf jeden Fall
thank you very much indeed	ganz herzlichen Dank
check out by three at the latest	spätestens bis drei das Zimmer räumen
the room can be made up	das Zimmer kann gemacht werden
in time	rechtzeitig

Verständnis- und Wortschatztest

a. I'm ..... to check out today but I'd like to ..... my stay. ☐ b. If you'll hold on a moment, I'll see if it can be ..... ☐ c. Would it ..... if you could ..... on till three o'clock? ☐ d. Yes, definitely. How much ..... that be? ☐ e. It'd be free of ..... ☐ f. Thank you very much ..... ☐ g. Could you please make ..... that you've checked out ..... three o'clock at the latest so the room can be ..... up in time for the next guests. ☐ h. To *extend* one's stay means to stay ..... ☐ i. To *check out* means to ..... ☐ j. To *retain* a room means to ..... ☐ k. If the hotel is rather *heavily booked*, it's .....

1. *to*-Infinitiv und *-ing*-Form nach Kettenausdrücken

Als Kettenausdrücke bezeichnen wir Wörter, an die ein Verb angehängt werden kann. Der Kettenausdruck kann ein Verb (a, d, e), ein Substantiv (b, f) oder ein Adjektiv (c, g) sein. Das angehängte Verb ist in den meisten Fällen ein *to*-Infinitiv (a–c) oder eine *-ing*-Form (d–g); ist es eine *-ing*-Form, so steht sie entweder allein (d) oder nach einer Präposition (e–g).

a. Kettenverb + *to*-Infinitiv:

He had/helped/managed/tried/wanted to bring the car to a halt.

b. Kettensubstantiv + *to*-Infinitiv:

There was no chance/opportunity to do it. It's the only way to do it.

c. Kettenadjektiv + *to*-Infinitiv:

They're bound/due/forced/unable to leave the area.

d. Kettenverb + *-ing*-Form:

I'd consider/enjoy/miss doing it.

e. Kettenverb + Präposition + *-ing*-Form:

I wouldn't look forward to / dream of / feel like going there.

f. Kettensubstantiv + Präposition + *-ing*-Form:

He gave the impression of / He had a reputation for being very selfish.

g. Kettenadjektiv + Präposition + *-ing*-Form:

I'm bad at / good at / sick of / used to saying no.

2. *Use(d) to*

Is flying safer today than it used to be?
Ist das Fliegen heute sicherer, als es „zu sein pflegte" / als es früher war?
Malta used to have a reputation for being "cheap and cheerful".
M. pflegte den Ruf zu haben / hatte früher den Ruf, billig und vergnügt zu sein.
Budget hotels used to be sleazy places.
Billighotels pflegten verkommene Etablissements zu sein / waren früher …

Frageform und verneinte Form werden meistens wie folgt gebildet:

She used to live here, didn't she? *Sie hat früher hier gewohnt, nicht wahr?*
Did(n't) she use to live here? *Hat sie (nicht) früher hier gewohnt?*
She didn't use to live here. *Sie hat hier früher nicht gewohnt.*

Dieses Verb *used to* darf nicht verwechselt werden mit dem Adjektiv *used to*, das in Lektion 4 vorkam:
They're now used to having two incomes.
Sie sind jetzt daran gewöhnt, zwei Einkommen zu haben.

1. Hängen Sie das Verb an einen Kettenausdruck an.

The pilot brought the plane to a halt. (manage)
The pilot managed to bring the plane to a halt.

a. The Royal was quite a good hotel. (used to)
b. It's a general trend. (seem)
c. The farmers are selling off their cattle. (have to)
d. We're moving to Basingstoke. (consider)
e. We're buying a new car. (plan)
f. I'm seeing her next week. (look forward to)
g. I'd stay at a budget hotel. (prefer)
h. She was very confident. (give the impression of)
i. Many young couples left the area. (be forced)
j. I've always travelled by train. (enjoy)
k. Work begins this morning. (be due)
l. Malta used to be "cheap and cheerful". (have a reputation for)
m. I have the dog around me all day. (be used to)
n. My parents would never have entertained in the kitchen. (dream of)

2. Setzen Sie Verben in der passenden Form ein.

a. The hotel I ..... at last night was comfortable, clean and efficient.
b. There was a nice coffee shop where I ..... an excellent breakfast.
c. When I went to the reception desk to ..... my key, I realized that I couldn't identify myself because I ..... my key card in my room.
d. I normally keep the card on me all the time because you also have to ..... it if you want to have a meal in the hotel restaurant ..... to your room account.
e. The man at the reception desk was very helpful. When I ..... him if I could ..... my room till about four o'clock, he let me have it free of charge.
f. Of course, by ..... the room so long you make it difficult for them ..... it up in time for the next guests.
g. When I travel, I try ..... those sleazy places with their smelly rooms and paper-thin walls.

3. Setzen Sie passende Entsprechungen für deutsch *bis* ein.

a. Could I keep the room ..... about four o'clock this afternoon?
b. Here is the forecast for southeast England ..... dusk on Sunday.
c. I work nine ..... five like most office people.
d. Please make sure that you've checked out ..... three at the latest.

4. Übersetzen Sie in Anlehnung an Text 1.

a. Als Handelsvertreter, der jedes Jahr so etwa 45 Wochen unterwegs ist, wünscht man ⟨sich⟩ ein Hotel, das ⟨einem⟩ ein sauberes Zimmer mit einem bequemen Bett, einem Farbfernseher und einem vernünftigen Badezimmer bietet.
b. Ich kann mir nicht leisten, im Hilton oder Sheraton zu wohnen – es muß schon ein preiswertes Hotel sein.
c. „Budget hotels" waren früher schmuddelige Etablissements mit miefigen Zimmern und hauchdünnen Wänden.
d. Die heutigen „budget hotels" bieten Bequemlichkeit, Sauberkeit und freundlichen Service zu einem vernünftigen Preis.
e. Sie haben kein Restaurant und keinen Zimmerservice, aber sie haben einen „coffee shop", wo man ein anständiges Frühstück bekommt.

11 Taxi!

Vom Taxifahren handeln die Texte dieser Lektion: Der erste eine wahre Geschichte von einer bald 1000 Kilometer weiten Taxifahrt durch England und Schottland, der zweite ein Dialog mit dem Fahrer in einem New Yorker Taxi, der dritte ein Informationstext über die Kunst des Taxifahrens in New York.
In der Tonaufnahme ist der erste Text – entsprechend der Herkunft von Dr. Cummings – mit einem leichten schottischen Akzent gesprochen. Im zweiten Text spricht der *taxi driver* mit amerikanischem, die Kundin dagegen mit einem „neutralen“ englischen Akzent. Der dritte Text wird im Stil einer amerikanischen Rundfunk- oder Fernsehreportage gelesen.

600 miles by taxi

FAMILY GP Dr Ian Cummings faced a real emergency when he arrived back at Gatwick Airport in the early morning and found himself stranded by the rail strike.

With no one to take surgery at his rural practice in Scotland, the desperate doctor did the only thing he could: he hailed a taxi.

Cabby Eddie Barnes was flabbergasted when the doctor told him his destination: Kilmorack in the Scottish Highlands.

But after a few minutes' haggling the taxi driver agreed to solve the doctor's dilemma, and for a round sum of £300 he set off on his first ever trip to Scotland.

They left Gatwick at 1 a.m. on Friday. Eleven weary hours later they pulled up outside the doctor's house just as the first patients began to queue up for the afternoon surgery.

Wortschatz

GP (= general practitioner) ***BE***	Arzt/Ärztin für Allgemeinmedizin
family doctor	Hausarzt; Hausärztin
face an emergency	mit einem Notfall konfrontiert sein
Gatwick Airport	(einer der 5 Londoner Flughafen)
be stranded	gestrandet sein; festsitzen
by the rail strike	durch den Eisenbahnerstreik
take surgery ***BE***	Sprechstunde halten
at his rural practice	in seiner Landpraxis
desperate	verzweifelt
hail a taxi	ein Taxi herbeiwinken/rufen/nehmen
cabby / cabbie / cab driver / taxi driver	Taxifahrer(in)
he was flabbergasted	er war platt
destination	Fahrtziel
in the Scottish Highlands	im schottischen Hochland
haggle	feilschen
agree to do something	sich bereit erklären, etw. zu tun
the doctor's dilemma	(Anspielung auf das gleichnamige Stück von Shaw [1906])
round sum	Pauschalbetrag
set off (– set – set)	aufbrechen
his first ever trip	die erste Fahrt seines Lebens
leave (– left – left) Gatwick	von Gatwick abfahren
weary	(sehr) müde; ermüdend
pull up outside the doctor's house	vor dem Haus des Arztes anhalten
queue up ***BE***	eine Schlange bilden; sich anstellen
the afternoon surgery ***BE***	die Nachmittagssprechstunde

Verständnis- und Wortschatztest

a. What's Ian Cummings' profession, and where's he from? □ b. What was the "emergency" he faced when he arrived at Gatwick? □ c. Why was he desperate to get home to Kilmorack? □ d. What was the only possible way of getting there? □ e. Why was the cabby flabbergasted? □ f. Had Eddie Barnes ever been to Scotland before? □ g. What time did they arrive, and what was the fare? □ h. Was the doctor back in time for his surgery?

Taking a cab in New York

A: The heliport on East 34th Street, please. D'you think you can make it in twenty minutes?

B: Sure – if we don't get stuck.

A: Hey. You're going west. Are you sure that's the shortest route?

B: You said the heliport, didn't you?

A: Yes – the one on East 34th Street.

B: Oh, I thought you said the one on the West Side. Sorry, I must have got you wrong.

A: Better get a move on now. If I miss the helicopter to Kennedy Airport, I'll never make my flight to Berlin.

B: We'll still get there in time, don't worry. (*A few blocks later:*) Just a few more blocks. The heliport's down there on the left. You'll have plenty of time. – Here we are now. That's four dollars sixty, and fifty cents for the bag – five dollars ten.

A: Here you are. Thanks a lot. Keep the change.

Wortschatz

heliport	Hubschrauberlandeplatz
East 34th Street	34. Straße, Ostseite
can you make it?	können Sie es schaffen?
sure	klar!
if we don't get stuck	wenn wir nicht steckenbleiben
hey!	he!
the shortest route	der kürzeste Weg
on the West Side	auf der Westseite (von Manhattan)
I must have got you wrong	ich muß Sie falsch verstanden haben
get a move on	sich beeilen
if I miss the helicopter	wenn ich den Hubschrauber verpasse
I'll never make my flight	schaffe ich meinen Flug nie
we'll still get there in time	wir kommen noch rechtzeitig hin
don't worry	machen Sie sich keine Sorgen
a few blocks later	ein paar (Quer-)Straßen später
down there on the left	da unten/hinten links
have plenty of time	viel Zeit haben
here we are now	so, da sind wir
that's four dollars sixty	das macht (dann) vier Dollar sechzig
bag	Tasche; Gepäckstück
thanks a lot	vielen Dank
here you are	(*wenn man jem. etw. reicht:*) bitte sehr
keep the change	(„behalten Sie das Wechselgeld") es stimmt so

Verständnis- und Wortschatztest

a. A heliport is a small airport for ..... ☐ b. One of New York's heliports is on ..... ☐ c. There's also a heliport on the ..... ☐ d. I thought you said "West Side". I must have ..... ☐ e. If I miss the helicopter, I'll never ..... my flight to Berlin. ☐ f. That's five ..... ten altogether. ☐ g. Here you are. Keep the .....

Taxis in New York: a few tips

New York taxis are painted bright yellow. If you want one, go to the edge of the sidewalk, wave your arm and hope for the best.
A cab that's available has the TAXI light on; ON RADIO CALL means it has been reserved by someone else; OFF DUTY means the driver is going home or returning to his garage.
Even if you don't know your way around, give the impression you know exactly where you're going, how to get there and how long it should take. It's also a good idea if you have a map to follow the route the driver is taking.
Make sure the driver doesn't "forget" to turn on the meter. That would be illegal and almost certainly to your disadvantage.
The driver must be able to change a $10 bill. Be prepared to pay a small extra charge for suitcases and for trips at night or on Sundays. Of course, you also have to pay all bridge and tunnel tolls. It's usual to tip the driver 15 to 20 per cent of the total fare.

Wortschatz

a few tips	ein paar Tips/Hinweise/Ratschläge
painted bright yellow	leuchtend gelb angestrichen
sidewalk *AE* / *BE* pavement	Bürgersteig; Gehsteig
the edge of the sidewalk	der Rand des Bürgersteigs
wave your arm	mit dem Arm fuchteln
available	verfügbar; frei
light	Licht; Lampe
on radio call	(*etwa:*) über Funk gerufen
reserved by someone else	von jem. anders reserviert
off duty	nicht im Dienst; außer Dienst
even if you don't know your way around	auch wenn Sie sich nicht auskennen
give the impression	den Eindruck erwecken
how to get there	wie man dort hinkommt
how long it should take	wie lange es dauern sollte
map	(Land-, Straßen-)Karte; (Stadt-)Plan
turn on the meter	die (Taxameter-)Uhr anstellen
illegal	illegal; gesetzwidrig
to your disadvantage	zu Ihrem Nachteil
change a $10 bill *AE* / *BE* note	einen Zehndollarschein wechseln
be prepared to pay	darauf eingestellt sein zu zahlen
a small extra charge	ein kleiner Zuschlag
suitcase	Koffer
toll	(Straßen-/Tunnel- *etc.*)Benutzungsgebühr
tip the driver	dem Fahrer ein Trinkgeld geben
the total fare	der Gesamtfahrpreis

Verständnis- und Wortschatztest

a. Another word for *taxi*? ☐ b. The British word for *sidewalk*? ☐ c. Another word for *against the law*? ☐ d. The American word for £10 *note*? ☐ e. The price you have to pay for a taxi ride is called the ..... ☐ f. The money you pay for using a bridge is called a .....

11 Erklärungen

1. Stützwort *one*

a. "You said the heliport, didn't you?" – "Yes, the one (= heliport) on East 34th Street."
Ja, der auf der 34. Straße, Ostseite.
b. "I thought you said the one (= heliport) on the West Side."
Ich dachte, Sie meinten den auf der Westseite.
c. New roads are being built and existing ones (= roads) widened.
Neue Straßen werden gebaut und bestehende (werden) verbreitert.

Um die Wiederholung eines Substantivs (*heliport, roads*) zu vermeiden, ersetzt man es nach Adjektiven (c) und *the* (a, b) durch *one(s)*. Entsprechend auch nach Wörtern wie *this/that* und *which*:

Which one do you mean – this one or that one?
Welchen meinst du – diesen hier oder den da?

2. *Can – be able to*

a. The driver can change a $10 bill.
Eine Zehndollarnote kann der Fahrer wechseln.
b. The driver must/should/will be able to change a $10 bill.
Eine Zehndollarnote muß/sollte/wird der Fahrer wechseln können.
c. The driver doesn't seem to be able to change a $10 bill.
Eine Zehndollarnote scheint der Fahrer nicht wechseln zu können.
d. Being able to change a $10 bill – I mean, that's the least you can expect, isn't it?
Eine Zehndollarnote wechseln zu können – ich meine, das ist doch das Wenigste, was man erwarten kann, oder?

Can ist ein „unvollständiges" Verb – z. B. kann man es nicht im Infinitiv (mit oder ohne *to*) oder in der *-ing*-Form gebrauchen. Die Beispiele b–d zeigen, wie *can* in solchen Fällen durch eine Konstruktion mit *be able to* ersetzt wird.

3. *To*-Infinitiv in relativsatzähnlicher Funktion

We are seeking aggressive, career-minded sales people to join (≈ who could/would join) our expanding sales force in West Germany ...
Wir suchen ... Vertreter für unseren expandierenden Außendienst ...

With no one to take (≈ who could/would take) surgery at his rural practice in Scotland, the doctor did the only thing he could ...
Da er niemanden hatte, der in seiner schottischen Landpraxis die Sprechstunde übernehmen konnte ...

Dieser eigentümliche Gebrauch des *to*-Infinitivs läßt sich nur unvollkommen durch eine andere Form ersetzen (daher das ≈) und hat auch keine direkte deutsche Entsprechung. In ähnlicher Verwendung findet sich der *to*-Infinitiv auch in Lektion 2 (vgl. S. 16):

There is nothing to replenish (≈ with which one can/could replenish) the rapidly diminishing stocks.
The only thing left to do (≈ that one can/could do) is pray.

1. Setzen Sie die folgenden Verben in der passenden Form ein.

agree, do, find, hail, know, pull, tell, wait, want

On his return from his holiday in Spain, Dr Ian Cummings ..... himself stranded at Gatwick Airport because of the rail strike. ..... that his patients ..... for him at his rural practice in Scotland, he ..... the only thing he could: he ..... a taxi. The cabby was flabbergasted when the doctor ..... him where he ..... to go: a little village in the Scottish Highlands 600 miles away. But after some haggling he ..... to make the trip for a bargain fare of £300, and eleven hours later they ..... up outside the doctor's house just in time for the afternoon surgery.

2. Setzen Sie ein passendes Verb im *to*-Infinitiv ein, und übersetzen Sie den Satz.

a. There was no one ..... surgery for him at his country practice in Scotland.
b. In a situation like that the only thing ..... is to take a taxi.
c. If you want an English atmosphere as well as a lot of sunshine, the place ..... your holiday is Malta.
d. If you don't know how to get tickets, the person ..... is Judy.
e. If you haven't got much money, the place ..... is a bed and breakfast.
f. We had no one ..... the dog with, so we stayed at home.
g. If you want a taxi, the number ..... is 565 5656.
h. I'm looking for a book ..... on a long train journey.
i. Many of them don't have a family ..... to for help.

3. *Können*. – Übersetzen Sie.

a. Du kannst deinen Urlaub hier verbringen.
b. Hier werden wir unseren Urlaub nicht verbringen können.
c. Er scheint nicht kommen zu können.
d. Wenn ich nicht kommen kann, rufe ich dich an.
e. Wir könnten dieses Problem lösen.
f. Wir hätten dieses Problem lösen können.
g. Wir müßten dieses Problem lösen können.
h. Jemand wie Sie muß solche Probleme lösen können.
i. Sie scheint das Problem nicht lösen zu können.
j. Ich konnte das Problem nicht lösen.

4. Übersetzen Sie.

a. „Könnten Sie mir bitte meinen Koffer geben?" – „Welcher ist Ihrer – dieser hier?" – „Nein, der da drüben."
b. Laß uns in ein Restaurant gehen. In der Dean Street ist ein gutes.
c. „Es gibt hier viele Restaurants." – „Aber nicht viele gute!" – „Ja, und die guten sind alle ziemlich teuer."
d. Nachdem wir ein paar Minuten ⟨miteinander⟩ gefeilscht hatten, einigten wir uns auf einen Fahrpreis von £300.
e. Meinen Sie, Sie können es in zwanzig Minuten schaffen?
f. Entschuldigen Sie, ⟨da⟩ muß ich Sie falsch verstanden haben.
g. Dieses Taxi ist von jemand anders bestellt worden.
h. Dieses Taxi muß von jemand anders bestellt worden sein.
i. Ich habe keine Ahnung, wie man da hinkommt.
j. Für die Koffer werden Sie einen kleinen Zuschlag zahlen müssen.

12 Thieves

Einbrecher im Haus, und ein Elfjähriger erschießt sie – Text 1 ist eine amerikanische Zeitungsmeldung, die auf ein Problem weist, das im Dialog des zweiten Textes angesprochen wird: das in den amerikanischen Medien immer wieder heiß diskutierte Recht auf Waffenbesitz. Text 3 – ebenfalls im Stil einer Zeitungsmeldung – bringt uns in eine entlegene kanadische Gegend: wieder die Geschichte eines Eigentumsvergehens, aber diesmal gleichsam *with a happy ending*.

In der Tonaufnahme sind die Texte 1 und 3 im Stil einer Reportage amerikanisch gesprochen, der zweite Text dagegen britisch – dieses Gespräch wird, wie unter anderem das *over there (= [da] drüben)* in der letzten Zeile andeutet, von Nichtamerikanern geführt.

Choose your weapon: A gun store in the United States

11-year-old shoots burglars

ELEVEN-YEAR-OLD Mike Bratton was alone in the house watching TV in his upstairs room when he realized that there were strangers downstairs. His immediate reaction was to try and get out of the house, but he couldn't because the intruders, two rough-looking men, were in the hall at the bottom of the stairs.

For a moment the boy didn't know what to do, but then he took the rifle he had got for Christmas, loaded it, slid down the stairs and shot the two men, who were just removing a video cassette recorder.

He then called 911. Later, when he learned the men were dead, he wept. The two burglars had been unarmed.

Most of the people in the rural one-store, one-church South Carolina town hailed Mike as "a brave little boy" who had done the right thing.

"He felt like his life was in danger," said the coroner. "He acted very wisely." And the sheriff said: "The boy would have been in danger if he hadn't had the gun. He acted in self-defense. It was justified killing."

Wortschatz

thief – thieves	Dieb – Diebe
shoot – shot – shot	schießen – schoß – geschossen
burglar	Einbrecher(in)
upstairs – downstairs	oben – unten (im Hause)
he realized	es wurde ihm bewußt; er bemerkte
stranger	Fremde(r)
intruder	Eindringling
rough	rauh; grob; hart
hall	Diele
at the bottom of the stairs	am Fuß / unteren Ende der Treppe
load the rifle	das Gewehr laden
slide – slid – slid	schleichen – schlich – geschlichen
shoot (– shot – shot)	erschießen (*auch* an-/niederschießen)
remove something	etw. entfernen/wegnehmen
video (cassette) recorder / VCR	Videorecorder
call 911 *AE* / *BE* dial 999	den Notruf wählen
he learned the men were dead	er erfuhr, daß die Männer tot waren
weep – wept – wept	weinen – weinte – geweint
unarmed	unbewaffnet
store *AE* / *BE* shop	Laden; Geschäft
hail someone	jem. bejubeln/preisen
a brave little boy	ein tapferer kleiner Junge
danger	Gefahr
coroner	(*Beamter, der Todesfälle untersucht, die nicht eindeutig eine natürliche Ursache haben*)
he acted very wisely	er hat sich sehr vernünftig verhalten
gun	(*Schußwaffe wie:*) Gewehr, Pistole
act in self-defense *AE* / *BE* -defence	in Notwehr handeln
justified	gerechtfertigt; begründet

Verständnis- und Wortschatztest (Text 1)

a. Mike was ..... TV in his room upstairs. ☐ b. When he ..... a noise from the hall downstairs, he ..... that there were burglars in the house. ☐ c. Looking down he saw two rough-looking men at the ..... of the stairs who were just ..... a video cassette recorder. ☐ d. For a moment the boy didn't know what to ....., but then he ..... the rifle he had ..... for Christmas, loaded it, ... down the stairs and ..... the two men. ☐ e. Then he ..... 911. ☐ f. Later, when he ..... that the two men were dead, he ..... ☐ g. The two burglars ..... unarmed.

Guns for everyone

A: Can you believe it – the coroner saying the boy acted wisely, and the sheriff even suggesting the boy might have been in greater danger if he hadn't had the gun. I'm not blaming the boy, of course ...

B: ... He shouldn't have been given a gun in the first place.

A: That's what we say, but there are parts of the United States where it's nothing unusual for a boy around the age of twelve to get his first shotgun and learn how to handle it.

B: Yes, you're right. You go into a house, and the first thing you see in the hallway is a gun rack.

A: The point is, those two unfortunate burglars would still be alive if that boy hadn't had a gun.

B: Thousands of other Americans would still be alive too if it wasn't so damn easy to get hold of a gun over there.

Wortschatz

suggest	unterstellen; behaupten
he might have been in danger	er hätte in Gefahr sein können; er wäre vielleicht in Gefahr gewesen
blame someone	jem. Vorwürfe machen
he shouldn't have been given a gun in the first place	man hätte ihm gar nicht erst ein Gewehr geben dürfen
handle a shotgun	mit einer Schrotflinte umgehen
in the hallway	im Flur
gun rack	Gewehrständer
the point is	das Wesentliche ist doch
unfortunate	unglücklich; unglückselig; arm
they would still be alive	sie würden noch leben / wären noch am Leben
if it wasn't so damn easy	wenn es nicht so verdammt einfach wäre
get hold of a gun	an ein Gewehr kommen

Verständnis- und Wortschatztest (Text 2)

a. You can't ..... the boy for shooting the burglars, can you? ☐ b. No, but it's nonsense for the sheriff to suggest that the boy might ..... in greater danger if he hadn't had the gun. ☐ c. That young boy should never have ..... a gun in the first place. ☐ d. The two burglars would still be alive if Mike ..... ☐ e. Yes, it's too easy in the US to get ..... of a gun.

Lake-shore resident rescues thief

LARRY PETERS, 43, was woken up shortly after midnight by cries for help from the waters of Okanagan Lake.

He threw his parka on and dashed out of his lake-shore home.

Noticing that his canoe was missing, he jumped into the only craft available, an old, leaky rowboat, which was partly filled with water.

Rowing as fast as he could, he reached the exhausted man just in time to save him from drowning in the cold, dark lake.

Later he learned that the man he saved had earlier stolen his canoe. A squall had come up, and the boat had overturned.

Peters said he wouldn't have hesitated even if he'd known that the man he was rescuing had taken his canoe. "It wouldn't even have crossed my mind," he said. "You don't think about it. You just do it."

Wortschatz

lake shore	Seeufer
resident	Bewohner(in); Anwohner(in)
rescue/save someone	jem. retten
wake someone up (– woke – woken)	jem. (auf)wecken
shortly after midnight	kurz nach Mitternacht
cry/cries for help	Hilferuf/-rufe
Okanagan Lake	(*See in der kanad. Provinz British Columbia*)
throw – threw – thrown	werfen – warf – geworfen
he threw his parka on	er warf sich seinen Parka über
dash out	hinausstürzen
his canoe was missing	sein Kanu war nicht mehr da
jump into a boat	in ein Boot springen
craft (*Plural* craft)	(*allg. Ausdruck für jede Art von Wasser-/Luft-/Raumfahrzeug*)
the only craft available	das einzig(e) verfügbare Boot
a leaky rowboat *AE* / *BE* rowing boat	ein leckes Ruderboot
partly filled with water	teilweise mit Wasser gefüllt
row	rudern
exhausted	erschöpft
save/rescue someone from drowning	jem. vor dem Ertrinken retten
steal – stole – stolen	stehlen – stahl – gestohlen
squall	plötzlicher, heftiger Wind(stoß); Bö
the boat had overturned	das Boot war gekentert
hesitate	zögern
it wouldn't (even) have crossed my mind	es wäre mir überhaupt nicht in den Sinn gekommen
you don't think about it	man überlegt sich's gar nicht
you just do it	man tut es einfach

Verständnis- und Wortschatztest

a. The residents of an area are the people who ..... in it. ☐ b. A thief is someone who ..... something from someone. ☐ c. The British word for *rowboat* is ..... ☐ d. A *canoe* is a kind of ....., a *parka* is a kind of ....., and a *squall* is a sudden strong ..... ☐ e. *Rescue* someone from drowning – another word for *rescue*?

1. Bedingungssätze

Typ 1: If I miss the helicopter, I won't make my flight.
Wenn ich den Hubschrauber verpasse, schaffe ich meinen Flug nicht.

Typ 2: If I missed the helicopter, I wouldn't make my flight.
Wenn ich den Hubschrauber verpaßte, würde ich meinen Flug nicht schaffen.

Typ 3: If I had missed the helicopter, I wouldn't have made my flight.
Wenn ich den Hubschrauber verpaßt hätte, („würde ich meinen Flug nicht geschafft haben") hätte ich meinen Flug nicht geschafft.

Für Englischlernende besonders schwierig ist Typ 3. Für diesen Typ bieten die Texte dieser Lektion Beispiele:

The boy would have been in danger if he hadn't had the gun.
Der Junge wäre in Gefahr gewesen, wenn er das Gewehr nicht gehabt hätte.

Peters wouldn't have hesitated even if he'd (= he had) known that the man had taken his canoe. *Peters hätte auch dann nicht gezögert, wenn er gewußt hätte, daß der Mann sein Kanu gestohlen hatte.*

Entsprechend auch der folgende Satz – allerdings mit *might* anstelle von *would*:

The boy might have been in greater danger if he hadn't had the gun.
Der Junge wäre vielleicht in größerer Gefahr gewesen, wenn er das Gewehr nicht gehabt hätte.

Das folgende Beispiel illustriert eine häufig vorkommende Mischung von Typ 2 (erste Hälfte) und 3 (zweite Hälfte):

The burglars would still be alive if the boy hadn't had a gun.
Die Einbrecher wären noch am Leben, wenn der Junge kein Gewehr gehabt hätte.

2. Vorvergangenheit (Plusquamperfekt)

a. They hailed Mike as a brave little boy who had done the right thing.
Sie lobten Mike als einen tapferen kleinen Jungen, der das Richtige getan hatte.
b. Later he learned that the man he saved had earlier stolen his canoe.
Später erfuhr er, daß der von ihm gerettete Mann zuvor sein Kanu gestohlen hatte.
c. He took the rifle he had got for Christmas.
Er nahm das Gewehr, das er zu Weihnachten bekommen hatte.

Wie im Deutschen gebraucht man diese „*had*-Form" für Handlungen, die zeitlich vor der „Erzählebene Vergangenheit" liegen: *had done* liegt vor *hailed* (a), *had stolen* vor *learned* (b) und *had got* vor *took* (c).
In (b) liegt allerdings nicht nur *had stolen*, sondern auch *saved* vor *learned*. „Logisch" richtig wäre also eigentlich: *Later he learned that the man he had saved had earlier stolen his canoe.* Auf ein solches stilistisch schwerfälliges Plusquamperfekt wird aber in der Regel dann verzichtet, wenn – wie hier – die Zeitverhältnisse auch ohne den Gebrauch der *had*-Form nicht mißzuverstehen sind.

1. Setzen Sie eine passende Form des eingeklammerten Verbs ein.

a. You (be) based in Frankfurt if you were to work for us.
b. If you (take) the helicopter, you'd get to the airport in time.
c. I (not hesitate) even if I had known that he'd stolen my canoe.
d. There would be less noise if people (not be) so inconsiderate.
e. If you (not fasten) your seat belt, you might have got a nasty knock.
f. We (have to) pay twice as much if we stayed at the Sheraton.
g. I (stay) here if I could find a job.
h. I (stay) here if I had been able to find a job.
i. If the burglars hadn't been in the hallway, Mike (be) able to get out of the house.
j. A lot of people would still be alive if it (not be) so easy to get a gun.
k. Those unfortunate burglars (still be) alive if that boy hadn't had a gun.
l. If the man (not take) the boat, he wouldn't have drowned.

2. Ersetzen Sie die Kurzform *'d* durch die Langform *had* oder *would*.

a. She isn't the type of girl who'd sell you something just to make a sale.
b. You know you'd be based in Frankfurt if you were to work for us.
c. Steve started work as a steward shortly after he and Sandra got married. He'd been made redundant from his previous job.
d. I'd like to go back to Scotland.
e. I wish we'd given as much thought to the sitting room as we did to planning the kitchen.
f. He wouldn't have hesitated even if he'd known that the man he was rescuing had taken his canoe.
g. I'd rather fly than drive any time.
h. She'd prefer to be able to converse without shouting.

3. Setzen Sie die passende Form des eingeklammerten Verbs ein.

a. (Notice) that his canoe was missing, he (jump) into the old rowboat.
b. (Row) as fast as he could, he (reach) the exhausted man just in time.
c. The youngsters drive up and down through country villages on their motorbikes (make) this horrible noise – it really (get) to me.
d. I enclose the photo I (take) of you and Bonnie (watch) TV in the evening.
e. The Republic of Malta (consist) of a small group of islands (lie) about 60 miles south of Sicily.
f. In the old days, the kitchen (be) a small and stuffy place, the windows (be) steamed up, and there (be) always washing (hang) from the clothesline.

4. Übersetzen Sie mit der *had*-Form.

a. Mike hatte die Einbrecher am Fuß der Treppe gesehen.
b. Er hatte sein Gewehr geladen und die beiden Männer erschossen.
c. Der Junge hatte das Gewehr zu Weihnachten bekommen.
d. Er war allein im Haus gewesen.
e. Die Einbrecher hatten versucht, einen Videorecorder zu stehlen.
f. Sie waren unbewaffnet gewesen.
g. Mike erzählte der Polizei, was passiert war.
h. Hatte der Junge in Notwehr gehandelt?
i. Nach Meinung (*according to*) des Sheriffs war es Notwehr gewesen.
j. Niemand hatte bemerkt, daß der Videorecorder fehlte.

13 Bridges

Der erste Text bringt eine Meldung, die es in sich hat – jedenfalls für New Yorker Pendler: eine der wichtigsten Brücken, die Manhattan mit den anderen Stadtteilen verbinden, ist wegen altersbedingter Schäden gesperrt worden: die Williamsburg Bridge. Im zweiten Text unterhalten sich Liz und Jim, verspätet im Büro angekommen, über diese Kalamität. Der dritte Text macht uns klar, daß die Williamsburg Bridge kein Einzelfall ist. In den USA sind viele tausend in die Jahre gekommene Brücken wegen mangelnder Wartung und überfälliger Untersuchungen potentiell nicht verkehrssicher – ein großes technisches und finanzielles Problem, das auch andere Industriestaaten haben.
In der Tonaufnahme sind alle drei Texte amerikanisch gesprochen.

NYC bridge closed

NEW YORK'S Williamsburg Bridge, one of America's busiest, was closed indefinitely Tuesday night after numerous defects – cracks, holes, and rust – were found on the span. Inspectors feared the bridge would collapse.

On Wednesday morning the people who travel daily across the bridge in 107,000 vehicles and 420 subway trains had to find other ways to get from Brooklyn to Manhattan and vice versa.

Most travelers took to other bridges, other subways, or even ferries. But some used the bridge's walkways, which were still open, to bicycle or walk across the East River.

"This is certainly one of the worst bridges we have," said a transportation official. "For 80 years, the bridge really hasn't been maintained."

The city will decide later whether to repair the bridge, at an estimated cost of $250 million, or replace it – for $500 million.

Wortschatz

NYC (= New York City)	(*es gibt auch New York State!*)
Williamsburg Bridge	(*1903 gebaute wichtige Brücke über den East River zwischen Manhattan und Brooklyn*)
a busy bridge	eine stark befahrene Brücke
indefinitely	auf unbestimmte Zeit
numerous defects	zahlreiche Mängel/Schäden/Fehler
cracks, holes, and rust	Risse, Löcher und Rost
the span of the bridge	der Brückenbogen
inspector	Prüfer(in); Prüfbeamte(r)
collapse	einstürzen
vehicle	Fahrzeug
and vice versa [vaɪsɪ ˈvɜːsə]	und umgekehrt
traveler ***AE*** **/** ***BE*** **traveller**	Reisende(r)
they took to other bridges	sie wichen auf andere Brücken aus
walkway	Gehweg; Fußgängerweg
bicycle (*als Verb meistens* cycle)	Fahrrad; radfahren; radeln
transportation ***AE*** **/** ***BE*** **transport**	Verkehr(swesen)
a transport(ation) official	(*etwa:*) ein(e) für das Verkehrswesen zuständige(r) Beamte(r)
maintain a bridge	eine Brücke warten / instand halten
decide	entscheiden
repair	reparieren
an estimated cost of $250 million	geschätzte Kosten in Höhe von 250 Millionen Dollar
replace something	etw. ersetzen

Verständnis- und Wortschatztest

a. Who is the Williamsburg Bridge used by? □ b. There was a danger that the bridge might ..... because of ..... □ c. What did travelers do when the bridge was closed? □ d. What was the decision the city had to make?

At the office at last

A: Sorry I'm late, Jim. It took me almost 90 minutes to get here.

B: Never mind, Liz. I only just arrived myself. It's complete chaos out there with the Williamsburg Bridge closed.

A: It sure is. I'll have to think of some other way of getting here if they don't fix that bridge soon. Maybe I'll walk. The walkways are still open.

B: It'd be good exercise, that's for sure, but I don't think you'd get here any faster. And you'd need comfortable shoes, of course. In fact, Joe took the ferry this morning. He said it was a nice ride, no hassles.

A: I don't know. Maybe one should rent an apartment here after all. But who can afford the rents in Manhattan?

Wortschatz

at the office at last	endlich im Büro
sorry I'm late	tut mir leid, daß ich zu spät komme
it took me almost 90 minutes	ich habe fast anderthalb Stunden gebraucht
never mind	macht nichts
I only just arrived myself	ich bin selber gerade erst gekommen
it's complete chaos	es herrscht totales Chaos
fix something	etw. reparieren / in Ordnung bringen
maybe I'll walk	vielleicht gehe ich zu Fuß
it'd (= it would) be good exercise	(*etwa:*) es wäre gut für die Gesundheit (exercise = Übung/Bewegung)
that's for sure	das steht fest
you'd (= you would) need comfortable shoes	du würdest bequeme Schuhe brauchen / du brauchtest bequeme Schuhe
in fact, Joe took the ferry this morning	(*etwa:*) Joe ist ja heute morgen mit der Fähre gekommen
a nice ride	eine angenehme Fahrt
no hassles	(*etwa:*) ging ganz reibungslos (hassle = Mühe/ „Theater")
rent an apartment *AE* / *BE* a flat	eine Wohnung mieten
maybe one should rent an apartment here after all	vielleicht sollte man doch hier eine Wohnung mieten
who can afford the rent?	wer kann sich die Miete leisten?

Verständnis- und Wortschatztest

a. Where does Liz work? □ b. Does she live in Manhattan? □ c. What happened to the Williamsburg Bridge? □ d. What about the walkways? □ e. ... if they don't *fix* that bridge soon – another word for *fix*? □ f. If Liz walked, she wouldn't get to the office any ..... □ g. Of course, walking is good ..... □ h. But Liz would need ..... shoes if she walked. □ i. How did Joe get across the East River? □ j. Renting an apartment in Manhattan would solve the transportation problem, but ..... □ k. Americans normally say *transportation* where British people say ..... □ l. British people don't speak of a *subway* train – they say ..... □ m. The British word for *apartment* is .....

Bridges under fire

"Thousands of US bridges may be dangerous," a transportation expert said yesterday.

The warning came at the end of a yearlong investigation into the collapse of a New York thruway bridge which killed ten motorists.

The probable cause of the collapse was failure by highway officials to replace large boulders around bridge piers, which led to erosion.

The expert said thousands of bridges had designs similar to the one that collapsed and they should all be checked immediately.

Wortschatz

(come) under fire	unter Beschuß (geraten)
they may be dangerous	sie sind möglicherweise gefährlich
transportation *AE* expert	Verkehrsexperte/-fachmann
warning	Warnung
an investigation into the collapse	eine Untersuchung des Einsturzes / der Einsturzursache
a yearlong investigation	eine Untersuchung, die ein Jahr dauerte; eine einjährige Untersuchung
thruway / throughway *AE*	Schnellstraße; Autobahn
the collapse killed ten motorists	bei dem Einsturz kamen zehn Autofahrer ums Leben
the probable cause	die wahrscheinliche Ursache
failure	(*etwa:*) Unterlassung, Versäumnis
highway	(*AE etwa:*) Bundesstraße
was failure by highway officials to replace ...	(*etwa:*) war die Tatsache, daß Straßenbaubeamte es versäumt hatten, ... zu ersetzen
boulder	Felsbrocken; großer Stein
bridge pier	Brückenpfeiler
lead – led – led	führen – führte – geführt
which led to erosion	was zu Erosion/Verwitterung führte
design (of a bridge etc.)	Konstruktion (einer Brücke etc.)
they should all be checked	sie sollten alle überprüft werden

Verständnis- und Wortschatztest

a. The large boulders around the bridge piers should have been ..... ☐ b. All bridges that have designs similar to the one that collapsed should be ..... immediately. ☐ c. A car is a type of ....., a ferry is a type of ....., and a thruway is a type of ..... ☐ d. People who travel regularly between their home and work are called ..... ☐ e. The stretch of water between Manhattan and Brooklyn is called the ..... ☐ f. A trip in a car, taxi, bus, etc. is also called a ..... ☐ g. If a bridge has a lot of cracks and holes, it is probably ..... ☐ h. Defects on bridges include ..... ☐ i. A motorist is someone who ..... ☐ j. A bridge inspector is a person who ..... ☐ k. A *yearlong* investigation is one that .....

13 Erklärungen

1. Indirekte Rede

Direkte Rede:
"Thousands of bridges have a design similar to the one that collapsed."
Indirekte Rede:
He said (that) thousands of bridges had a design similar to the one that collapsed.
Er sagte, Tausende von Brücken hätten eine ähnliche Konstruktion wie die eingestürzte.

Direkte Rede:
"The bridge will collapse."
Indirekte Rede:
Inspectors feared (that) the bridge would collapse.
Prüfer befürchteten, daß die Brücke einstürzen würde.

Beachten Sie in der indirekten Rede die Zeitverschiebung gegenüber der direkten Rede. Steht das Berichtsverb wie hier in der Vergangenheit (*said*, *feared*), so „rutscht" das Verb des berichteten Satzes um eine Zeitstufe in die Vergangenheit: *have* → *had*, *will* → *would* etc.
So auch in diesen Beispielen aus früheren Lektionen:

"The men are dead." – Later he learned that the men were dead.
"87 per cent (have) once held a job." – A survey of 1,000 homeless people found that 87 per cent had once held a job.

Steht das Verb der direkten Rede in der Vergangenheit, so kann die Zeitverschiebung unterbleiben, sofern ein Mißverstehen der zeitlichen Beziehungen ausgeschlossen ist:

Direkte Rede: "It was a nice ride."
Indirekte Rede nach der „Verschiebungsregel" eigentlich:
He said it had been a nice ride.
Die Aussage ist aber auch ohne Zeitverschiebung nicht mißzuverstehen:
He said it was a nice ride.

2. Superlativ (Steigerungs-Höchststufe)

Sehr häufig ist die Struktur Superlativ + Substantiv + Relativsatz:

This is certainly one of the worst bridges we have.
This is the worst drought I've ever seen.
Belgrave Road in Victoria is the best I can do.

Rufen Sie sich auch noch einmal die verschiedenen Arten der Bildung des Superlativs ins Gedächtnis zurück:

Bei kurzen Wörtern Anhängen von *-est*: *short – shortest* etc.
Stummes End-*e* entfällt: *late – latest* etc.
Verdopplung des Endkonsonanten: *big – biggest* etc.
Bei zweisilbigen Adjektiven wird *-y* zu *-i-*: *busy – busiest* etc.

Bei längeren Wörtern mit *most*: *important – most important* etc.

Unregelmäßig: *bad – worst* etc.

1. Setzen Sie in die indirekte Rede.

She said: "I'll probably take the ferry the next time I come."
She said she'd probably take the ferry the next time she came.

a. He said: "I'll probably walk."
b. Jim said: "The Williamsburg Bridge is closed."
c. He said: "It's an extremely busy bridge."
d. Liz said: "It took me almost 90 minutes to get here."
e. Her boss said: "I only just arrived myself."
f. Someone said: "The walkways are still open."
g. Janet said: "I'm thinking of renting an apartment in Manhattan."
h. I told her: "People like us can't afford the rents in Manhattan."
i. The press were told: "Failure to replace the boulders around the piers led to erosion."
j. City officials said: "We'll decide later whether the bridge will be repaired or replaced."
k. The boy said: "I was alone in the house."
l. The sheriff told me: "You did the right thing."
m. The coroner said: "The boy acted wisely."
n. His mother said: "I'll never forget that night."
o. Janet said: "I know what happened."

2. Setzen Sie einen passenden Superlativ ein.

a. Please make sure that you've checked out by three at the .....
b. The Williamsburg Bridge is one of the ..... bridges in the USA.
c. Pneumatic drills and all the roadworks that are going on – those are the things that annoy me .....
d. Noisy children and noisy neighbours in general are the ..... cause of trouble and annoyance in my experience.
e. Malta has the ..... climate of all the English-speaking countries in Europe.
f. I'm in a hurry – are you sure this is the ..... route?
g. The Savoy is one of the ..... hotels in London.
h. The rail strike isn't our ..... problem.
i. Concorde is one of the ..... planes in the world.
j. The bridge is full of cracks, holes and rust – it's one of the ..... bridges we have.

3. Übersetzen Sie.

a. Die Brücke ist auf unbestimmte Zeit gesperrt worden.
b. Experten befürchteten, die Brücke könnte einstürzen.
c. Dies ist gewiß eine der schlimmsten Brücken, die wir haben.
d. Seit achtzig Jahren ist an der Brücke nichts getan (*maintain*) worden.
e. Die Stadt wird später entscheiden, ob sie die Brücke repariert oder ersetzt.
f. Hunderttausende von Pendlern müssen andere Wege finden, um von Brooklyn nach Manhattan zu kommen.
g. Ich weiß nicht, was ich tun werde. Vielleicht werde ich zu Fuß gehen.
h. Mit der Fähre ist es eine schöne Fahrt.
i. Oder man könnte mit dem Fahrrad über den East River fahren.
j. Vielleicht sollte man doch hier in Manhattan eine Wohnung mieten.
k. Könntest du dir die Mieten hier leisten? Ich nicht!

14 Illiteracy

Ein Briefträger „hortet“ Postsendungen, deren Adressen er nicht lesen kann. Diese in Text 1 erzählte wahre Geschichte aus dem Norden Englands weist auf ein in vielen Ländern bestehendes Problem, über das im dialogartigen Text 2 individuelle Erfahrungen mitgeteilt und im *background*-Text 3 Informationen gegeben werden.
In der Tonaufnahme wird Text 1 entsprechend seiner regionalen Herkunft mit einem leichten nordenglischen Akzent gesprochen; in Text 2 ist die Aussprache neutralenglisch, in Text 3 amerikanisch.

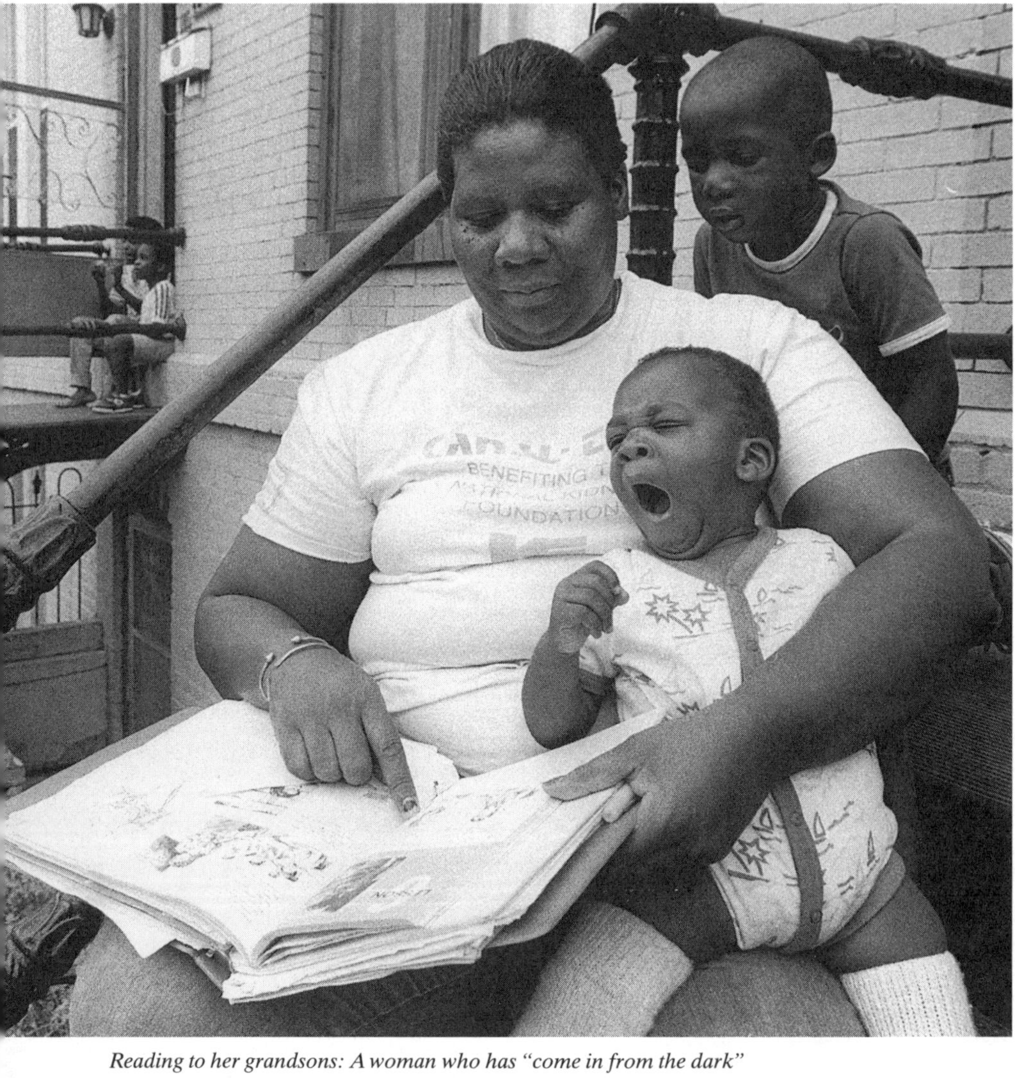

Reading to her grandsons: A woman who has "come in from the dark"

Postman with a reading problem

A TYNESIDE postman hid sacks of letters for seven years because he could not read properly. He could manage simple addresses, but the more difficult family and place names baffled him.

His secret was discovered in a routine clear-out when the mail fell out of his locker.

The postman had not revealed his problem because he feared he would be fired.

At first the Post Office suspected that theft was the motive, but none of the letters had been opened.

A Post Office spokesman said: "Apart from this lapse he was regarded as a good worker and for the past five years of his employment successfully delivered 100,000 letters a year. Strangely enough, we have had no complaints about him."

Although delaying the mail is a criminal offence, no action was taken against the postman, who has resigned and found a new job.

Wortschatz

illiteracy	Analphabetentum, Analphabetismus (= Schreib- und Leseunkundigkeit)
postman	Briefträger; (Post-)Zusteller
Tyneside	(Gebiet zwischen Newcastle und der Küste)
hide – hid – hidden	verstecken – versteckte – versteckt
sacks of letters	Säcke mit Briefen
he could not read properly	er konnte nicht richtig lesen
he could manage simple addresses	einfache Adressen schaffte er
they baffled him	sie überforderten ihn
discover a secret	ein Geheimnis entdecken
a routine clear-out	eine routinemäßige Ausräumung
fall – fell – fallen	fallen – fiel – gefallen
locker	(verschließbares) Schrank(fach); Spind
reveal something	etw. zu erkennen geben
fire someone	jem. entlassen
the Post Office	die Post(behörde)
suspect (that)	den Verdacht haben(, daß)
theft	Diebstahl
motive	Motiv; Beweggrund
none of the letters	keiner der Briefe
apart from this lapse	abgesehen von dieser Verfehlung
regard someone as	jem. ansehen als
for the past five years	während der letzten fünf Jahre
employment	Beschäftigung
deliver letters	Briefe zustellen
strangely enough	seltsamerweise
although	obwohl; obgleich
delay the mail	die Post verzögern
criminal offence *BE* / *AE* offense	strafbare Handlung
take action against someone	gegen jem. (gerichtlich) vorgehen
resign	kündigen

Verständnis- und Wortschatztest (Text 1)

a. What was the postman's problem? □ b. What did he do with the letters whose addresses he couldn't read? □ c. Why had he not revealed his problem? □ d. Why could the Post Office have taken action against the postman?

Is illiteracy a problem in this country?

A: No, I don't think so. Some people don't read as well as one would expect but I'd be surprised if there were many people who can't read the headlines in the popular papers.

B: I suspect there are millions who can't read properly. In my line of work – I'm a police officer – I often have to read statements back to people, and I've seen a lot of adults actually sign their names with an "X".

C: And there are many people who can't read or write apart from signing their names.

D: I'm not surprised there's widespread illiteracy. There's no respect for the three Rs in schools today.

E: Some of my patients can't even read the labels on their medicine. I think it's a serious problem. There should be more programmes available to teach adults how to read and write their own language.

Wortschatz

this country	(meint immer das Land, in dem der/die Sprechende sich befindet)
as well as one would expect	so gut, wie man erwarten möchte
surprised	überrascht
headline	Schlagzeile
the popular papers	die Boulevardzeitungen
in my line of work	in meinem Beruf
police officer	Polizeibeamte(r)
statement	Aussage; Protokoll
read something back to someone	jem. etw. noch einmal vorlesen
actually	tatsächlich
sign one's name	(mit seinem Namen) unterschreiben
widespread	weitverbreitet
respect	Respekt; Achtung
the three Rs (= reading, [w]riting, [a]rithmetic)	Lesen, Schreiben und Rechnen
label	Etikett; Aufschrift
medicine	Arznei; Medikament; Medizin
a serious problem	ein ernstes Problem
there should be more programmes *BE* / *AE* programs available	es sollte mehr Programme geben
teach adults how to read	Erwachsenen das Lesen beibringen

Verständnis- und Wortschatztest (Text 2)

a. Name some of the popular papers in this country, Britain, or the USA. □ b. How do people usually sign documents if they can't write? □ c. What are *the three Rs*? □ d. What's speaker E's profession?

A problem more common than alcoholism

"Functional illiterates" are people who can't read simple texts such as the destination sign on a bus, the address on a letter, a headline in a newspaper or the instructions on a parking meter or pay phone. It has been estimated that in the United States one out of five adults may be functionally illiterate; the same is probably true of many other highly developed countries.

People who can't read or write are ashamed of their disability and try to disguise it. This makes it difficult to help them. Those who face up to their handicap and seek help are offered adult-education classes or individual tutoring by volunteers.

Not being able to read or write can deeply affect a person's self-respect, career prospects, social relations and enjoyment of life. "Becoming able to read is like coming in from the dark," says an adult who was formerly illiterate.

Wortschatz

common	weitverbreitet; häufig
alcoholism	Alkoholismus; Alkoholkrankheit
functional illiterate	(jem., dessen Lese- u. Schreibfähigkeit nicht für Grundsituationen in Alltag u. Beruf ausreicht)
instructions	Hinweise; Gebrauchsanweisung
parking meter	Parkuhr
pay phone	Münzfernsprecher
highly developed country	hochentwickeltes Land
they're ashamed of their disability	sie schämen sich ihrer Behinderung
disguise something	etw. verbergen/verschleiern
face up to a handicap	sich zu einer Behinderung bekennen
seek help	Hilfe suchen / in Anspruch nehmen
adult education	Erwachsenenbildung
adult-education classes	Erwachsenenunterricht, -kurse
individual tutoring	Privatunterricht
volunteer	Freiwillige(r)
affect something deeply	sich stark auf etw. auswirken; etw. stark beeinträchtigen
self-respect	Selbstachtung
career prospects	Berufsaussichten
social relations	gesellschaftliche Beziehungen
enjoyment of life	Lebensfreude
come in from the dark	aus der Dunkelheit hereinkommen
who was formerly illiterate	der/die früher Analphabet(in) war

Verständnis- und Wortschatztest

a. What percentage of the US population is estimated to be functionally illiterate? ☐ b. What makes it difficult to help people who are illiterate? ☐ c. What is done to help adults who are illiterate? ☐ d. Another word for *disability*? ☐ e. *Career* prospects – a word that could replace *career* in this context? ☐ f. The destination sign on a bus tells you ..... ☐ g. The instructions on a pay phone tell you how.....

14 Erklärungen

1. Gebrauch des Bindestrichs

adult-education classes	*aber:* classes in adult education
a remote-control TV	*aber:* a TV with remote control
a limited-service hotel	*aber:* a hotel with limited service
a lake-shore home	*aber:* a house on a/the lake shore
clay-pigeon shooting	*aber:* shooting at clay pigeons
a one-church town	*aber:* a town with one church
an eleven-year-old boy	*aber:* a boy of eleven years

Werden Wortzusammensetzungen wie *adult education* oder *clay pigeon* gleich einem Adjektiv vor ein Substantiv gestellt, so werden sie bei sorgfältiger Schreibweise durch einen Bindestrich verbunden.
Auch zusammengesetzte Adjektive wie die folgenden werden in aller Regel mit Bindestrich geschrieben:

long-haul   long-term   low-priced   paper-thin   tax-free

Bei vielen Wortzusammensetzungen schwankt auch der sorgfältige Sprachgebrauch zwischen Bindestrichsetzung und Zusammenschreibung:

a clear-out / a clearout
car-pooling / carpooling (*auch* car pooling *wäre richtig*)
non-alignment / nonalignment
over-confident / overconfident
a thank-you letter / a thankyou letter

Bei ausgeschriebenen Bruchzahlen ist (beachten Sie allerdings die Ausnahme) die Schreibung mit Bindestrich üblich:

two-thirds   three-quarters   one-sixth   one-twentieth
(*Aber wenn eine der beiden Zahlen bereits einen Bindestrich enthält, entfällt der Bindestrich zwischen Zähler und Nenner:*)
one twenty-third   two twenty-fifths   twenty-one forty-eighths

2. *Could = könnte/konnte*

A Tyneside postman hid sacks of letters for seven years because he could not read properly. ... *weil er nicht richtig lesen konnte.*
He could manage simple addresses, but the more difficult family and place names baffled him. *„Einfache Adressen konnte er bewältigen ...“*

Bei diesen Sätzen kann kein Zweifel darüber aufkommen, daß *could* sich auf die Vergangenheit bezieht, also dem deutschen *konnte* entspricht. Aber wie wäre es mit folgendem Satz?

I could help her.

So wie es in diesem Satz steht, könnte *could* nur als „Möglichkeit in der Gegenwart“ verstanden werden: *Ich könnte ihr helfen.* Die Vergangenheit müßte man dagegen mit Hilfe von *be able to* (vgl. S. 70) ausdrücken:

I was able to help her. *Ich konnte ihr helfen.*

1. Vervollständigen Sie den Text.

For seven years a postman ..... hundreds of letters and cards in his locker because he could not ..... well enough to make out the addresses. He did not ..... his problem because he feared he would be ..... His secret was ..... in a routine clear-out at the sorting office when the undelivered mail ..... out of his locker. Now he has ....., leaving the Post Office to send on ..... that's up to seven years old. Despite his ....., the man, who has not been named, ... to deliver 100,000 letters a year and was regarded ..... a good worker. "Strangely ....., we have had no complaints ..... him," said a Post Office spokesman. "..... of the letters were opened. They hadn't ..... left the building." He added: "Delaying the mail is a criminal ....., but no action will be ....." New postmen are now being given a written test to ..... they can read.

2. Setzen Sie ins Passiv.

They discovered his secret. – His secret was discovered.

a. They regarded him as a good worker.
b. They took no action against the postman.
c. He hid the letters in his locker.
d. He hadn't opened the letters.
e. He hasn't signed the statement.
f. Experts have estimated that one out of five adults may be illiterate.
g. He feared they would fire him.
h. We must teach these people how to read and write properly.

3. Mit oder ohne *-ly*?

a. He can't even read (simple) addresses.
I (simple) can't read this address.
b. She's always been quite (successful) at disguising this disability.
She's always disguised this disability quite (successful).
c. It's (strange) that we never had any complaints about him.
(Strange) enough we never had any complaints about him.
d. You haven't eaten (proper), that's why you're feeling weak.
What you need is a (proper) meal, then you'll feel better.
e. It's a problem that should be taken very (serious).
It's certainly a very (serious) problem in this country.
f. We can offer you a class or (individual) tutoring.
You can be taught together with others or (individual).
g. Her disability had a (deep) effect on her character.
Not being able to read or write (deep) affected her self-respect.

4. Übersetzen Sie.

a. Ich könnte die Briefe eine Zeitlang verstecken.
b. Ich konnte die Briefe eine Zeitlang verstecken.
c. Sie wußte, daß man sie nicht entlassen konnte.
d. Wir hatten den Verdacht, er habe die Briefe gestohlen, aber er konnte alles erklären.
e. Keiner der Briefe war geöffnet worden.
f. Ich wäre überrascht, wenn Sie das lesen könnten.
g. Wir brauchen Leute, die Erwachsenen das Lesen und Schreiben beibringen können.
h. Wir werden von einer Frau unterrichtet, die früher selbst Analphabetin war.

15 Language

Von Sprache allgemein, vom Englischen und vom Sprachenlernen handeln die Texte dieser Lektion. In der Tonaufnahme sind alle drei Texte mit britischen Akzenten gesprochen. Am Ende des dritten Textes finden Sie diesmal zwei Spalten von Wörtern, die Sie einander zuordnen sollen: links sogenannte Euphemismen (d. h. verhüllende, beschönigende Ausdrücke) und rechts die normalen Wörter, die die Dinge unverblümt beim Namen nennen (*call a spade a spade*). Deutsche Euphemismen wären z. B. *Heimgang* für *Tod, preiswert* für *billig, Raumpflegerin* für *Putzfrau, Senioren* für *alte Menschen* und *transpirieren* für *schwitzen*. Fallen Ihnen noch weitere Beispiele ein?

Where Chinese is the first language: New York's Chinatown

The world language

English, spoken by roughly 700 million people, is the closest thing to a world language. It has replaced French as the language of diplomacy and German as the language of science. It is the language of technology and international business, of radio and television, of advertising and film, of pop music, sport and tourism.
English is not only spoken by the most people, it also has the most words – something between 500,000 and a million. But to get along in English, it is enough to know a few thousand of the words most frequently used.
English exists in many different varieties. People from the south of England, Scots from Aberdeen, and Americans from Texas all speak with different accents, and when a Londoner and a New Yorker use the word *subway*, they mean different things. But when Oscar Wilde remarked that "the English have everything in common with the Americans except the language", and when a British cinema owner advertised an American film "with English subtitles", they were of course exaggerating. English speakers from Britain and America, from Australia and New Zealand, from southern Asia and Africa can all understand each other in spite of any regional peculiarities their English may have.

Wortschatz

roughly 700 million people	rund 700 Millionen Menschen
is the closest thing to a world language	kommt einer Weltsprache am nächsten
the language of diplomacy	die Sprache der Diplomatie
science	(Natur-)Wissenschaft(en)
the language of technology	die Sprache der Technologie/Technik
international business	(das) internationale Geschäftsleben
advertising	(die) Werbung
get along in English	im Englischen zurechtkommen
variety	(Spiel-)Art; Variante
Scots from Aberdeen	Schotten aus Aberdeen
accent	Akzent; Aussprache
subway	*AE* U-Bahn / *BE* Fußgängerunterführung
Oscar Wilde	(*1854 Dublin, †1900 Paris)
remark	bemerken; konstatieren
have something in common	etwas gemeinsam haben
advertise a film	für einen Film Reklame machen
exaggerate	übertreiben
New Zealand	Neuseeland
southern Asia	Südasien
in spite of regional peculiarities	trotz regionaler Besonderheiten

Verständnis- und Wortschatztest

a. How many people speak English? □ b. What used to be the language of diplomacy? □ c. How many words are there in English, and how many do you need to get along in English? □ d. Name some varieties of English. □ e. Where's Aberdeen? □ f. Was Oscar Wilde an *English* writer? □ g. You see the sign SUBWAY in a London street. What does it indicate?

Learning English

A: How long have you been learning English?

B: Oh, I don't know ... I'd say about four years, apart from the English I had at school.

A: So you didn't have to start from scratch when you took up English again?

B: Well, I did start from the beginning, actually. I didn't seem to remember much of what I'd learnt at school, but it gradually came back. So I suppose I got ahead faster than I would have done without my school English.

A: Your English is very good. How did you manage to learn it so well?

B: My first teacher kept telling us that learning a foreign language was simply a matter of practice. So I made sure I got some practice every day. I listened to tapes and to the radio, I watched English and American films on TV and on video, I grabbed every opportunity of talking with English-speaking visitors. I did a lot of reading – first simple readers, then books and newspapers. I wrote letters in English to people I had met ...

Wortschatz

start from scratch	ganz von vorn anfangen
take up English again (– took – taken)	wieder mit Englisch anfangen
I did start from the beginning, actually	an sich habe ich schon von vorn angefangen
learn – learnt/learned – learnt/learned	lernen – lernte – gelernt
it gradually came back	es kam allmählich wieder
I got ahead faster	ich kam schneller voran
manage to do something	es schaffen, etw. zu tun
teacher	Lehrer(in)
keep doing something (– kept – kept)	etw. immer wieder tun
it's simply a matter of practice *BE* / *AE* practise	es ist einfach eine Sache der Übung / Übungssache
listen to tapes	sich Tonbänder anhören
grab the opportunity	die Gelegenheit ergreifen
visitor	Besucher(in)
I did a lot of reading	ich habe viel gelesen
simple readers	einfache Lektüren (*d. h. Hefte mit einfachen Texten*)
write a letter to someone (– wrote – written)	jem. einen Brief schreiben
meet people (– met – met)	Leute/Menschen treffen/kennenlernen

Verständnis- und Wortschatztest

a. Talk about ways you can practise your English. – I can practise my English by ... ☐ b. *Start from scratch* – another expression for this? ☐ c. *Take up* English. Another expression for *take up*? ☐ d. Our teacher *kept telling* us ... – another expression for *kept telling*? ☐ e. *Grab* the opportunity of doing something – another word for *grab*?

Euphemisms

When people are trying to be polite or tactful, they often say things indirectly. In other words, they avoid calling a spade a spade – they use euphemistic language. Instead of giving someone a blunt "no", for example, they may answer "I'll think about it", and to get away from someone they've run into in the street they might say "We really must get together for lunch one of these days" without actually meaning it.

On the left are 10 frequently used euphemisms. Can you match them with the straightforward words on the right?

adult (book/film)	loved one	dead person	sex
bathroom	pass away	die	steward(ess)
flight attendant	previously owned	housewife	strike
homemaker	put to sleep	kill	toilet
industrial action	sunset years	old age	used

Wortschatz

euphemism	Euphemismus; beschönigender Ausdruck
polite	höflich
tactful	taktvoll
(in)direct(ly)	(in)direkt
avoid doing something	es vermeiden, etw. zu tun
call a spade a spade	„einen Spaten einen Spaten nennen"; die Dinge beim Namen nennen
euphemistic language	(eine) beschönigende Ausdrucksweise
a blunt "no"	ein unverblümtes „nein"
run into someone (– ran – run)	jem. zufällig treffen
they might say	sie könnten sagen
get together for lunch	sich zum (Mittag-)Essen treffen
match the A words with the B words	die A-Wörter den B-Wörtern zuordnen
the straightforward words	(*etwa:*) die Wörter, die das Gemeinte direkt ausdrücken
homemaker	Hausfrau (*aber auch* Hausmann, *weshalb dieser neutrale Ausdruck heute mitunter vorgezogen wird*)
take industrial action	in den Ausstand treten
the loved one	(*etwa:*) der/die liebe Verblichene
pass away	hinscheiden; entschlafen
previously owned	(„schon einmal besessen")
put to sleep	(ein Tier) einschläfern
sunset	Sonnenuntergang
die	sterben
housewife	Hausfrau
old age	das Alter (als letzter Lebensabschnitt)
toilet	Toilette
used	gebraucht

15 Erklärungen

1. Betonung, Verstärkung, Hervorhebung bewirkende Wörter und Strukturen

a. Betonendes *do*:

Accidents do happen. *Unfälle passieren nun einmal.*
He does seem to know about it. *Er scheint tatsächlich/wirklich davon zu wissen.*
Well, I did start from the beginning, actually.
(Etwa:) Na ja, an sich habe ich tatsächlich von vorne angefangen.

b. Betonende *-self*-Pronomen:

I only just arrived myself. *Ich bin selber gerade erst gekommen.*
Can't you do it yourself? *Kannst du es nicht selber machen?*

c. Verstärkende Adverbien:

It was a completely different kind of place then. *... ein völlig anderer Ort.*
It really gets to me. *Das nervt/wurmt mich vielleicht.*
I thoroughly enjoyed my stay. *Ich habe meinen Aufenthalt sehr genossen.*
I sure didn't realize it. *(AE) Ich habe es wirklich nicht gemerkt.*
You know damn well what I mean. *Du weißt doch ganz genau, was ich meine.*
Thank you very much indeed. *Vielen herzlichen Dank.*

d. *So* oder *such*:

She's so friendly and helpful. *Sie ist (ja) so freundlich und hilfsbereit.*
She's got such enthusiasm. *Sie ist so voller Begeisterung.*

e. Besondere Wortstellung:

(Normal betont:) We must really get together one of these days.
(Stärker betont:) We really must get together one of these days.

f. Einleitendes *it is* / *it was* und Relativsatz:

It was you who told me that. *Du warst es doch, der mir das gesagt hat.*
It was you who put Debbie's name up for the competition.
Sie waren es doch, die Debbie für den Wettbewerb vorgeschlagen hat.

g. Ausrufesatz:

Isn't it awful! *Ist das nicht furchtbar!*
What a nightmare! *Was für ein Alptraum!*

2. *Must – have to* (vgl. *can – be able to*, S. 70 u. 88)

Gegenwart: You must / have to start from scratch. *Du mußt von vorn anfangen.*
Vergangenheit: I had to start from scratch. *Ich mußte von vorn anfangen.*
Nach *will/would*: I'll/I'd have to start from scratch.
Ich werde/würde von vorn anfangen müssen.
To-Infinitiv/*-ing*-Form: I don't like to have to / having to start from scratch.
Ich habe es nicht gern, von vorn anfangen zu müssen.

Der Gebrauch von *must* ist im wesentlichen auf die Gegenwart beschränkt. In anderen Zeiten oder Formen wird es u. a. durch *have to* ersetzt.

1. Vervollständigen Sie den Text.

English is the ..... thing to a world language. It has ..... French as the language of diplomacy and German as the language of science. English is spoken by the ..... people and is also the language with the ..... words. ..... English has a vocabulary of over 500,000 words, you can get ..... well if you know a few thousand of the words most ..... used.
There are many ..... varieties of English, but on the whole English speakers from all over the world can all understand ..... other in spite of any regional ..... their English may have.
Learning English is very much a .... of practice. ..... to tapes and to the radio, ... English and American films, and ..... with English-speaking visitors are all excellent ..... of practising your English.
In any language, people use euphemisms if they want to say something ..... rather than call a spade a spade.

2. Heben Sie die unterstrichenen Elemente besonders hervor, betonen bzw. verstärken Sie sie. Gebrauchen Sie Adverbien wie *certainly, completely, exactly, highly, indeed, so, such, sure, thoroughly, very,* verstärkendes *do* oder die Form des Ausrufesatzes.

a. You know <u>what to do</u>.
b. <u>It's awful</u>.
c. There have been <u>many</u> changes.
d. She's a <u>nice girl</u>.
e. Other salesgirls <u>could learn a thing or two from her</u>.
f. Malta was a <u>different</u> place in those days.
g. Inter Motors is a <u>successful</u> company.
h. I <u>enjoyed</u> my recent stay at your house.
i. <u>Thank you very much</u>.
j. I <u>love you</u>, Claire.
k. I <u>didn't realize</u> I was going that fast.
l. You <u>knew</u> that there was a speed limit of 55 on that highway.

3. Setzen Sie eine englische Entsprechung von *müssen* ein.

a. We really ..... get together for lunch one of these days.
b. So you didn't ..... start from scratch when you took it up again?
c. I'll ..... think of some other way of getting here if they don't fix that bridge soon.
d. I don't see why I should ..... listen to other people's music just because *they* feel like listening to it.
e. She's got such enthusiasm, you only ..... walk past her counter to want to stop, even if you weren't planning to buy anything.
f. The taxi driver ..... be able to change a $10 bill.
g. They haven't had any rain for months in some parts. The farmers are ..... sell off their cattle, the crops are ruined and there are fires all over the place.

4. Übersetzen Sie.

a. Englisch, das von rund 700 Millionen Menschen gesprochen wird, kommt einer Weltsprache am nächsten.
b. Englisch ist die Sprache mit den meisten Wörtern.
c. Um im Englischen zurechtzukommen, muß man ein paar Tausend der am häufigsten gebrauchten Wörter kennen.
d. Wir haben eine Menge gemeinsam – mit Ausnahme der Sprache natürlich!
e. Wir verstehen uns doch, oder?
f. Sie sagt uns ständig, daß es einfach eine Sache der Übung ist.

16 Holiday chaos

Urlaubszeit, Fluglotsenstreik, Chaos an den Charterflughäfen – die Texte dieser Lektion behandeln eine solche Situation aus englischer Sicht und liefern uns so nützliches Sprachmaterial zum Thema Urlaubsreise. Text 1 ist ein Lagebericht, wie man ihn zur Reisezeit im Rundfunk hören oder in der Zeitung lesen kann. Text 2 ist ein Dialog „vor Ort", und Text 3 vermittelt eine kleine Kostprobe des Kleingedruckten in Reiseprospekten und -verträgen.
In der Tonaufnahme sind alle drei Texte mit britischen Akzenten gesprochen.

Chaos at the airport: Holidaymakers wait for their flights

Thousands wait for sunshine flights

ALL OVER Britain thousands of people have been spending another night stranded at airports as delays to charter flights to Europe continue. Some people have been waiting in departure lounges for 30 hours.

The enormous holdups are being caused by air-traffic controllers striking in several European countries, but tight scheduling by charter airlines, overcrowded airspace and congested airports are also being blamed for the chaos.

As one expert put it, "the whole European flight system is near breaking point".

At Gatwick, Britain's busiest holiday airport, the airport authorities have provided family bedding areas and extra washing facilities for the more than 2,000 people kept in the terminal overnight. Food bars are open 24 hours a day.

Britain's Tourism Minister, John Lee, urged people to forget the Continent and back British resorts instead. He said: "I'm taking my family to Scotland. Anyone who pays to wait for 24 hours or more in an airport lounge needs their head testing."

Wortschatz

they were stranded at the airport	sie saßen am Flughafen fest
as delays continue	während die Verspätungen fortbestehen
charter flights to Europe	Charterflüge nach Europa
departure lounge	Abflughalle
the enormous holdups	die enormen Verspätungen
air-traffic controller	Fluglotse
in several European countries	in mehreren europäischen Ländern
schedule flights (etc.)	Flüge (etc.) planen
tight scheduling	(*etwa:*) gedrängte Flugpläne
overcrowded airspace	überfüllter Luftraum
congested airports	überfüllte/verstopfte Flughäfen
as one expert put it	wie ein Experte es ausdrückte
is near breaking point	steht kurz vor dem Zusammenbruch
busy	verkehrsreich
the airport authorities	die Flughafenbehörden
provide bedding areas	Schlafbereiche einrichten
extra washing facilities	zusätzliche Waschmöglichkeiten
terminal	(Flughafen-)Abfertigungsgebäude
urge someone to do something	jem. auffordern, etw. zu tun
back British resorts	britische Urlaubsorte unterstützen
instead	statt dessen
anyone who does that needs their head testing	jeder, der das tut, sollte „sich am Kopf untersuchen lassen“

Verständnis- und Wortschatztest

a. What kind of flights are being delayed? □ b. Who is causing the delays? □ c. Sunshine flights are flights to ..... □ d. Another word for *delays*? □ e. Another word for *congested*? □ f. Another expression for *he needs his head testing*?

16 Text 2

In the departure lounge

A: If we hadn't gone charter we wouldn't be in this mess. The scheduled flights are all dead on time.

B: But they cost a fortune too. And we would've had to make all our own bookings.

A: How long have we been waiting now? Twelve – fourteen hours? If they'd only let you know what's going on. They just tell you to hang around and listen to the announcements.

B: Yes, why don't they say "There's going to be a delay of so and so many hours" so you can go and have lunch or something. It'd make it a lot easier to put up with.

C: We were supposed to fly at 6.30 this morning. There was no information until nine o'clock. At midday they said we'd be put on a bus for Luton to fly at three. Then they said it would be 4.30 from here.

A: It's a bloody shambles, that's what it is ...

Wortschatz

go charter (– went – gone)	mit Charter fliegen; einen Charterflug nehmen
mess	Durcheinander; Schlamassel
scheduled flight	Linienflug
dead on time	pünktlich auf die Minute
make all our own bookings	alle Buchungen selbst vornehmen
let someone know what's going on	jem. Bescheid sagen, was los ist
hang around (– hung – hung)	warten
listen to the announcements	auf die Ansagen achten
so you can go and have lunch	so daß man essen gehen kann
or something	oder irgendwas / so was
easier to put up with	leichter hinzunehmen / zu ertragen
we were supposed to fly at 6.30	wir sollten um 6.30 Uhr abfliegen
there was no information until nine o'clock	erst um neun Uhr gab es eine Information / hat man uns etwas gesagt
put someone on a bus for Luton	jem. in einen Bus nach Luton setzen
Luton	(Stadt und Flughafen 45 km NW von London)
a shambles	(*etwa:*) ein heilloses Durcheinander
it's a bloody shambles (Bloody *wird im Standardenglisch* ['blʌdɪ] *gesprochen; die Aussprache mit* [ʊ] *in der Tonaufnahme findet sich in nordbritischen Akzenten.*)	(*etwa:*) es ist ein verdammtes Chaos

Verständnis- und Wortschatztest

a. Why are the charter flights being delayed? ☐ b. Are scheduled flights being delayed too? ☐ c. Where are the passengers waiting? ☐ d. How long have they been waiting? ☐ e. Why can't they go and have lunch or something? ☐ f. The charter flights are delayed, but the scheduled flights are ..... ☐ g. But, of course, a scheduled flight is much ..... than a charter flight. ☐ h. Another word for *hang around*? ☐ i. Another word for *midday*? ☐ j. It's a bloody *shambles* – another word for *shambles*?

A look at the small print

If you don't take out insurance, there is a paragraph in the "booking conditions" of your package holiday which makes sure you cannot hold the tour operator responsible if there is any kind of delay:
"The company accepts no responsibility for loss or additional expenses due to delay or changes in air, road, rail, sea or other services or arising from quarantine, sickness, civil disturbance, strikes, lockouts or weather or any other conditions. Any such loss will have to be borne by the passenger, with possible reimbursement under certain circumstances because of Delay Insurance Cover."

Wortschatz

the small print	das Kleingedruckte
take out insurance (– took – taken)	eine Versicherung abschließen
paragraph	Absatz (in einem Text)
booking conditions	„Buchungs-"/Reisebedingungen
package holiday	Pauschalreise
hold someone responsible (– held – held)	jem. zur Verantwortung ziehen; sich an jem. halten
tour operator	Reiseveranstalter
accept no responsibility	keine Verantwortung übernehmen
loss	Verlust
additional expenses	zusätzliche Kosten
due to delay	durch Verspätung verursacht
changes in air/rail/sea services	Veränderungen im Flug-/Eisenbahn-/Schiffsverkehr
arise from (– arose – arisen)	sich ergeben aus/durch
quarantine	Quarantäne
sickness	Krankheit
civil disturbance	Unruhen; Störungen der öffentlichen Ordnung
lockout	Aussperrung
weather conditions	Witterungsverhältnisse
any such loss	jeder solche Verlust
bear – bore – borne	tragen
with possible reimbursement	bei eventueller Entschädigung
under certain circumstances	unter bestimmten Umständen
Delay Insurance Cover	Versicherungsschutz gegen Verspätung

Verständnis- und Wortschatztest

a. A paragraph in the booking conditions makes ..... that the tour operator can't be ..... responsible if there are delays because of strikes or lockouts. ☐ b. The only way to protect yourself against additional expenses is to ..... insurance. ☐ c. Delays may be ..... to such things as strikes, lockouts, weather ..... or civil disturbance. ☐ d. Losses ..... from delays normally have to be ..... by the passenger. ☐ e. Under certain ..... reimbursement is possible because of Delay Insurance ..... ☐ f. Try to think of words that mean roughly the same as the following: *make sure*, any *kind* of delay, *due to delays*, *sickness*, *strikes*.

1. Gebrauch der Zeiten

a. Thousands of people have been spending another night at airports.
Tausende von Menschen haben eine weitere Nacht auf Flughäfen verbracht.
b. Thousands of people have spent another night at airports.
Tausende von Menschen haben eine weitere Nacht auf Flughäfen verbracht.

c. I'm taking my family to Scotland. *Ich fahre mit meiner Familie nach Schottland.*
d. I'm going to take my family to Scotland. *Ich werde ... nach Schottland fahren.*
e. I'll take my family to Scotland. *Ich werde ... nach Schottland fahren.*

f. If we hadn't gone charter, we wouldn't be in this mess.
Wenn wir nicht Charter gebucht hätten, wären wir nicht in diesem Schlamassel.
g. If we hadn't gone charter, we wouldn't have got into this mess.
Wenn wir nicht Ch. gebucht hätten, wären wir nicht in diesen Schlamassel geraten.

In den Sätzen (a) und (b) geht es um den Unterschied zwischen Verlaufsform des Perfekts (a) und einfacher Form des Perfekts (b):
Satz (a) stellt die Handlung (*have been spending*) als sich aus der Vergangenheit in die Gegenwart erstreckend – also noch andauernd – dar, wird also etwa an dem auf die Nacht folgenden Morgen gesprochen (Nachrichten!), während die Reisenden immer noch auf den Flughäfen warten.
Satz (b) berichtet einfach die Tatsache (*have spent*), ohne etwas darüber auszusagen, ob die Reisenden immer noch warten oder nicht.
Die Sätze (c), (d), (e) beziehen sich auf die Zukunft. Die Verlaufsform *am taking* (c) drückt aus, daß die Handlung (seit einiger Zeit) geplant ist; *am going to take* (d) betont die gegenwärtige Absicht; *'ll take* (e) – sonst häufig die neutrale, „ungefärbte" Zukunftsform – deutet hier an, daß der Entschluß gerade spontan gefaßt wurde.
Der Bedingungssatz (f) ist formal eine Mischung von Typ 3 (erste Hälfte) und Typ 2 (zweite Hälfte), während (g) in beiden Teilen ein Bedingungssatz vom Typ 3 ist – vergleichen Sie dazu S. 76.

2. *Some – any*

a. Some people have been waiting for 30 hours.
Manche Leute warten nun schon seit dreißig Stunden.
b. There aren't any holidaymakers waiting at the airports at the moment.
Im Augenblick warten auf den Flughäfen keine Urlauber.
c. Are there any holidaymakers still waiting at the airports?
Warten noch Urlauber auf den Flughäfen?

d. There was something on TV about it. *Darüber war etwas im Fernsehen.*
e. There wasn't anything on TV about it. *Im Fernsehen war nichts darüber.*
f. Was there anything on TV about it? *War darüber was im Fernsehen?*

Some steht bei bejahtem Sinn (a, d); *any* steht bei verneintem (b, e) oder fragendem (c, f) Sinn. In bejahten, nichtfragenden Aussagen dagegen heißt *any* so etwas wie *jede (x-beliebige) / irgendeine / irgendwelche*:

Any such loss will have to be borne by the passenger.
Jeder solche Verlust muß durch den Reisenden getragen werden.
Anyone who pays to wait for 24 hours or more in an airport lounge needs their head testing. *Jeder/Jemand, der dafür bezahlt, daß ...*

1. Setzen Sie *some* oder *any* oder Zusammensetzungen mit diesen Wörtern ein.

a. ..... showers are likely this evening and overnight.
b. They haven't had ..... rain for months in ..... parts.
c. I'd rather fly than drive ..... time.
d. You feel you don't have ..... privacy in your own home any more.
e. Have you got ..... spare change on you?
f. Bring along ..... documents that may be relevant to your application.
g. You cannot hold the tour operator responsible if there is ..... kind of delay.
h. ..... people don't read as well as one would expect.
i. I wasn't planning to buy ....., actually.
j. Debbie isn't the type of girl who'd sell you ..... just to make a sale.
k. Did you sell ..... today?
l. The stage is ..... I've been keen on for a long time.
m. Is there ..... you're particularly keen on?
n. I don't know ..... who got hurt travelling by air.
o. I actually know ..... who lives there.

2. Bilden Sie jeweils einen Bedingungssatz entsprechend dem ersten oder dem zweiten Beispiel.

we / not go charter // we / not get into this mess If we <u>hadn't gone</u> charter, we <u>wouldn't have got</u> into this mess.
we / not go charter // we / not be in this mess If we <u>hadn't gone</u> charter, we <u>wouldn't be</u> in this mess.

a. it / not be a package holiday // it / cost a fortune
b. we / take a scheduled flight // we / not have to wait for 20 hours
c. we / go to Scotland // we / not be sitting here
d. you / not go to have lunch // you / hear the announcement
e. we / take out insurance // we / get some sort of reimbursement
f. the boy / not have a gun // those two unfortunate burglars / still be alive
g. the film / not have German subtitles // I / not understand it
h. you / walk // you / get here faster
i. the captain / not manage to bring the plane to a halt // we / all be dead now
j. people / be told what was going on // they / not be so angry

3. Übersetzen Sie.

a. Wir warten nun schon seit 20 Stunden.
b. Wodurch werden diese enormen Verspätungen verursacht?
c. Wenn wir einen Linienflug genommen hätten, wären wir nicht in diesem Schlamassel.
d. Ein Linienflug hätte ein Vermögen gekostet.
e. Und wir hätten alle Buchungen selber machen müssen.
f. Wie lange warten wir jetzt schon?
g. Es wäre leichter gewesen, wenn man uns gesagt hätte, was los ist.
h. Wir sollten heute morgen um sechs Uhr dreißig fliegen.
i. Wenn wir eine Versicherung abgeschlossen hätten, hätten wir vielleicht (*might*) einen Teil unseres Geldes zurückbekommen.
j. Wir hätten das Kleingedruckte lesen sollen.

17 Older drivers

In den Vereinigten Staaten ist ein einmal erworbener Führerschein nicht unbegrenzt gültig, sondern muß in regelmäßigen Abständen (in den meisten Bundesstaaten 4 Jahre) verlängert werden. Die Bedingungen für die Verlängerung sind je nach Staat unterschiedlich; häufig ist ein Sehtest, vielfach auch eine schriftliche Prüfung, mitunter aber auch weder Test noch Prüfung vorgeschrieben. In einigen wenigen Staaten werden jugendliche oder ältere Autofahrer besonders überprüft. Das Für und Wider besonderer Tests für ältere Autofahrer wird immer wieder diskutiert. Die Texte dieser Lektion enthalten 1. einen Unfallbericht (Zeitungsmeldung), 2. eine Zusammenfassung des aktuellen Diskussionsstandes und 3. persönliche Äußerungen zu dieser Frage. In der Tonaufnahme sind alle drei Texte mit amerikanischen Akzenten gesprochen, der erste im Stil einer Meldung im Regionalfunk, der zweite in der Art eines Kommentars zu einer Fernseh- oder Rundfunkdokumentation, der dritte in gewöhnlicher Alltagssprache.

Two men hurt in car crash

TWO MEN were treated at St. Francis Medical Center Monday for injuries they suffered in a collision at the junction of Illinois Route 89 and Rutland Road in Marshall County. Both were released after treatment.

Terry Hufford, 35, of Toluca, was driving north on Route 89 when his car was hit by a camper driven by Byron Jenkins, 73, of Texas. Jenkins, who was headed south, realized too late that a car in front of him had stopped to make a left turn. Jenkins lost control when he braked and swerved into the northbound lane, state police said.

Hufford was ticketed for not wearing his seat belt. Jenkins was ticketed for failure to reduce speed and using the wrong lane, state police said.

Wortschatz

car crash	(Auto-)Zusammenstoß; Autounfall
treat	behandeln
medical center *AE* / *BE* centre	(*besonders in Namen:*) Krankenhaus
injury	Verletzung
suffer injuries	Verletzungen erleiden
collision	Zusammenstoß
junction	(Straßen-)Kreuzung
Illinois Route 89	(*etwa:*) Illinois-Staatsstraße 89 (Illinois = Bundesstaat der USA)
county	(*AE etwa:*) (Land-)Kreis
release (from hospital)	(aus dem Krankenhaus) entlassen
Toluca	(Stadt mit 1470 Einw. in Illinois)
camper	Wohnmobil
his car was hit by a camper	sein PKW stieß mit einem Wohnmobil zusammen
he was headed south	er fuhr in Richtung Süden
a car in front of him	ein Wagen vor ihm
lose – lost – lost	verlieren – verlor – verloren
he lost control	er verlor die Kontrolle
he braked	er bremste
he swerved into the northbound lane	er („schwenkte") geriet auf die nach Norden führende Fahrspur
he was ticketed	er bekam ein Strafmandat
wear his seat belt (– wore – worn)	den Sitzgurt anlegen; angeschnallt sein
for failure to reduce speed	weil er seine Geschwindigkeit nicht vermindert hatte
use the wrong lane	die falsche Fahrspur benutzen

Verständnis- und Wortschatztest

a. Where exactly did the accident happen? ☐ b. How many people were involved, and who were they? ☐ c. Did they suffer serious injuries? ☐ d. Who was probably to blame for the accident, and why? ☐ e. How old was the person who caused the accident? ☐ f. Another word for *crash*? ☐ g. Another word for *medical center*? ☐ h. Instead of "Hufford was *ticketed*" one could also say .....

Regular testing for older drivers?

With the US population getting older, the percentage of older motorists is rising. Statistics show that drivers over 65 are involved, per mile driven, in considerably more accidents than those aged between 25 and 65.
To sift out those who are no longer fit to drive, some states now require people over 65 to take periodic tests to get their licenses renewed. In some cases, this involves no more than an eye test, but in others it means driving tests and medical checkups.
Many Americans want all older motorists to be tested regularly, but others argue that such a practice would be discriminatory. A point often made in discussing the problem is that in areas without adequate public transportation a car means freedom and independence, particularly for older people. Losing the right to drive therefore seriously affects a person's self-respect and quality of life.

Wortschatz

regular testing	regelmäßig Prüfungen/Tests
rise – rose – risen	steigen – stieg – gestiegen
statistics show	Statistiken zeigen/belegen
are involved in accidents	sind in Unfälle verwickelt
per mile driven	pro gefahrener Meile (= ca. 1,6 km)
considerably more	erheblich mehr
aged between 25 and 65	im Alter von 25 bis 65
sift out	aussieben
no longer fit to drive	nicht mehr fahrtauglich
require someone to do something	von jem. verlangen, daß er etw. tut
take periodic tests	sich regelmäßig prüfen lassen
to get their licenses *AE* / *BE* licences renewed	um ihre Führerscheine verlängert zu bekommen
it involves an eye test	es bedeutet einen Augentest
driving test	Fahrprüfung
medical checkup	ärztliche Untersuchung
test someone regularly	jem. regelmäßig prüfen/testen
such a practice	so eine Praxis/Verfahrensweise
discriminatory	diskriminierend
a point often made	ein Argument, das oft vorgebracht wird
adequate public transportation *AE* / *BE* public transport facilities	ausreichende öffentliche Verkehrsmittel
freedom	Freiheit
the right to drive	das Recht, Auto zu fahren
it affects a person's self-respect	es beeinträchtigt die Selbstachtung eines Menschen
quality of life	Lebensqualität

Verständnis- und Wortschatztest

In the US, the percentage of older motorists is ..... Drivers over 65 are ..... in more accidents than those aged 25 to 65. Many people ..... that those who are no longer ..... to drive should be ..... out. They want drivers over 65 to ..... periodic tests to ..... their licenses renewed.

What do you think of elderly drivers?

A young man: Their reflexes are often slower, they don't see as well as they used to – they should be tested at least once a year to make sure they're still fit to drive.
A senior citizen: I haven't noticed many bad elderly drivers. They may drive slower than some of these young hot rodders. It's these teenagers that need testing more frequently, not the elderly drivers.
A motorcycle officer: When you stop them to give them a ticket, they're often not aware that they've broken the law. They tell you that they've driven for years, that they're very competent drivers, that they couldn't possibly have done anything wrong.
A middle-aged woman: Of course some older drivers have problems, but so do individuals in the other age groups. On the whole, I think they drive more responsibly than young people. Testing them more often than other drivers wouldn't be fair ...

Wortschatz

what do you think of elderly drivers?	wie denken Sie über ältere (Auto-)Fahrer?
their reflexes are slower	sie reagieren langsamer
at least once a year	mindestens einmal jährlich
senior citizen	ältere(r) (Mit-)Bürger(in)
hot rod *Slang*	(„heiße Stange") frisiertes Auto
hot rodder *Slang*	Fahrer(in) eines frisierten Wagens; Raser(in)
they need testing more frequently	sie sollten häufiger geprüft werden
motorcycle officer *AE*	(Verkehrs-)Polizist(in) mit Motorrad
they're not aware they've broken the law	ihnen ist nicht klar, daß sie gegen die Gesetze verstoßen haben
break – broke – broken	brechen – brach – gebrochen
a very competent driver	ein(e) sehr gute(r) Fahrer(in)
do something wrong (– did – done)	etw. falsch machen
a middle-aged woman	eine Frau in mittleren Jahren
an individual	ein einzelner; eine Einzelperson
age group	Altersgruppe
on the whole	im großen (und) ganzen
drive responsibly	verantwortungsbewußt fahren

Verständnis- und Wortschatztest

a. When you're old, you don't see as well as you ..... to. ☐ b. If you can't see properly, you're not ..... to drive. ☐ c. Older drivers usually drive ..... than younger ones. ☐ d. The old lady was not ..... that she had broken the law. ☐ e. She said: "I can't possibly have done ..... wrong." ☐ f. Some older drivers have problems, but so ..... people in the other age groups. ☐ g. *Elderly* drivers – another word for *elderly*? ☐ h. Another expression for *senior citizens*? ☐ i. Instead of drive *slower* you could also say drive ..... ☐ j. A *hot rodder* is someone who drives ..... ☐ k. A *motorcycle officer* is ..... ☐ l. A very *competent* driver is a ..... ☐ m. A *middle-aged* person is someone who .....

17 Erklärungen

1. Komparativ (Steigerungs-Höher- od. Mehrstufe)

Häufig steht der Komparativ in Verbindung mit *than*:

Is flying safer today than it used to be?
It involves no more than an eye test.
Roads are more congested than they were ten years ago.
They may drive slower than some of these young hot rodders.
I think they drive more responsibly than young people.
Testing them more often than other drivers wouldn't be fair.

Rufen Sie sich noch einmal die verschiedenen Arten der Bildung des Komparativs ins Gedächtnis zurück:

Bei kurzen Wörtern Anhängen von *-er*: *great – greater* etc.
Stummes End-*e* entfällt: *safe – safer* etc.
Verdopplung des Endkonsonanten: *hot – hotter* etc.
Bei zweisilbigen Adjektiven wird *-y* zu *-i-*: *early – earlier* etc.

Bei längeren Wörtern mit *more*: *expensive – more expensive* etc.
Alle *-ly*-Adverbien sind „längere Wörter": *deeply – more deeply* etc.

Unregelmäßig: *good – better* etc.

2. *Do* und *so/nor/neither* als „Stellvertreter"

Accidents do happen, and when they do (= when they "happen"), it can make all the difference whether you know exactly what to do.
Unfälle passieren nun einmal, und wenn sie es tun …

I wish we'd given as much thought to the sitting room as we did (= as we "gave") to planning the kitchen. *Ich wünschte, wir hätten dem Wohnzimmer soviel Überlegung gewidmet wie der Planung der Küche.*

I suppose I got ahead faster than I would have done (= than I would have "got ahead") without my school English.
Ich bin wohl schneller vorangekommen, als ich es ohne mein Schulenglisch wäre.

Die Beispiele zeigen, wie ein verbaler Ausdruck durch eine Form von *do* wieder aufgenommen werden kann. Die eingeklammerten Umschreibungen deuten jeweils an, wofür *do* stellvertretend steht; sie sind keine idiomatisch gleichwertigen Alternativen.
In dem folgenden Satz steht stellvertretendes *do* in Verbindung mit rückweisendem *so*:

Of course some older drivers have problems, but so do individuals in the other age groups (= inviduals in the other age groups have problems too).
Natürlich haben manche älteren Fahrer Probleme, aber das gilt auch für einzelne Angehörige der anderen Altersgruppen.

Wird statt auf einen bejahten auf einen verneinten Sachverhalt bestätigend zurückverwiesen, so steht statt *so* entweder *nor* oder *neither*:
Of course the older drivers don't have this problem, but nor/neither do individuals in the other age groups (= individuals in the other age groups don't have this problem either).

1. Ergänzen Sie die fehlenden Verben.

Two men were ..... at St. Francis Medical Center Monday for injuries they ..... in a collision at the junction of Illinois Route 89 and Rutland Road in Marshall County. Both were ..... after treatment. Terry Hufford, 35, of Toluca, was ..... north on Route 89 when his car was ..... by a camper ..... by Byron Jenkins, 73, of Texas. Jenkins, who was headed south, ... too late that a car in front of him had ..... to make a left turn. Jenkins ..... control when he braked and swerved into the northbound lane, state police said. Hufford was ticketed for not ..... his seat belt. Jenkins was ticketed for failure to reduce speed and ..... the wrong lane, state police said.

2. Setzen Sie *so/nor/neither* oder eine Form von *do* ein.

a. You don't know him as well as Doris .....
b. She doesn't like you, but I .....
c. I didn't think I'd lose but I .....
d. We hear of more crashes than we ever ..... in the past.
e. He didn't get there as quickly as he would have ..... if the roads hadn't been so congested.
f. He drives very competently, and ..... does his wife.
g. "He looks like a ghost." – "..... would you if you hadn't slept for 48 hours."
h. I didn't break the law. ..... did any of the people who worked with me.
i. I didn't like it and ..... did my wife.
j. He didn't reduce speed, ... did the driver of the other car.

3. Bilden Sie jeweils einen Vergleichssatz entsprechend den Beispielen.

loud music / annoying / traffic noise
Loud music is more annoying than traffic noise.
Loud music is less annoying than traffic noise.
Loud music is(n't) as annoying as traffic noise.

a. charter flights / expensive / scheduled flights
b. flying / dangerous / travelling by car
c. a pneumatic drill / noisy / motorbike
d. a jukebox / bad / a barking dog
e. a senior citizen drives / slow(ly) / a young hot rodder
f. watching TV / interesting / playing cards
g. at eighty you have / slow reflexes / at eighteen
h. a friendly salesperson / usually successful / an aggressive one
i. on the whole, old hotels / nice / ultramodern ones

4. Übersetzen Sie.

a. Fahrer über 65 sind weit häufiger in Unfälle verwickelt.
b. Von Fahrern über 65 wird verlangt, daß sie sich regelmäßig testen lassen.
c. Mit siebzig sieht man nicht so gut wie früher.
d. Ich fahre seit fünfzig Jahren – ich kann unmöglich etwas falsch gemacht haben.
e. Ältere Fahrer sollten regelmäßig getestet werden, aber diese jugendlichen Raser sollten es auch.
f. Im großen ganzen fahren ältere Autofahrer verantwortungsbewußter als junge Leute.

18 Working mothers

Sollten Mütter nur für ihre Kinder da sein, oder können sie ruhig auch arbeiten gehen? In Text 1 äußert sich dazu eine Betroffene, Text 2 bringt die Meinung eines australischen Geistlichen, und in Text 3 hören Sie Stimmen aus einer Fernsehdiskussion.
In der Tonaufnahme spricht eine Frau aus dem Londoner Raum den ersten Text und eine Männerstimme mit leichtem australischen Akzent den zweiten; im dritten Text hören Sie „neutrale“ britische Stimmen.

A mother

I'd like to go back to work. I think it's a very good idea for mothers to work, if you can be organized enough, just for the stimulus it would give. You see, being at home you've got no deadlines any more. Getting up in the morning to look after the baby and do housework is different from getting up and going to work, and perhaps dressing up to go somewhere special.
What I'd like to do is buy a house, so we've got more room, and go to work perhaps mornings, or something like that. And with my salary I'd have a girl in – an au pair perhaps – just for the company it'd give me while Paul's away, and also to look after the baby mornings so I can go to work and at least be doing something other than chores. I don't think Sarah would suffer if we had that sort of arrangement.

Wortschatz

if you can be organized enough	(*etwa:*) wenn man alles gut im Griff hat
just for the stimulus it would give	einfach wegen der Anregung, die es einem geben würde
you've got no deadlines any more	man hat keine Termine mehr
get up in the morning (– got – got / *AE auch* gotten)	morgens aufstehen
look after the baby	sich um das Baby kümmern
do housework	den Haushalt machen
dress up	sich feinmachen; sich schön anziehen
go somewhere special	ausgehen
or something like that	oder so was
have a girl in	sich ein (Haus-)Mädchen nehmen
au pair (girl)	Au-pair-Mädchen (das ohne oder bei geringer Bezahlung, gegen Unterkunft u. Verpflegung, im Haushalt hilft)
just for the company it'd give me	nur um der Gesellschaft willen
do something other than chores	etw. anderes als Hausarbeit machen
Sarah would suffer	Sarah würde darunter leiden
if we had that sort of arrangement	wenn wir es so regeln/machen würden

Verständnis- und Wortschatztest

a. What kind of work is this woman doing at the moment? □ b. What would she like to do? □ c. She'd like to go out to work just for the ..... it would give. □ d. What would she use the salary for? □ e. What kind of home does she have? □ f. What kind of home would she like to have, and why? □ g. What would be the advantage of having an au pair? □ h. If you're very organized, you have everything under ..... □ i. A ..... is a time by which a job etc. must be finished. □ j. She doesn't like doing the *chores* – another word for *chores*? □ k. The money you're paid for your job each month is your ..... □ l. A foreign girl who lives with a family looking after the children and helping with the housework is called an ..... □ m. People usually dress ..... when they go out to dinner.

An Australian clergyman speaking on Mother's Day

What children desperately need are some old-fashioned mums with some unconditional love, some wholesome home cooking and some precious time set aside each day to read bedtime Bible stories, ending with a prayer and a kiss.

Mothers need to start taking their children to Sunday school and church each Sunday, even if it means leaving Dad at home watching his rehashed sport on TV or drinking and gambling with his mates at the club.

Wortschatz

an Australian clergyman	ein australischer Geistlicher/Pfarrer
Mother's Day	Muttertag
need something desperately	etw. dringend benötigen
old-fashioned	altmodisch
mum *BE* / *AE* mom	Mutti; Mami
unconditional	bedingungslos; vorbehaltlos
wholesome home cooking	gesunde Hausmannskost
precious	wertvoll; kostbar
set time aside (– set – set)	Zeit „abzweigen"/freihalten/einplanen
bedtime story	Gutenachtgeschichte
Bible	Bibel
ending with a prayer	abschließend mit einem Gebet
kiss	Kuß
they need to start taking their children to Sunday school	sie sollten damit anfangen, ihre Kinder in die Sonntagsschule zu bringen
even if it means leaving Dad at home	auch wenn das bedeutet, daß man (den) Papi zu Hause läßt
the rehashed sport on TV	(*etwa:*) die Sportaufzeichnungen im Fernsehen (rehash = aufwärmen)
gamble	(um Geld etc.) spielen
his mates	seine Kumpel/Kumpane
at the club	im Klub/Verein

Verständnis- und Wortschatztest

Können Sie die fehlenden Wörter aus dem Gedächtnis einsetzen? Wenn nicht, lesen und hören Sie bitte den zweiten Text noch ein- oder zweimal, bevor Sie sich auf die nachstehende Aufgabe konzentrieren.

An Australian ..... speaks on Mother's Day. What children ..... need are some old-fashioned mums with some ..... love, some ..... home cooking and some ..... time set aside each day to read bedtime Bible stories, ending with a ..... and a kiss.

Mothers ..... to start taking their children to Sunday school and church each Sunday, ... if it means leaving Dad at home watching his ..... sport on TV or drinking and ..... with his mates at the club.

A discussion panel

A: I don't like the idea of a woman going out to work if she's got small children.

B: What if she needs the money?

A: I can't quarrel with that, of course – if there's no husband, or if he's ill or poorly paid, that's a different matter.

C: Often it's just to have money for things they wouldn't be able to afford on one income – a second car, expensive holidays ...

B: It's a personal thing, isn't it? I mean you have a right to decide for yourself how you want to live your life, don't you?

A: But it's the children who suffer.

B: You don't have to be with your children all the time to be a good mother. – And there may be a grandmother around.

C: If you're lucky!

B: Still, I say if a woman's frustrated at home, by all means let her go out and find herself a job. Children are adaptable. They'll get more benefit from a half-time mother who's contented than from a full-time one who's totally frustrated.

Wortschatz

discussion panel	Diskussionsrunde
quarrel with something	an etw. etw. auszusetzen haben
ill or poorly paid	krank oder schlecht bezahlt
that's a different matter	das ist (ganz) etw. anderes
things they wouldn't be able to afford on one income	Dinge, die sie sich von einem Einkommen nicht leisten könnten
it's a personal thing	es ist Privatsache
you have a right to decide for yourself	man hat das Recht, selber zu entscheiden
there may be a grandmother around	vielleicht ist ja auch noch eine Großmutter da
if you're lucky	wenn man Glück hat
still	(*hier:*) trotzdem
frustrated	frustriert
by all means let her go out	sie soll ruhig rausgehen
and find herself a job	und sich eine Stelle suchen
adaptable	anpassungsfähig
get more benefit from something	aus etw. mehr Nutzen ziehen; mehr von etw. haben
half-time/full-time (job *etc.*)	Halbtags-/Ganztags-(stelle *etc.*)
contented	zufrieden
totally frustrated	total frustriert

Verständnis- und Wortschatztest

a. A *discussion panel* is a ..... of people who ..... something. ☐ b. If you can *afford* something, you have enough ..... ☐ c. Your *grandmother* is your ..... ☐ d. The opposite of *frustrated* could be ..... ☐ e. What's the difference between a *full-time* and a *half-time* mother? ☐ f. Another word for *mother*, and another word for *children*?

1. Großschreibung

an airline spokesman – a British Airways spokesman
the southern states – the (United) States (of America)
a post office (= *ein Postamt*) – the Post Office (= *die Postbehörde, die „Bundespost“*)
there have been two world wars – the Second World War
she's a shop assistant – she's Shop Assistant of the Year
a day in (the) summer – a Saturday in June
a local cinema owner – a British cinema owner

Namen und namenähnliche Bezeichnungen im weitesten Sinn werden im Englischen groß geschrieben. Abweichend vom Deutschen werden auch von Namen abgeleitete Adjektive (*Britain → British, Europe → European* etc.) groß geschrieben.
Bei Grenzfällen schwankt die Schreibweise, je nachdem ob die Vorstellung „Name“ oder „normales Substantiv“ überwiegt: *Are you coming by Tube/tube? He doesn't like Yuppies/yuppies. It's somewhere in the South/south of England. Where's Dad/dad?*
Gern wird Großschreibung auch zur Heraushebung bzw. zur Betonung des „Institutionscharakters“ benutzt:

We are seeking aggressive, career-minded Sales People to join our expanding sales force in West Germany.
The Management and the Staff of the Royal Hotel welcome you and hope you will enjoy your stay.
If you wish to extend your stay, please give our Reception as much notice as possible.
Any loss will have to be borne by the passenger, with possible reimbursement under certain circumstances because of Delay Insurance Cover.

2. *-ing*-Konstruktion als adverbiale Bestimmung

Being at home you've got no deadlines any more.
Wenn man zu Hause ist, hat man keine Termine mehr.
Noticing that his canoe was missing, he jumped into an old, leaky rowboat.
Da/Als er sah, daß sein Kanu nicht da war, sprang er in ein altes, leckes Ruderboot.

Mike Bratton was alone in the house watching TV.
Mike Bratton war allein zu Hause und sah fern.
They drive up and down through country villages making this horrible noise.
Sie fahren durch kleine Dörfer und machen dabei diesen scheußlichen Lärm.
I feel very safe flying. *Ich fühle mich vollkommen sicher, wenn ich fliege.*

... even if it means leaving Dad at home watching his rehashed sport on TV.
... auch wenn das bedeutet, daß man Papi zu Hause läßt, wo er sich im Fernsehen seinen wiederaufgewärmten Sport ansehen kann.

With the US population getting older, the percentage of older motorists is rising.
Da die US-Bevölkerung älter wird, nimmt auch die Zahl der älteren Autofahrer prozentual zu. / Das Durchschnittsalter der amerikanischen Bevölkerung steigt, und mit ihm nimmt auch der Anteil älterer Kraftfahrer zu.

1. Was ist groß zu schreiben? Schreiben Sie die Sätze in korrigierter Form ab.

a. on mother's day dad will read the children some stories from the bible.
b. two men were treated at st. francis medical center monday for injuries they suffered in a collision at the junction of illinois route 89 and rutland road in marshall county.
c. on tv last night, tourism minister john lee urged holidaymakers to forget the continent and back british resorts instead.
d. with the williamsburg bridge closed, commuters are having to find other ways of travelling across the east river from brooklyn to manhattan and vice versa.
e. family gp dr ian cummings from kilmorack in the scottish highlands faced a real emergency when he arrived back at gatwick airport and found himself stranded by the rail strike.
f. in southwest london, work on the a309 kingston bypass at the claygate lane roundabout has been causing long delays for drivers heading into central london, and in the west end berkeley square, berkeley street and hay hill are closed because of a fire.

2. Setzen Sie die Verben in eine passende Form. (Erzählzeit soll stets die Vergangenheit sein.)

a. (Row) as fast as he could, he (reach) the exhausted man just in time (save) him from (drown).
b. (Throw) on his parka, he (dash) out of the house (see) what (happen).
c. (Face) financial ruin and unable (pay) for extra animal feed, farmers (sell) livestock in the hope that the extra income (help) (see) them through until the rain (come).
d. (Realize) that there (be) strangers in the house, he (take) his rifle, (load) it and (slide) down the stairs.
e. (Fear) that the bridge (collapse), they immediately (close) it to all traffic.
f. (Fear) that she (be) fired, she (not reveal) her problem.
g. Not (know) what (do), she (sit) down and (weep).
h. Yesterday he (spend) the afternoon (drink) and (gamble) with his mates at the club.
i. I enclose the photo I (take) of you and Bonnie (watch) TV in the evening.
j. With thousands of people (wait) at airports, the government finally (decide) (act).
k. In the first year of our marriage, with my wife (work) nine to five and me (work) nights, we hardly ever (have) time for each other.

3. Übersetzen Sie.

a. Wir würden gern ein Haus kaufen, damit wir mehr Platz haben.
b. Ich glaube, es wäre eine gute Idee, wenn ich wieder arbeiten ginge.
c. Ich glaube nicht, daß es für Sarah von Nachteil wäre (*suffer*), wenn ich vormittags arbeiten ginge.
d. Wenn wir beide arbeiteten (*with ... -ing*), hätten wir Geld für Dinge, die wir uns von *einem* Gehalt nicht leisten können.
e. Man hat doch das Recht, selber zu entscheiden, wie man sein Leben führen will, oder nicht?
f. Dieser Geistliche möchte, daß alle Mütter ihren Kindern vorm Schlafengehen Geschichten aus der Bibel vorlesen.
g. Und sonntags sollen sie mit ihnen in die Kirche gehen.

19 Health

Von Krankheit, Arzt und Arznei ist in dieser Lektion die Rede, von häufig genannten Symptomen und dem, was man gegen sie tun kann. Text 1 berichtet in Form einer Zeitungsmeldung von einem interessanten Umfrageergebnis, Text 2 ist ein realistischer Dialog in einer Arztsprechstunde, und Text 3 gibt *background information* zum Thema *stress* – seit den fünfziger Jahren gehört das letztere englische Wort ja auch zum deutschen Sprachbestand.
In der Tonaufnahme klingt Text 1 wie eine britische Rundfunk- oder Fernsehmeldung. Text 2 vermittelt die Atmosphäre einer britischen Arztpraxis, während Text 3 von einer Amerikanerin gesprochen ist.

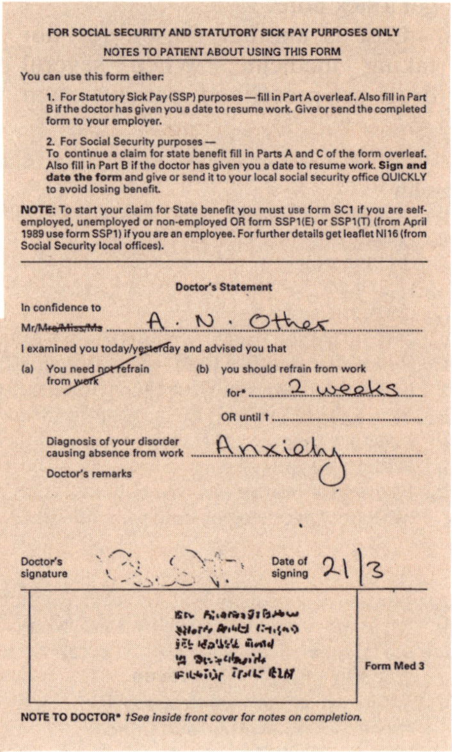

FOR SOCIAL SECURITY AND STATUTORY SICK PAY PURPOSES ONLY

NOTES TO PATIENT ABOUT USING THIS FORM

You can use this form either:

1. For Statutory Sick Pay (SSP) purposes — fill in Part A overleaf. Also fill in Part B if the doctor has given you a date to resume work. Give or send the completed form to your employer.

2. For Social Security purposes — To continue a claim for state benefit fill in Parts A and C of the form overleaf. Also fill in Part B if the doctor has given you a date to resume work. **Sign and date the form** and give or send it to your local social security office QUICKLY to avoid losing benefit.

NOTE: To start your claim for State benefit you must use form SC1 if you are self-employed, unemployed or non-employed OR form SSP1(E) or SSP1(T) (from April 1989 use form SSP1) if you are an employee. For further details get leaflet NI16 (from Social Security local offices).

Doctor's Statement

In confidence to

Mr/~~Mrs/Miss/Ms~~ A. N. Other

I examined you today/~~yesterday~~ and advised you that

(a) You need ~~not~~ refrain from ~~work~~

(b) you should refrain from work for* 2 weeks

OR until †

Diagnosis of your disorder causing absence from work Anxiety

Doctor's remarks

Doctor's signature

Date of signing 21/3

Form Med 3

NOTE TO DOCTOR* †*See inside front cover for notes on completion.*

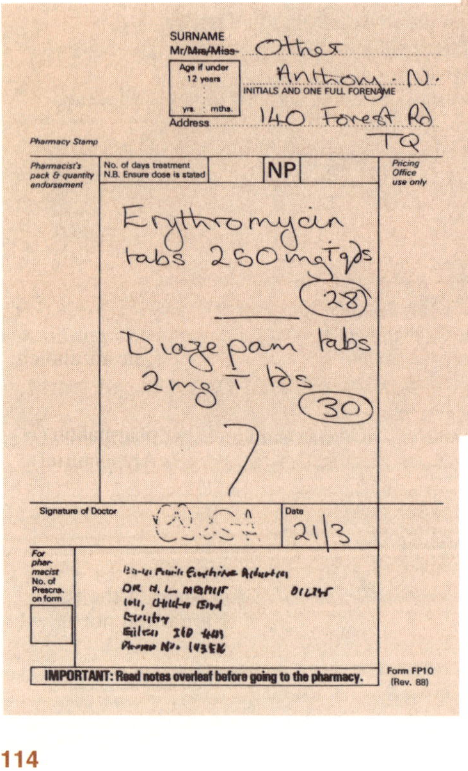

SURNAME Mr/~~Mrs/Miss~~ Other

Age if under 12 years — yrs. mths.

Anthony. N.
INITIALS AND ONE FULL FORENAME

Address 140 Forest Rd
TQ

Pharmacy Stamp

Pharmacist's pack & quantity endorsement

No. of days treatment N.B. Ensure dose is stated

NP

Pricing Office use only

Erythromycin tabs 250 mg T qds (28)

Diazepam tabs 2 mg T tds (30)

Signature of Doctor

Date 21/3

For pharmacist No. of Prescns. on form

IMPORTANT: Read notes overleaf before going to the pharmacy.

Form FP10 (Rev. 88)

What the doctor may give you:
A prescription and a sick note

Patients go easy on drugs

ONE PATIENT in five does not pick up medicine prescribed by the doctor, a British survey has revealed.

Some people don't collect their prescriptions because their main purpose in going to the doctor is to get a sick note.

Cost is another reason for not taking medicine. When several drugs are prescribed, patients often ask which is the most important and take only that one.

Other patients are worried by the side effects of drugs.

Among the drugs patients don't bother to pick up are antibiotics and the "mind drugs". This could mean they are prescribed too often and money could be saved by cutting down on the number of prescriptions.

Wortschatz

health	Gesundheit
go easy on something	sich mit etw. zurückhalten
drug	Medikament; Arzneimittel
one patient in five	einer von fünf Patienten
pick up medicine	eine Arznei (ab)holen
prescribe medicine	Medizin / eine Arznei verschreiben
reveal	enthüllen; offenbaren; zeigen
a survey has revealed	hat eine Umfrage ergeben
prescription	Verschreibung; Rezept
collect a prescription	eine (verschriebene) Arznei abholen
purpose	Zweck
their main purpose in going to the doctor	der Hauptzweck ihres Arztbesuchs
sick	krank
sick note *BE*	(eine Art) Krankmeldung (muß bei Krankheit von über 7 Tagen Dauer von einem Arzt unterschrieben sein)
get a sick note	sich krank schreiben lassen
be worried by something	sich über etw. Sorgen machen
side effects	Nebenwirkungen
they don't bother to pick them up	sie machen sich nicht die Mühe, sie abzuholen; sie holen sie einfach nicht ab
antibiotic – antibiotics	Antibiotikum – Antibiotika
mind drug	(*umgangssprachl. für:*) Psychopharmakon (= auf die Psyche einwirkendes Arzneimittel)
save money	Geld sparen
cut down on something	etw. einschränken

Verständnis- und Wortschatztest

a. What percentage of prescriptions are not collected? ☐ b. What are some of the reasons why patients don't pick up medicine? ☐ c. What drugs in particular are often not taken? ☐ d. Another word for *drug*? ☐ e. Another expression for *take less* drugs? ☐ f. Another expression for *collect* medicine? ☐ g. *Mind drugs* have an ..... on the mind. ☐ h. How else can you express *cut down on the number of prescriptions*?

At the doctor's

D: Well, Mr Murray, what's the trouble?

P: I've just been feeling terrible for some time.

D: What do you mean by "feeling terrible"?

P: Oh, I sleep badly, I'm tired, depressed. I have difficulty concentrating. And I sometimes get this pain in my stomach.

D: Do you have the pain at night?

P: Yes. I wake up with it and can't get to sleep again.

D: How's your appetite?

P: Quite good usually. But when I feel really low, I can't eat anything.

D: Have you got any worries?

P: Well, yes, mainly at work. You see, the company I work for has been taken over, and the young chap who's my boss now is constantly finding fault with my work ...

Wortschatz

at the doctor's	beim Arzt
what's the trouble?	wo fehlt's?
feel terrible	sich miserabel/mies fühlen
for some time	seit einiger Zeit
what do you mean by that?	was meinen Sie damit?
I sleep badly	ich schlafe schlecht
tired	müde
depressed	deprimiert; niedergeschlagen
I have difficulty concentrating	es fällt mir schwer, mich zu konzentrieren
pain	Schmerz(en)
stomach	Magen; Bauch
I have a pain in my stomach	ich habe Magen-/Bauchschmerzen
wake up – woke up – woken up	aufwachen – aufwachte – aufgewacht
I wake up with it	ich wache davon auf
I can't get to sleep	ich kann nicht einschlafen
how's your appetite?	wie ist Ihr Appetit?
when I feel low	wenn's mir schlecht geht; wenn ich down bin
have you got any worries?	haben Sie (irgendwelche) Sorgen?
mainly at work	hauptsächlich auf der Arbeit / im Büro
the company I work for	die Firma, für die ich arbeite
the company has been taken over	die Firma ist aufgekauft worden
the young chap	der junge Mann
boss	Chef(in)
find fault with something	an etw. was auszusetzen haben
he's constantly finding fault with my work	er nörgelt ständig an meiner Arbeit rum

Verständnis- und Wortschatztest

a. What's the patient's name? ☐ b. Why has he gone to see his doctor? (Symptoms?) ☐ c. What may be causing his problems? ☐ d. Another word for *low* in *feeling low*?

Stress

Anything that forces a person to react is stress, so a certain amount of stress is normal, indeed necessary. "Complete freedom from stress is death," says a well-known expert.
But too much stress can lead to illness. People who are exposed to more stress than they can cope with may develop headaches, backache, high blood pressure, stomach ulcers and heart disease.
People suffering from stress are often advised to reduce their work load or organize their time better, not to take things too seriously, to leave time for laughter, relaxation, meditation and regular exercise, to spend time with their family and friends, to eat sensibly, and to cut down on coffee, alcohol and cigarettes.

Wortschatz

force a person to react	jem. zu einer Reaktion zwingen
a certain amount of stress	ein gewisses Maß an Belastung
normal, indeed necessary	normal, ja sogar notwendig
complete freedom from stress	völliges Freisein von Belastung
death	(der) Tod
a well-known expert	ein namhafter Experte/Fachmann
it can lead to illness (– led – led)	es kann zu Krankheit führen
be exposed to stress	Streß/Belastungen ausgesetzt sein
cope with problems	mit Problemen fertigwerden
more than they can cope with	mehr als sie bewältigen können
develop an illness	sich eine Krankheit zuziehen
headaches (*sonst nur Einzahl*)	häufige/chronische Kopfschmerzen
backache	Rückenschmerzen
heart disease	Herzerkrankungen
suffer from stress	unter Streß leiden; überbeansprucht sein
advise someone to do something	jem. raten, etw. zu tun
reduce their work load	ihre Arbeitslast / arbeitsmäßige Belastung verringern
organize their time better	ihre Zeit besser einteilen
take things too seriously	(die) Dinge zu ernst/schwer nehmen
leave time for something	sich Zeit für etw. lassen
laughter and relaxation	Lachen und Entspannung
meditation	Meditation
regular exercise	regelmäßige Bewegung
friends	Freunde; Bekannte
eat sensibly	vernünftig essen
cut down on coffee and alcohol	weniger Kaffee und Alkohol trinken
cut down on cigarettes	weniger rauchen

Verständnis- und Wortschatztest

a. A certain amount of stress is ....., but too much stress can ..... ☐ b. People who are exposed to too much stress often develop ..... ☐ c. Patients suffering from stress are advised to ..... ☐ d. Another expression for *cut down on* in *cut down on coffee*?

1. Stellung des Objekts bei zusammengesetzten Verben (*phrasal verbs*)

a. Why didn't you pick up the medicine?
b. Why didn't you pick up the medicine Dr Day prescribed for your cough?

---

c. Why didn't you pick the medicine up?
d. Why didn't you pick it up?

Zusammengesetzte Verben sind z. B. *bring up, point out, sell off, take over, write down*. Haben sie – wie *pick up (= abholen)* in den Beispielen a–d – ein Objekt, so kann dieses grundsätzlich auf das Verb folgen (a–b) oder vom Verb „eingerahmt" sein (c–d). Dabei sind folgende Gesetzmäßigkeiten zu beobachten:
Ist das Objekt sehr lang (b), so verbietet sich die „Einrahmung".
Ist das Objekt ein Personalpronomen (d), so wird es immer „eingerahmt".
Ein kurzes Objekt wie *the medicine* erlaubt beide Stellungen (a und c), je nachdem ob das Objekt *the medicine* (a) oder das Verb *pick up* (c) betont werden soll:
a. = *Warum hast du die Arznei nicht abgeholt?*
c. = *Warum hast du die Arznei nicht abgeholt?*

2. *To*-Infinitiv nach Verb + Objekt

a. Anything that forces a person to react is stress.
Alles, was einen Menschen zwingt zu reagieren, ist Streß.
b. They require drivers over 65 to take periodic tests.
Sie verlangen von Autofahrern über 65, daß sie sich regelmäßig testen lassen.
c. They just tell you to hang around and listen to the announcements.
Die sagen einem bloß, man soll warten und auf die Ansagen achten.
d. Many Americans want all older motorists to be tested regularly.
Viele Amerikaner wollen, daß sich alle älteren Kraftfahrer regelmäßig testen lassen.

Für diese im Englischen häufige Konstruktion gibt es im Deutschen nur selten – etwa wie in (a) – eine direkte Entsprechung. Besonders ungewöhnlich klingt sie für das deutsche Sprachempfinden bei einem Verb wie *want* (d), ist aber gerade hier im Englischen sehr häufig: What do you want me to do? *„Was willst du, daß ich tue?" / Was soll ich tun?*
You don't want me to tell her that, do you? *Du willst doch nicht, daß ich ihr das sage, oder?*

3. *Have* als Vollverb und Hilfsverb

a. Do you have the pain at night? *Haben Sie die Schmerzen nachts?*
b. I don't have the pain at night. *Nachts habe ich die Schmerzen nicht.*

---

c. Have you got any worries? *Haben Sie irgendwelche Sorgen?*
d. She hasn't got any sales experience. *Sie hat keine Verkaufserfahrung.*

In (c) wäre genausogut *Do you have any worries?* möglich und in (d) *She doesn't have any sales experience.*
Umgekehrt läßt sich aber in (a) *Do you have* nicht durch *Have you got* ersetzen, und in (b) kann es statt *I don't have* nicht *I haven't got* heißen, da die *have got*-Konstruktion weitgehend auf die Bedeutung *have = besitzen* beschränkt ist, *have* in (a) und (b) aber so etwas wie *get/feel* heißt: *Do you get/feel the pain at night? I don't get/feel the pain at night.*
Im Zweifel sollten Sie also bei *have* der *do*-Konstruktion den Vorzug geben – Sie können dann nichts falsch machen: *Does she have a car?*, *What time do you have breakfast?*, *I don't have enough money, Budget hotels don't have restaurants* etc.

1. Vervollständigen Sie den Text.

A British survey has ..... that 20 per cent of patients do not pick up medicine ..... by the doctor. Asked why they didn't bother to ..... their prescriptions, some people said their main purpose ..... to the doctor was to get a sick note. Others cited cost as a reason for not ..... medicine, and a third group was ..... by the side effects of drugs. Foremost among the drugs that patients didn't pick up ..... antibiotics and the so-called mind drugs, which could ..... they are prescribed too often and money could be saved by ..... on the number of prescriptions.

2. Setzen Sie die folgenden zusammengesetzten Verben entsprechend den Beispielen in passender Weise ein: *bring up, find out, make up, point out, put up, sell off, sift out, take out, take up, throw on, turn on, wake up, write down, write out.*

He ..... the stairs and shot the burglar. He slid down the stairs and shot the burglar.
I like to have the TV in my bedroom to ..... me to sleep. I like to have the TV in my bedroom to get me off to sleep.

a. Her husband was killed in the war, so she had to ..... her three children alone.
b. It was you who ..... Debbie's name for the competition.
c. We need to ..... the room in time for the next guests.
d. They ..... him shortly after midnight.
e. So you didn't have to start from scratch when you ..... English again?
f. To make sure he didn't forget, she ..... everything for him.
g. The flight attendant always ..... the location of emergency exits in the aircraft.
h. I don't know why it always takes so long to ..... the ticket.
i. Before going to the interview, you should try to ..... as much as possible about the company you're applying to.
j. If you don't ..... insurance, there's no way you can hope for reimbursement.
k. The drought was so severe that many farmers had to ..... their cattle.
l. Make sure the cabby doesn't "forget" to ..... the meter.
m. ..... his parka he dashed out of the house.
n. There are lots of old people who are no longer fit to drive, but it isn't easy to ..... them.

3. Übersetzen Sie.

a. Ich fühle mich seit einiger Zeit schrecklich.
b. Die Firma, bei der ich arbeite, hat den Besitzer gewechselt (ist übernommen worden), und mein neuer Chef hat ständig was an meiner Arbeit auszusetzen.
c. Der Arzt will nicht, daß ich irgendein Medikament nehme.
d. Er riet mir, mich mehr zu entspannen.
e. Er sagte mir, ich solle die Dinge nicht so ernst nehmen, mehr Zeit mit meiner Familie verbringen und ⟨den⟩ Alkohol⟨konsum⟩ einschränken.
f. Natürlich könnten wir viel Geld sparen, wenn wir (*by ...-ing*) mit Alkohol, Zigaretten und Arzneimitteln sparsamer umgingen.

„Radio“, das Generalthema dieser Lektion, wird in drei Texten angesprochen: 1. Ausschnitte aus einer Nachrichtensendung, 2. Dialog über die Wichtigkeit des Hörenübens für das Englischlernen, 3. Informationstext über die BBC.
Die Bedeutung des Englischhörens kann in der Tat kaum überbewertet werden. Hauptquellen für „Hörtexte“ sind – abgesehen von den Audiocassetten zu diesem Lehrbuch und vom persönlichen Gespräch mit Englischsprachigen: Rundfunk (vor allem der von Sprache und Programmgestaltung her vorzüglich geeignete BBC World Service), Fernsehen (insbesondere die englischsprachigen Kabel- und Satellitensender), Video (großes kommerzielles Angebot englischsprachiger Spiel- und Dokumentarfilme).
In der Tonaufnahme werden alle drei Texte in neutralem britischen Englisch gesprochen.

London Calling,
the programme monthly
of the BBC World Service

From the 9 a.m. news

The Prime Minister of New Zealand, Mr David Lange, has been admitted to hospital in Wellington with a heart condition. He is not in danger and is said to be comfortable. He is expected to be back at work in about a fortnight. Mr Lange, who is 45, has been ill with flu for the past week. He had been suffering from chest pains, which have now been diagnosed as angina.
A team of Royal Marines have broken the record for circumnavigating Britain by boat. The men arrived back in Plymouth earlier this morning, taking about five and a half hours off the previous fastest time. They hope to have raised more than a hundred thousand pounds for the Royal National Lifeboat Institution.
An attempt to stage an illegal car race on the M25, London's orbital motorway, has failed. The police believe it was to have been held late last night, but a Scotland Yard spokesman said the publicity, and advice that was issued earlier, appeared to have prevented what he called an irresponsible race. Little is known about the organizers except that they placed an advertisement in a London newspaper with a box number for replies. The plan was for up to 25 owners of high-performance cars to race along the 117-mile motorway around the capital.

Wortschatz

the Prime Minister of New Zealand	der Premierminister von Neuseeland
admit someone to hospital	jem. ins Krankenhaus einliefern
Wellington	(Hauptstadt von Neuseeland)
with a heart condition	mit Herzbeschwerden
he's comfortable	es geht ihm den Umständen entsprechend gut
in about a fortnight	in etwa vierzehn Tagen
he's ill with flu	er ist an Grippe erkrankt
suffer from chest pains	an Schmerzen in der Brust leiden
diagnose	diagnostizieren
angina (pectoris)	Angina pectoris; Stenokardie
marines	Marine(infanterie)soldaten
circumnavigate an island	eine Insel umfahren/umschiffen
Plymouth	(Hafenstadt in SW-England)
raise money	Geld aufbringen
Royal National Lifeboat Institution	(*entspricht etwa der Deutschen Gesellschaft zur Rettung Schiffbrüchiger, DGzRS*)
an attempt to do something	ein Versuch, etw. zu tun
stage an illegal car race	ein illegales Autorennen veranstalten
M25 (= Motorway 25) *BE*	Autobahn 25
orbital motorway *BE*	Autobahnring
fail	fehlschlagen
hold (– held – held)	abhalten; veranstalten
Scotland Yard	(*die Londoner Polizei, die aber auch gewisse überregionale Aufgaben hat*)
publicity	Publicity; öffentl. Aufsehen
advice	Rat(schlag), Ratschläge (*stets als Einzahl und ohne* an *konstruiert!*)

issue advice	(*etwa:*) Empfehlungen ausgeben
appeared to have prevented it	schienen es verhindert zu haben
irresponsible	unverantwortlich
the organizers	die Veranstalter
place an advertisement in a newspaper	eine Anzeige in einer Zeitung aufgeben
box number	Chiffre(nummer)
reply	Antwort; Zuschrift
high-performance car	Hochleistungsauto/-wagen
race (along)	(entlang)rasen/jagen
capital	Hauptstadt

Verständnis- und Wortschatztest (Text 1)

a. Why has Mr Lange been admitted to hospital? □ b. The Royal Marines team *circumnavigated* Britain – what does that mean? □ c. What does the text tell you about the M25?

Learning by listening

A: I wish we had more undubbed English-language films on television.

B: So do I. Most of the time the dubbing ruins the film completely.

A: Always the same voices, and it all sounds so unnatural.

B: A London cockney, an Irishman, and an American hillbilly – they all talk like a German radio announcer.

A: It's a shame, really – it'd be such good practice watching a film in the English original.

B: I listen to the radio a lot, actually – the BBC World Service and Radio 4. It's amazing how much you can learn just by listening to the news ...

Wortschatz

I wish we had	ich wünschte, wir hätten
dub a film	einen Film synchronisieren
voice	Stimme
it all sounds so unnatural	es klingt alles so unnatürlich
cockney	Cockney (= Sprecher[in] des Londoner Stadtdialekts)
an Irishman	ein Ire
hillbilly ***AE***	Hinterwäldler (aus den Bergen „jwd")
radio announcer	Rundfunksprecher(in)
it's a shame, really	es ist wirklich eine Schande
I listen to the radio a lot, actually	(*etwa:*) weißt du, ich höre viel Radio
it's amazing	es ist erstaunlich/verblüffend

Verständnis- und Wortschatztest (Text 2)

a. She prefers a ..... foreign film to one with subtitles. □ b. But if you ask me, in most cases the ..... ruins the film completely. □ c. It seems the dubbing studios always use the same ..... □ d. And it all ..... so unnatural – everyone speaking like a German radio ..... □ e. It really is a ..... we can't watch English films in the original. □ f. It's ..... how much you can learn by ..... a film in English.

The British Broadcasting Corporation (BBC)

The BBC runs two television channels (BBC1, BBC2) as well as a number of radio networks (Radio 1, Radio 2, Radio 3, Radio 4, Local Radio, and the BBC World Service).
Radio 4, which can be received in certain parts of Germany, is an excellent medium for news and comment. It also offers general entertainment and information: plays and readings, comedy shows, panel games and magazine programmes. Since Radio 4 concentrates on the spoken word, it broadcasts hardly any music.
The high-quality programmes of the BBC World Service can be received worldwide, mostly on short wave but also on medium and long wave and – in Berlin – on VHF.

Wortschatz

broadcast – broadcast – broadcast	senden – sendete – gesendet
corporation	Gesellschaft; Körperschaft; Anstalt
British Broadcasting Corporation (BBC)	(1922 gegr., seit 1927 staatl. finanzierte britische Rundfunkgesellschaft)
run something	etw. betreiben
television channel	Fernsehkanal, -programm
as well as	sowie; wie auch
a number of radio networks	eine Reihe von Rundfunksendern
receive a station	einen Sender empfangen
in certain parts of Germany	in bestimmten Teilen Deutschlands
excellent	ausgezeichnet
medium – media	Medium – Medien
news and comment	Nachrichten und Kommentar(e)
general entertainment	allgemeine Unterhaltung
information (*keine -s-Mehrzahl!*)	Information(en)
(radio) play	Hörspiel
reading	Lesung
comedy show	(humoristische) Unterhaltungssendung
panel game	Quiz(programm); Ratespiel
magazine programme *BE* / *AE* program	Magazinsendung
since Radio 4 concentrates on the spoken word	da sich Radio 4 auf das gesprochene Wort konzentriert
Radio 4 broadcasts hardly any music	Radio 4 sendet fast keine Musik
high-quality programme *BE* / *AE* program	qualitativ hochwertiges Programm
can be received worldwide	können in der ganzen Welt empfangen werden
mostly on short wave	hauptsächlich auf Kurzwelle
medium wave – long wave	Mittelwelle – Langwelle
VHF (= very high frequency)	UKW (= Ultrakurzwelle)

Verständnis- und Wortschatztest

a. What does *BBC* stand for? ☐ b. How many national radio networks does the BBC run? ☐ c. Does Radio 4 broadcast a lot of music? ☐ d. Can Radio 4 be received everywhere in Germany? ☐ e. *VHF* is short for ..... ☐ f. Can the BBC World Service be received worldwide on VHF? ☐ g. What's the opposite of *the spoken word*?

20 Erklärungen

1. Gebrauch der Perfektformen

a. They have broken the record for circumnavigating Britain by boat.
Sie haben den Rekord für die Umseglung Großbritanniens gebrochen.
b. Mr Lange has been ill with flu for the past week.
Mr Lange ist seit einer Woche grippekrank.
c. He has been admitted to hospital with a heart condition.
Er ist wegen Herzbeschwerden in ein Krankenhaus eingeliefert worden.
d. He had been suffering from chest pains.
Er hatte an Schmerzen in der Brust gelitten.
e. They hope to have raised more than a hundred thousand pounds.
Sie hoffen über hunderttausend Pfund aufgebracht zu haben.
f. The race was to have been held late last night.
Das Rennen hatte gestern am späten Abend „abgehalten werden sollen".

a. Gebrauch des Perfekts (present perfect simple) für abgeschlossene, aber nicht „datierte" Handlungen. Wäre die Handlung „datiert", so müßte die Vergangenheitsform (Präteritum, past tense) stehen: *They broke the record only last week. (= Sie haben den Rekord erst vergangene Woche gebrochen.)*
b. Gebrauch des Perfekts (present perfect simple) für aus der Vergangenheit in die Gegenwart dauernde Handlungen. Ein Verb wie *suffer* (anstelle von *be*) würde in der Verlaufsform (present perfect progressive) stehen: *He has been suffering from chest pains for the past week. (= Er leidet seit einer Woche an Schmerzen in der Brust.)*
c. Gebrauch des Perfekts wie in (a), aber im Passiv.
d. Gebrauch des Perfekts wie in (b), aber um eine Zeitstufe in die Vergangenheit versetzt (past perfect progressive) – die Handlung erstreckt sich also aus der Vorvergangenheit in die Vergangenheit.
e. Infinitiv des Perfekts (perfect infinitive).
f. Wie (e), aber im Passiv.

2. *To*-Infinitiv nach passiven Verben

He is expected to be back in about a fortnight.
Er wird in etwa vierzehn Tagen zurück erwartet.
He is said to be comfortable.
Es soll ihm (den Umständen entsprechend) gut gehen.
People over 65 are required to take periodic tests.
Von Personen über 65 wird verlangt, daß sie sich regelmäßig testen lassen.

3. *To*-Infinitiv nach einer *for*-Konstruktion

The plan was for up to 25 cars to race along the motorway.
Der Plan sah vor, daß bis zu 25 Wagen die Autobahn entlangrasen sollten.
I could arrange for you to stay on till three o'clock free of charge.
Ich könnte es einrichten, daß Sie das Zimmer bis drei Uhr kostenlos behalten.
I think it's a very good idea for mothers to go out to work.
Ich finde es sehr gut, wenn Mütter arbeiten gehen.
In the US it's nothing unusual for a boy around the age of twelve to get his first shotgun and learn how to handle it.
In den USA ist es keineswegs ungewöhnlich, wenn ein Junge mit etwa zwölf Jahren seine erste Schrotflinte bekommt und lernt, wie man damit umgeht.

1. Ergänzen Sie die Verben in der passenden Form.

An attempt (stage) an illegal car race on the M25, London's orbital motorway, has (fail). The police believe it was to (hold) late last night, but a Scotland Yard spokesman said the publicity, and advice that (issue) earlier, appeared to (prevent) what he called an irresponsible race. Little is (know) about the organizers except that they (place) an advertisement in a London newspaper with a box number for replies. The plan was for up to 25 owners of high-performance cars (race) along the 117-mile motorway around the capital.

2. Geben Sie „ich auch"-Antworten.

"I wish we had more English-language films on television." – "So do I."
"I've learnt a lot by listening to the BBC World Service." – "So have I."

a. "I listen to the radio a lot." –
b. "I've got the flu." –
c. "I arrived last night." –
d. "I'm going back to work tomorrow." –
e. "I prefer watching films in the original." –
f. "I can understand that." –
g. "I'm cutting down on cigarettes." –
h. "I'll take a bus." –
i. "I'd like to go back to work." –
j. "I had a lot of problems with her." –
k. "I've seen it before somewhere." –
l. "I always have lunch at work." –

3. Setzen Sie die folgenden Verben in der passenden Form ein.

break, expect, have, hold, raise, say, suffer, tell

a. She's ..... to be very ill.
b. He's ..... to be back on Monday.
c. He's ..... from chest pains for some time.
d. They hope to ..... more than a hundred thousand pounds by ..... the record.
e. I wish we ..... a faster car.
f. I wish you ..... us more about it.
g. The race was to ..... yesterday, but the police prevented it.

4. Übersetzen Sie.

a. Dies ist die schlimmste Dürre, die ich je erlebt habe.
b. Bis jetzt sind wir in Australien, Neuseeland und dem Fernen Osten gewesen.
c. Ich habe schon den ganzen Tag Kopfschmerzen.
d. Er hat sein ganzes Leben in diesem Dorf gewohnt.
e. Wie lange lernen Sie schon Englisch?
f. Sie scheint es nicht gelesen zu haben.
g. Es kann sein, daß sie es nicht gelesen hat.
h. Ich muß Sie falsch verstanden haben.
i. Wir hätten alle tot sein können.
j. Man hätte ihm kein Gewehr geben sollen.
k. Ich hätte nicht gezögert, auch wenn ich es gewußt hätte.

21 Films

Vom Film (*[motion] pictures, films, movies*) handelt diese Lektion. In Text 1 geht es um die Frage: Sind die Kinofilme besser oder schlechter geworden? Text 2 ist ein Dialog vor einem Kinobesuch. Text 3 bietet ein paar Fakten zur Geschichte des Films. In der Tonaufnahme von Text 1 hören Sie zwei amerikanische, in der von Text 2 zwei britische Stimmen; Text 3 wird nach Art einer amerikanischen Rundfunk- oder Fernsehreportage gelesen.

Winner of five Oscars: Kramer vs. Kramer

Are today's movies better than yesterday's?

Bruce: Don't you think movies are a lot better today than they were a couple of decades ago?
Carol: I don't know. There's so much sex and violence in today's movies.
Bruce: But that's why people like them – they show life as it is.
Carol: That's what the movie people say. And the young kids who see the films – they go away thinking that life's all about fighting and drugs.
Bruce: But what goes on in the movies is what's happening on the streets.
Carol: Yes, because the kids watch all those violent movies and then they go out and get into trouble.
Bruce: Still, I think on the whole today's films are better than the Hollywood oldies. Maybe not always contentwise, but the photography and special effects are definitely better.
Carol: That's true, I suppose.
Bruce: They're more entertaining somehow, to me at least. If I had the choice of watching today's movies or those of the fifties or sixties, I'd pick today's movies – at yesterday's prices.

Wortschatz

movie (*umgangssprachl., bes. AE*)	Film
a couple of decades ago	vor ein paar Jahrzehnten
violence	Gewalt(tätigkeit)
that's why people like them	deshalb gefallen sie den Leuten
they show life as it is	sie zeigen das Leben, wie es ist
the young kids	die Kinder/Jugendlichen
life's all about fighting and drugs	im Leben geht es nur um Kampf und Drogen
what goes on in the movies	was sich in den Filmen abspielt
happen	passieren; geschehen
watch a movie	sich einen Film ansehen
violent	gewalttätig; brutal
get into trouble	Dummheiten machen
the Hollywood oldies	die alten Hollywood-Filme
contentwise	(„inhaltsmäßig") was den Inhalt angeht
photography	(*Film:*) Aufnahmetechnik
special effects	Tricks
definitely better	ohne Frage / ganz bestimmt besser
that's true, I suppose	das stimmt wohl
they're more entertaining somehow	sie sind irgendwie unterhaltsamer
to me at least	für mich jedenfalls
if I had the choice	wenn ich die Wahl hätte
pick	(aus)wählen; nehmen

Verständnis- und Wortschatztest

a. What doesn't Carol like about today's movies? ☐ b. According to the movie people, today's films show life ..... ☐ c. In Carol's view young people are wrongly led to believe that life's all about ..... ☐ d. Carol believes that watching violent films may cause children to get into ..... ☐ e. Bruce thinks that the photography and special ..... are better in today's films. ☐ f. Give expressions from the text that mean the same as the following: *ten years* ago, young *children*, the *old Hollywood films*, *choose* a *film*.

Going to the movies

A: It's getting late.

B: It's starting to rain too. What are we going to do with the rest of the evening?

A: Go and see a film?

B: Yes, why not. But is there anything worth seeing?

A: Nothing special among the new films as far as I know. But I noticed that *Kramer vs. Kramer* is showing at the Classic. Just this evening I think.

B: I saw it when it first came out but I wouldn't mind seeing it again. A great film – good dialogue, tremendous acting. Did you see it?

A: No, I didn't as a matter of fact, but I've heard a lot of good things about it. It won several Oscars at the time, didn't it?

B: Yes ... but if we want to make it to *Kramer vs. Kramer* we'd better hurry. It starts at 8.30. Shall we take the Tube?

Wortschatz

go to the movies	ins Kino gehen
it's getting late	es („wird") ist spät
it's starting to rain too	es fängt auch an zu regnen
the rest of the evening	der Rest des Abends / angebrochene Abend
is there anything worth seeing?	gibt es irgend was, das sich zu sehen lohnt?
nothing special	nichts Besonderes
as far as I know	soviel ich weiß
Kramer vs. (= versus) Kramer	Kramer gegen Kramer (US-Film von 1979, mit Dustin Hoffman und Meryl Streep)
it's showing at the Classic	er läuft im Classic
just this evening	nur heute abend
I wouldn't mind seeing it again	ich hätte nichts dagegen, ihn noch einmal zu sehen
good dialogue	guter Dialog
tremendous acting	(„tolle Schauspielerei") klasse Schauspieler
no, I didn't as a matter of fact	(*etwa:*) nein, eben nicht
win – won – won	gewinnen – gewann – gewonnen
Oscar (***Spitzname für vergoldete Statuette, die offiziell* Academy Award = Akademiepreis *heißt***)	(seit 1927 jährlich vergebener US-Filmpreis für Spitzenleistungen in div. Bereichen der Filmkunst)
if we want to make it	wenn wir es schaffen wollen
we'd (= we had) better hurry	wir sollten uns (besser) beeilen

Verständnis- und Wortschatztest

a. There's too much violence in today's *movies*. Another word for *movies*? ☐ b. Another word for *movies* in: Let's go to the *movies*. ☐ c. *King Kong* is *showing* at the Classic. Another expression for *showing*? ☐ d. *What are we going to do* with the rest of the evening? What could you say instead of *What are we going to do*? ☐ e. Other words for *great*, *good*, and *tremendous* in: A *great* film – *good* dialogue, *tremendous* acting. ☐ f. *Kramer vs. Kramer* won several *Oscars*. – Another word for *Oscars*? ☐ g. Another way of saying *We'd better hurry*? ☐ h. Shall we take the *Tube*? What would an American say?

Movies past and present

Motion pictures have been around since the beginning of the twentieth century. By 1910 the "star system" had come into being, and after 1913 Hollywood became the movie capital of the United States.
After 1927 sound films took over, and in the 1930s and 40s – the industry's heyday – Hollywood's powerful studios turned out something like 500 feature films each year.
By 1956 the cinema had lost the battle against TV, and the Hollywood studios began producing series and commercials for television.
Since then the number of cinemas, as well as their size, has decreased dramatically. Fewer people go to the movies, but those who do tend to be more sophisticated than the mass audiences of the 1930s and 40s. As a result, there are fewer and, on average, better films made nowadays; and since all the good films of the past are regularly shown on TV or available on video, it may well be said that today's world is a movie buff's paradise.

Wortschatz

past and present	(in) Vergangenheit und Gegenwart
motion picture	(Kino-)Film
they have been around since ...	es gibt sie schon seit ...
the twentieth century	das zwanzigste Jahrhundert
the "star system"	(= die Herausstellung von Filmstars)
come into being	entstehen
sound film	Tonfilm
they took over from silent films	sie lösten die Stummfilme ab
the (film) industry's heyday	die Glanzzeit/Blütezeit der (Film-)Industrie
Hollywood's powerful studios	die mächtigen (Film-)Studios von Hollywood
turn out 500 films per year	jährlich 500 Filme herausbringen
feature film	Spielfilm
lose a battle (– lost – lost)	eine Schlacht verlieren
produce series and commercials	Serien und Werbespots produzieren
the size of a cinema	die (räumliche) Größe eines Kinos
the number has decreased dramatically	die (An-)Zahl ist drastisch gesunken
fewer people	weniger Menschen/Leute
they tend to be more sophisticated	sie („neigen dazu, ... zu sein") sind in der Regel anspruchsvoller
the mass audiences of the 1930s	das Massenpublikum der dreißiger Jahre
as a result	die Folge (davon) ist, daß
on average	im Durchschnitt
nowadays	heutzutage
available on video	als Videocassette erhältlich
it may well be said	man kann wohl sagen
movie buff	Filmfan(atiker[in]); Filmnarr

Verständnis- und Wortschatztest

a. When was the first sound film made? ☐ b. When did Hollywood become less powerful, and why? ☐ c. Differences between today's movie audiences and those of the 1940s?

1. Fügungen mit dem -'s-Genitiv

Steve's salary	*Steves Gehalt*
the doctor's house	*das Haus des Arztes*
the bridge's walkways	*die Gehwege der Brücke*
New York's tens of thousands of homeless	*New Yorks Zehntausende von Wohnungslosen*
New York's Williamsburg Bridge	*die New Yorker Williamsburg Bridge*
London's Regent's Park	*der Londoner Regent's Park*
Hollywood's powerful studios	*die mächtigen (Film-)Studios von Hollywood*
woman's fight against noise	*„Kampf einer Frau gegen den Lärm"*
Mother's Day	*(der) Muttertag*
driver's license *AE*	*Führerschein*
extending one's stay	*„Verlängerung des Aufenthalts"*
everybody's favourite room	*jedermanns Lieblingszimmer*
today's Daily Mail	*die heutige Daily Mail*
yesterday's prices	*die Preise von gestern*

Die deutschen Übersetzungen veranschaulichen die unterschiedlichen Beziehungen, die durch diese Konstruktion ausgedrückt werden. Die unter (2) dargestellte *of*-Fügung hat mitunter – aber keineswegs immer! – eine gleiche oder ähnliche Bedeutung. Soweit die beiden Konstruktionen in der Isolation austauschbar sind (z. B. *the doctor's house – the house of the doctor*), wird bei der Anwendung im Satz doch in der Regel die eine oder die andere Fügung eindeutig bevorzugt, wie etwa in folgendem Beispielpaar:

Eleven weary hours later they pulled up outside the doctor's house just as the first patients began to queue up for the afternoon surgery.

She pointed out the house of the doctor who had saved her mother's life.
Sie zeigte auf das Haus des Arztes, der ihrer Mutter das Leben gerettet hatte.

2. Fügungen mit *of*

the Prime Minister of New Zealand	*der Premierminister von Neuseeland*
owners of high-performance cars	*Besitzer von Hochleistungsautos*
this kind/type/sort of person	*diese Art von Mensch*
the movie capital of the United States	*die Filmhauptstadt der Vereinigten Staaten*
the beginning of the 20th century	*der Beginn des 20. Jahrhunderts*
the collapse of a bridge	*der Einsturz einer Brücke*
the south of England	*der Süden Englands*
the quality of life	*die Lebensqualität*
the 25th of June	*der 25. Juni*
a couple / a lot of showers	*ein paar / viele Regenschauer*
a certain amount of stress	*ein gewisses Maß an Streß*
two sacks of letters	*zwei Säcke mit Briefen*
the village of Wayford	*das Dorf Wayford*
the Republic of Malta	*die Republik Malta*

1. Setzen Sie die Verben in der passenden Form ein.

a. Too many young people today think that life is about (fight) and (sell) drugs.
b. She believes that (watch) violent films may cause children (get) into trouble.
c. If I (have) the choice of (watch) today's movies or those of the past, I'd pick today's movies at yesterday's prices.
d. Are there any new films worth (see) at the moment?
e. I noticed that *Kramer vs. Kramer* (show) at the Classic.
f. I saw *Kramer vs. Kramer* when it first (come) out but I wouldn't mind (see) it again.
g. *Kramer vs. Kramer* (win) several Oscars, ... it?
h. Motion pictures (be) around since the beginning of the twentieth century.
i. By 1910 the "star system" (come) into being, and after 1913 Hollywood (become) the movie capital of the United States.
j. By 1956 the cinema (lose) the battle against TV, and the Hollywood studios (begin)(produce) series and commercials for television.

2. Adjektiv (ohne *-ly*) oder Adverb (mit *-ly*)?

a. Many of the good films of the past are (regular) shown on TV or (easy) (available) on video.
b. It's a (tremendous) interesting film. – The acting's (real) (excellent).
c. In the 1960s the number of cinemas decreased (dramatic).
d. We've seen a (dramatic) increase in (violent) TV films in (recent) years.
e. An attempt to stage an (illegal) car race on the M25 has failed.
f. They would have acted (irresponsible), even (illegal), if they had done that.
g. They talk rather (unnatural) in this film – a bit like radio announcers, don't you think?
h. Don't you think the dialogue sounds rather (unnatural)?
i. It's (amazing) how much you can learn just by listening to the radio.
j. She's learnt the language (amazing) (quick), hasn't she?
k. Her (main) purpose in going to the doctor was to get a sick note.
l. She went to the doctor (main) to get a sick note.
m. I've been feeling (terrible) for some time.
n. I've been feeling (terrible) depressed for some time.
o. We're never (complete) free from stress, are we? – No, (complete) freedom from stress is death.
p. She's such a (serious) person, always takes things so (serious).

3. Übersetzen Sie.

a. Er ist einer von New Yorks Zehntausenden von Wohnungslosen.
b. Ich rufe wegen Ihrer Anzeige in der heutigen Daily Mail an.
c. Was machen wir mit dem Rest des Abends?
d. Kinofilme gibt es schon seit Beginn des zwanzigsten Jahrhunderts.
e. Die Zahl der Unfälle ist in den letzten Jahren gestiegen (*go up*).
f. Die Republik Malta ist ein Mitglied (*member*) des Commonwealth.
g. Herrn Burstocks Familie lebt seit 170 Jahren in dem Dorf Wayford in Somerset.
h. In den letzten zwanzig Jahren hat sich die Lebensqualität dramatisch verbessert (*sich verbessern = improve*).
i. Wir haben in den letzten Wochen eine Menge Probleme gehabt.

22 Food

Ums Essen geht es in den Texten dieser Lektion: der erste handelt vom Hafer und anderer Gesundheitskost; der zweite hat eine Tischreservierung in einem Restaurant zum Thema; der dritte geht der Frage nach, ob es so etwas wie schadstofffreie Lebensmittel überhaupt noch gibt.

In der Tonaufnahme wird Text 1 mit amerikanischem Akzent gelesen; in Text 2 spricht Mrs Freeman mit britischem, der italienische Gastronom aber mit leichtem italienischen Akzent; Text 3 hören Sie in einer neutralen britischen Aussprache (Rundfunkreporterin).

Changing eating habits

In his famous *Dictionary of the English Language* of 1755, Dr Samuel Johnson defined *oats* as "a grain, which in England is generally given to horses, but in Scotland supports the people". Today it's not only the Scots that are fond of oats – just about everybody is eating oats nowadays, and the cereal companies are creating new oat-based products all the time.
Apart from making people "happy, healthy and regular", as one commercial suggests, the grain is believed to bring down the blood cholesterol level, thus reducing the risk of heart attacks and strokes.
The popularity of oatmeal and oat bran is a sign of our health-conscious times. Consumers are looking for food which is high in fibre and low in fat, sugar and salt. If possible, it should be "additive-free" and "organically grown".
Many people are dieting to control their cholesterol intake and lose weight. They're switching from whole milk to low-fat milk, from butter to margarine, from white bread to wholemeal bread, and from ice cream to fruit.

Wortschatz

eating habits	Eßgewohnheiten
dictionary	Wörterbuch
Dr Samuel Johnson	(1709–84, engl. Lexikograph)
define a word	ein Wort definieren/erklären
oats	Hafer(flocken)
grain	Getreide; Korn
horse	Pferd
support someone	jem. unterhalten/ernähren
be fond of something	etw. gern haben/essen; etw. mögen
just about everybody	so ziemlich jeder
cereal	Getreideprodukt
create a product	ein Produkt schaffen/kreieren
oat-based	auf Haferbasis
healthy	gesund
regular	(*hier bezügl. Verdauung:*) regelmäßig
bring down the cholesterol level	den Cholesterinspiegel senken
thus	und auf diese Weise; und so
reduce a risk	ein Risiko vermindern
heart attacks and strokes	Herzanfälle und Schlaganfälle
popularity	Popularität; Beliebtheit
oatmeal *AE* / *BE* porridge	Haferbrei
oat bran	Haferkleie
health-conscious	gesundheitsbewußt
consumer	Konsument(in); Kunde, Kundin
food high in fibre *BE* / *AE* fiber	faserreiche/ballaststoffreiche Kost
low in fat, sugar and salt	mit geringem Fett-, Zucker- und Salzgehalt
additive-free	frei von Zusätzen
organically grown	aus organischem/biologischem Anbau
she's dieting	sie lebt diät
to control their cholesterol intake	um ihre Cholesterinaufnahme im Rahmen zu halten

lose weight (– lost – lost)	(„Gewicht verlieren") abnehmen
switch from A to B	sich von A auf B umstellen
whole milk and low-fat milk	Vollmilch und fettarme Milch
wholemeal bread	Vollkornbrot
ice cream or fruit	Eis(krem) oder Obst

Verständnis- und Wortschatztest (Text 1)

a. Why have oats become so popular? □ b. What kind of food do health-conscious people generally prefer? □ c. The cereal companies are *developing* new oat-based products all the time – another word for *developing*?

Booking a table at a restaurant

A: Piccadilly Restaurant. Good morning.
B: Good morning. My name's Freeman. I'd like to book a table for lunch-time today.
A: Yes, madam. How many would that be for?
B: For six. Can you give us a table upstairs?
A: Yes of course, madam. A table for six upstairs for Mrs …
B: Freeman.
A: Mrs Freeman. That's all right, madam. About what time d'you think you'll be arriving?
B: Oh, about twelve thirty, I should think. By the way, you do have some vegetarian dishes on the menu …?
A: We do indeed, madam. You'll find quite a variety of vegetarian quiches, salads, pasta, pizzas …
B: Good. Thank you … goodbye.
A: Goodbye.

Wortschatz

book a table	(sich) einen Tisch reservieren (lassen)
about what time will you be arriving?	wann etwa werden Sie kommen?
you do have … (do *betont!*)	Sie haben doch …
vegetarian dishes	vegetarische Gerichte
menu	Speisekarte
we do indeed	aber natürlich; selbstverständlich
quite a variety of salads	eine große Auswahl an Salaten
quiche	(oben offene Teigtasche mit Käse-, Gemüse-, Ei- *etc.* Füllung)
pasta	Nudelgerichte

Verständnis- und Wortschatztest (Text 2)

a. *Book* a table at a restaurant – another word for *book*? □ b. If *lunch* is the midday meal, what's the evening meal called? □ c. What's a *vegetarian*? □ d. What's the word for *a list of dishes you can order from in a restaurant*? □ e. *Quite a variety of* vegetarian salads, pasta and so on – another expression for *quite a variety of*? □ f. What kinds of *pasta* can you think of?

How pure is pure?

Supermarket shelves are stacked with all sorts of foods with large labels proclaiming "No artificial colourings or flavourings added".

But the question is: is there really such a thing as additive-free food? Experts say there is not. While there might not be any chemicals added to the product, they point out that before any food is harvested it will almost certainly have been contaminated with pesticides.

Even organic food will have some nitrates in it because of the residues in the soil. But the level is much lower and the food itself is better – not only for the person who eats it but also for the environment.

Wortschatz

pure	rein (d. h. ohne Zusatzstoffe)
supermarket shelves are stacked with all sorts of foods	auf den Regalen der Supermärkte stapeln sich alle möglichen Lebensmittel (stack = Stapel)
label	Aufschrift; Aufkleber; Etikett
proclaim	proklamieren; verkünden; erklären
artificial colourings *BE* / *AE* colorings	künstliche Farbstoffe
flavouring *BE* / *AE* flavoring	Aromastoff
no ... added	ohne Zusatz von ...
chemical	Chemikalie; chemischer Stoff
while there might not be any chemicals added to the product	wenn dem Produkt vielleicht auch keine chemischen Stoffe hinzugefügt wurden
point out that ...	darauf hinweisen, daß ...
before any food is harvested	bevor Nahrungsmittel geerntet werden
contaminate with pesticides	durch Schädlingsbekämpfungsmittel verunreinigen; mit ... verseuchen
organic food	Lebensmittel aus organischem/biologischem Anbau; Biokost
nitrate	Nitrat
residues in the soil	Rückstände im Boden
the nitrate level	der Nitratanteil/-gehalt
the environment	die Umwelt

Verständnis- und Wortschatztest

a. Food is called *pure* if nothing artificial has been ..... ☐ b. But even in food that has not been artificially coloured or flavoured there may be ..... of pesticides from the ..... ☐ c. If food has been ..... with pesticides, it is, strictly speaking, not ..... ☐ d. Food that has been organically ..... is better both for the person who eats it and for the ..... ☐ e. In our supermarkets the shelves are ..... with all sorts of foods. ☐ f. The ..... on the packet said: "No artificial colourings or flavourings added". ☐ g. *Pure* food – another word for *pure*? ☐ h. The shelves were *stacked with* all sorts of foods – another expression for *stacked with*? ☐ i. All *sorts* of food – another word for *sorts*? ☐ j. What do you call a *person who buys goods and services*?

Fünf Möglichkeiten, die Zukunft auszudrücken (vgl. S. 100, 1c–e)

Will (bzw. die Kurzform *'ll*) ist die am häufigsten vorkommende und „neutralste" Ausdrucksform für die Zukunft. Wie die Übersetzungen (b, d, e) zeigen, entspricht der englischen *will*-Zukunft im Deutschen oft die Gegenwart:

a. We'll have to wait and see. *Wir werden abwarten müssen.*
b. It will stay mostly cloudy tomorrow. *Morgen bleibt es überwiegend bewölkt.*
c. I'll see if it can be arranged. *Ich will mal sehen, ob es sich machen läßt.*
d. Maybe I'll walk. *Vielleicht gehe ich zu Fuß.*
e. I'm sure / I think / I hope you'll like it.
Ich bin sicher / Ich glaube / Ich hoffe, daß es dir gefällt.
f. She doubts they'll be able to manage. *Sie bezweifelt, daß sie zurechtkommen werden.*

Eine Zukunftsaussage mit *be going to* betont gegenwärtige Absicht (Beispiele a–c) oder Gewißheit (d):

a. We're going to have lunch at the Piccadilly Restaurant.
Wir werden im Piccadilly Restaurant (zu Mittag) essen.
b. I'm not going to carry something as heavy as that.
Ich habe nicht die Absicht, so was Schweres zu tragen.
c. What are we going to do with the rest of the evening?
Was machen wir mit dem angebrochenen Abend?
d. There's going to be a delay of 45 minutes.
Es wird eine Verspätung von 45 Minuten geben.

Die Verlaufsform der Gegenwart als Ausdruck einer zukünftigen Handlung betont das Element der Planung:

I'm taking my family to Scotland. *Ich fahre mit meiner Familie nach Schottland.*
Are you coming by Tube? *Kommst du mit der U-Bahn?*

Auch die Konstruktion *will be -ing* wird in der Nichtfrageform (a–b) für Aussagen über geplante Zukunftshandlungen gebraucht; als Frageform (c–d) wirkt sie distanzierter, unaufdringlicher und damit höflicher als *be going to* oder die Verlaufsform der Gegenwart:

a. We'll be arriving at about half past twelve.
Wir werden so gegen halb eins (an)kommen.
b. I'll be taking my family to Scotland.
Ich werde mit meiner Familie nach Schottland fahren.
c. Will you be coming by Tube?
Werden Sie mit der U-Bahn kommen/eintreffen?
d. About what time d'you think you'll be arriving?
Um welche Zeit werden Sie etwa kommen/eintreffen?

Für Handlungen oder Ereignisse, die aufgrund eines Fahrplans, Terminplans, Programms usw. eintreten werden, steht oft die einfache Form der Gegenwart:

The movie starts at 8.30. *Der Film fängt um halb neun an.*
My plane leaves at 10.15 from Heathrow.
Mein Flugzeug geht um 10.15 Uhr von Heathrow.
My driving test is tomorrow. *Meine Fahrprüfung ist morgen.*

1. Vervollständigen Sie den Text.

In the 1980s, oat bran ..... the darling of health-conscious Americans. "Oat bran sells .....self," said the manager of a New York supermarket. The big ..... companies were quick to cash in on the oat-bran trend. Dozens of new oat-bran products were ..... in a hurry and the TV commercials were full of people who smilingly told you oat bran had not only ..... them "happy, healthy and regular" but also ..... their cholesterol level. Thanks to oat bran they ..... live to be a hundred and ten. For them, heart attacks and strokes had ..... a thing of the past. But food gurus warned that simply ..... oat bran to one's diet was not enough. They ..... people generally to eat food ..... was high in fibre and ..... in fat, sugar and salt.

2. Vervollständigen Sie die Sätze so, daß sie sich auf die Zukunft beziehen. Soweit mehr als eine Formulierung möglich ist, werden die Bedeutungsunterschiede im Schlüssel (S. 174–175) erklärt.

a. This evening it (remain) rather cloudy, and it (be) a mild and humid night everywhere.
b. The farmers are selling off their livestock in the hope that the extra income (help) to see them through until the rain (come).
c. I look forward to my next visit to London and (let) you know the date in good time.
d. Keith Rayner has quit the BBC. He (be) an actor.
e. If I (not get) more money, I (quit).
f. There (be) chaos when they (close) the Williamsburg Bridge.
g. It (not take) you more than forty minutes if you (go) by Tube.
h. The repair work on the A339 (begin) tomorrow morning.
i. You (not mind) the dog, ... you?
j. (You need) me this afternoon, sir?
k. If I (miss) the helicopter to Kennedy Airport, I (not make) my flight to Berlin.
l. When (you pay) us the money back?
m. You can keep it till I (get) back from my holiday.
n. I can see we (be) great friends.
o. I (have to) think of some other way of getting here if they (not fix) that bridge soon.
p. The interview (be) at 10.30 tomorrow morning.
q. Have you forgotten that I (fly) to New York tomorrow?

3. Übersetzen Sie.

a. Die Lebensmittelkonzerne entwickeln ständig neue Produkte.
b. Von Haferkleie wird angenommen, daß sie den Cholesterinspiegel senkt.
c. Viele Menschen leben diät, um abzunehmen.
d. Sie haben sich von Butter auf Margarine und von Weißbrot auf Vollkornbrot umgestellt.
e. Das Piccadilly Restaurant hat eine Vielfalt von vegetarischen Gerichten auf der Speisekarte.
f. In den Supermärkten gibt es alle möglichen Lebensmittel, von denen gesagt wird, daß sie frei von Zusätzen seien.
g. Aber Experten haben darauf hingewiesen, daß heute fast alle Lebensmittel durch Schädlingsbekämpfungsmittel verunreinigt sind.
h. Sogar in Lebensmitteln aus organischem Anbau sind Nitrate.
i. Allerdings ist der Nitratgehalt viel niedriger, und die Lebensmittel selbst sind besser – nicht nur für die Menschen, die sie essen, sondern auch für die Umwelt.

23 Waste

Von Abfällen und den durch sie verursachten Umweltproblemen handelt diese Lektion. Text 1 ist eine eher kuriose *human-interest story*, wie sie in einer englischen Zeitung berichtet wurde. In Text 2 unterhalten sich zwei Leute über die Verschmutzung der New Yorker Strände und ihre Ursachen. Text 3 handelt in allgemeiner Form von den Abfallproblemen der modernen Industriegesellschaft und skizziert mögliche Beiträge zu ihrer Lösung.
In der Tonaufnahme wird Text 1 von britischen Stimmen gesprochen; Text 2 hören Sie als amerikanischen Alltagsdialog; Text 3 wird etwa wie in einer Magazinsendung des amerikanischen Rundfunks oder Fernsehens gelesen.

Dustmen dump bride's presents

BRIDE ALISON Bell was shattered when her wedding presents were carted away – by dustmen.

Alison, 21, and her husband Martin had stored the gifts in their yard while they decorated their new home. They had carefully placed about £1000 worth of cutlery, crockery and glasses in cartons. But when they went out to bring them back in, the boxes had gone.

Heartbroken, Alison said last night: "A neighbour told us she saw the refuse collectors taking them. We put in a claim for compensation, but the council's insurers more or less told us the cartons shouldn't have been left near the dustbin."

Wortschatz

waste	Abfall; Abfälle
dustman *BE* / *AE* garbage man	Müllmann
dump something	(*eigentl.*:) etw. abladen/(ab)kippen
bride	Braut
dustmen dump bride's presents	(*hier etwa:*) Müllabfuhr nimmt Hochzeitsgeschenke mit
she was shattered	sie war „am Boden zerstört"
wedding present	Hochzeitsgeschenk
cart away	abtransportieren; davonschaffen
they had stored the gifts in the yard	sie hatten die Geschenke im Hof untergebracht/abgestellt
decorate a room	ein Zimmer tapezieren und/oder streichen
place things in cartons	Sachen in (Papp-)Kartons unterbringen
cutlery	(Eß-)Besteck
crockery	(*bes.* irdenes) Geschirr
the boxes had gone	die Kartons waren weg
heartbroken	todunglücklich; untröstlich
the refuse collectors *BE* / *AE* garbage collectors	die (Leute von der) Müllabfuhr
she saw them taking them	sie sah, wie sie sie mitnahmen
put in a claim for compensation (– put – put)	einen Schadenersatzantrag stellen; eine Entschädigung beantragen
the council's insurers	die Versicherung (des Stadt-/Gemeinderats) der Stadt/Gemeinde
leave – left – left	lassen – ließ – gelassen
dustbin *BE* / *AE* garbage can	Mülltonne

Verständnis- und Wortschatztest

a. Where did Alison and Martin store their wedding presents? □ b. Why didn't they leave them in the house? □ c. Why did the dustmen think they were refuse? □ d. Do you think the couple received compensation? (Why or why not?) □ e. Alison was *shattered* – another word that has a similar meaning to *shattered*? □ f. The dustmen *carted* the presents away – another word for *carted*? □ g. Wedding *presents* – another word for *presents*? □ h. Another British word for *dustmen*? □ i. Another word for *carton*?

Medical waste on N.Y. beaches

A: Temperatures are in the nineties, it's vacation time, and the beaches are closed. It's outrageous.

B: It's a scandal. For weeks we've had these reports of hospital waste being washed ashore. People are scared. They wouldn't go on the beaches even if they were open.

A: Syringes, blood vials, decayed organs, corpses of laboratory rats – it's disgusting.

B: They say it comes from midnight dumpers.

A: Of course it does. You can't legally dump garbage of that sort directly offshore just like that. What I don't like is that there's no way the hospitals can be held responsible. They say, "We've turned the stuff over to the garbage collectors, we've paid them to dispose of it, and what happens then isn't our business."

B: The hospitals ought to check where their medical waste goes.

A: Exactly. It should be up to them to make the disposal companies show they're disposing of the waste properly. And there should be harsher punishments. People who dump that kind of waste are dangerous criminals and should be treated as such.

Wortschatz

N.Y. (= New York)	(Stadt und Bundesstaat der USA)
beach	Strand
temperatures are in the nineties	(90–100° Fahrenheit = 32–38° Celsius)
vacation *AE* / *BE* holiday(s)	Urlaub; Ferien
outrageous	unerhört
report	Bericht
hospital waste is washed ashore	Klinikmüll wird an Land gespült
people are scared	die Leute haben Angst
syringe	(Injektions-)Spritze
vial	(Glas-)Fläschchen; Phiole
decay	(*Fleisch:*) verwesen
corpses of laboratory rats	Kadaver von Versuchsratten
disgusting	widerlich; ekelhaft
midnight dumpers	Leute, die Abfälle/Müll auf illegale Weise beseitigen
dump garbage *AE* / *BE* refuse/rubbish	Müll/Abfälle abkippen/verklappen
directly offshore	direkt vor der Küste
you can't dump it just like that	man kann es nicht einfach abkippen
we've turned the stuff over to them	wir haben ihnen das Zeug übergeben
dispose of waste	Abfälle beseitigen/entsorgen
they ought to check	sie müßten nachprüfen/überprüfen
it should be up to them to ...	es müßte ihnen obliegen / sie müßten verpflichtet sein, zu ...
disposal company	Entsorgungsunternehmen
dispose of the waste properly	die Abfälle ordnungsgemäß entsorgen
harsher punishments	strengere/empfindlichere Strafen
dangerous criminals	gefährliche Verbrecher
and should be treated as such	und sollten entsprechend behandelt werden

Verständnis- und Wortschatztest (Text 2)

a. Why are the beaches closed? □ b. Where did the waste come from, who dumped it, where was it dumped? □ c. Who is acting illegally – the hospitals or the dumpers? □ d. How could illegal dumping like this be made more difficult?

The garbage problem

There was a time when people didn't give much thought to the garbage they produced. They just put it in the garbage can and forgot about it. But that has changed. Industrialized countries are running out of landfills to dump the garbage in. Our garbage has to be shipped to faraway places, it has to be burned or recycled – at horrendous cost.
Garbage has become one of our greatest problems. What can we do about it? We can try to produce less of it. There's a lot of wrapping, packaging and bottling being done that's really quite unnecessary. We can encourage the use of biodegradable and recyclable packaging. We can help to make recycling work by separating food, glass, metal, and paper when we throw things away. We can take an active interest in our community's waste management. We can help to persuade those who are uninformed that the cheapest solution is not always the best.

Wortschatz

put it in the garbage can (– put – put)	es in die Mülltonne tun/werfen
industrialized country	Industrieland, -nation
we're running out of landfills	wir haben bald keine Müllkippen/Deponien mehr
ship to faraway places	an weit entfernte Orte transportieren/bringen (ship *bezieht sich auf jede Art von Transportmittel*)
burn (– burnt/burned – burnt/burned)	verbrennen
recycle	wiederaufbereiten; wiederverwerten
at horrendous cost	bei/unter horrenden Kosten
wrap something	etw. einwickeln
package something	etw. verpacken
bottle something	etw. (in Flaschen) abfüllen
encourage the use of something	die Verwendung von etw. fördern
biodegradable	biologisch abbaubar
recyclable packaging	für Recycling geeignete Verpackung
help to make recycling work	mithelfen, damit das Recycling funktioniert
separate	trennen
our community's waste management	die Abfallwirtschaft in unserer Gemeinde/Stadt/Gesellschaft
persuade someone that ...	jem. davon überzeugen, daß ...
the cheapest solution	die billigste Lösung

Verständnis- und Wortschatztest (Text 3)

a. Why has garbage become such a problem? □ b. How is garbage being disposed of nowadays? □ c. What are some possible answers to the garbage problem? □ d. What are some other words for *garbage* and *garbage can*?

1. Synonyme (= bedeutungsähnliche oder -gleiche Ausdrücke)

Wenn wir sagen, daß zwei Ausdrücke synonym sind, so meinen wir, daß sie die gleiche oder eine ähnliche Bedeutung haben. Meist ist es möglich, sie in bestimmten Textzusammenhängen gegeneinander auszutauschen, ohne daß sich der Sinn der Aussage wesentlich ändert. Beispiele für synonyme Ausdrucksmöglichkeiten:

Bride Allison Bell was shattered/shocked/heartbroken when her wedding presents/gifts were carted/taken/driven away by dustmen *BE* / refuse collectors *BE* / garbage men *AE* / garbage collectors *AE*.
Alison and Martin had stored/placed/put/stacked the gifts in their yard while they decorated / redecorated / renovated / did up their new home / house / flat *BE* / apartment *AE*.
They had carefully placed/packed/put about £1000 worth of cutlery, crockery and glasses in cartons / (cardboard) boxes.
But when they went out to bring them back in, the boxes had/were gone / had disappeared / were no longer there.

Beim Formulieren von Aussagen treffen wir ständig Entscheidungen zwischen verschiedenen synonymen Ausdrucksmöglichkeiten. Oft sind diese Entscheidungen auch grammatischer Art wie in den folgenden Beispielen:

(*Aktiv*) A neighbour told us she saw the refuse collectors taking them.
(*Passiv*) A neighbour told us she saw them being taken by the refuse collectors.

(*Passiv*) The council told us the cartons shouldn't have been left near the dustbin.
(*Aktiv*) The council told us we shouldn't have left the cartons near the dustbin.

We're running out of landfills to dump the garbage in.
We're running out of landfills in which to dump the garbage.
We're running out of landfills where we can dump the garbage.

2. *Should – ought to – must*

There should be / ought to be harsher punishments.
Es müßte strengere Strafen geben.
Midnight dumpers should be / ought to be treated as dangerous criminals.
Leute, die Abfälle illegal beseitigen, müßten/sollten als gefährliche Verbrecher behandelt werden.
The hospitals ought to check where their medical waste goes.
Die Krankenhäuser müßten (eigentlich) überprüfen, wo ihre Abfälle hinkommen.

The driver must be able to change a $10 bill.
Der Fahrer muß in der Lage sein, einen Zehndollarschein zu wechseln.
The driver should be able to change a $10 bill.
Der Fahrer sollte in der Lage sein, einen Zehndollarschein zu wechseln.
The driver ought to be able to change a $10 bill.
Der Fahrer müßte eigentlich in der Lage sein, einen Zehndollarschein zu wechseln.

Should und *ought to* sind in der Bedeutung *sollte/müßte* häufig austauschbar, aber *ought to* klingt stärker, nachdrücklicher als *should*.

1. Vervollständigen Sie den Text.

When Alison and Martin ..... that their wedding presents had been ..... away by the dustmen, they immediately phoned the council and ..... them what had happened. The council people said they would ..... for the missing presents, but the search turned out to ..... unsuccessful. When the couple ..... a claim for compensation, they were ..... they had no one but themselves to blame because the cartons shouldn't have been ..... near the dustbin. A council spokesman said later: "Our men had no reason to ..... that these materials were anything ..... rubbish." Yesterday, Alison was busy ..... thank-you letters for the ..... gifts. Asked how she felt about the whole thing, she .....: "It's terrible to ..... that all these lovely gifts have ended up at the rubbish dump without ever ..... used."

2. Setzen Sie die folgenden Sätze vom Aktiv ins Passiv oder vom Passiv ins Aktiv.

a. Can you believe it! The dustmen have taken away our wedding presents.
b. We had stored the gifts in cartons in the yard.
c. A neighbour of ours saw the refuse collectors taking them away.
d. We put in a claim for compensation, but the council's insurers told us the cartons shouldn't have been left near the dustbin.
e. Temperatures are in the nineties, and they've closed most of the beaches.
f. Garbage of that sort shouldn't be dumped directly offshore.
g. There's no way anyone can hold the hospitals responsible.
h. Nobody knows what happens when we've turned the stuff over to the garbage collectors.
i. We pay the garbage collectors to dispose of it.
j. We don't know if the waste has been disposed of properly.
k. In many cases, our garbage has to be shipped to faraway places.
l. We must encourage the use of recyclable packing.

3. *If*-Sätze. Setzen Sie die fehlenden Wörter ein.

a. They wouldn't go on the beach even if it ..... open.
b. If we ..... to make it to *Kramer vs. Kramer* we'd better hurry.
c. I don't think she'd suffer if we ..... that sort of arrangement.
d. If they ..... only let you know what's going on.
e. If we .....n't gone charter we wouldn't be in this mess.

4. Übersetzen Sie.

a. Eine Nachbarin sah, wie die Müllabfuhr die Kartons mitnahm.
b. Man hätte die Kartons nicht in der Nähe der Mülltonne lassen dürfen.
c. Wir hören nun schon seit Wochen davon, daß Klinikmüll an Land gespült wird.
d. Es gibt keine Möglichkeit, die Krankenhäuser zur Verantwortung zu ziehen.
e. Sie sagen: „Was die Abfuhrunternehmen mit den Abfällen machen, ist nicht unsere Sache."
f. Die Krankenhäuser müßten nachprüfen, was mit den Abfällen geschieht.
g. Die Abfuhrunternehmen müßten gezwungen werden nachzuweisen (*show*), daß sie die Abfälle ordnungsgemäß entsorgen.
h. Für „midnight dumpers" müßte es strengere Strafen geben.
i. Leute, die solche Abfälle ins Meer kippen, sollten als gefährliche Verbrecher behandelt werden.

24 Religion

Wie alle anderen Bereiche des menschlichen Lebens hat auch der der Religion seine besondere Sprache. Die Texte dieser Lektion vermitteln dazu einige Schlüsselwörter und Informationen. So benennt Text 1 die wichtigsten in den englischsprachigen Ländern vertretenen Religionen und religiösen Gruppen und gibt Grundinformationen zur Religion in England und Amerika. Text 2 vermittelt Ihnen einen Eindruck von der gottesdienstlichen Sprache: die (auch aus manchen Filmen) bekannten Worte des Treuegelöbnisses aus der Trauungszeremonie der anglikanischen Kirche. Dieser Text ist über 450 Jahre alt; Sie lesen ihn hier allerdings in einer 1980 offiziell modernisierten Fassung. Text 3 skizziert einige Fragen und Probleme, die in den christlichen Kirchen in unserer Zeit diskutiert werden.
In der Tonaufnahme werden Text 1 und 3 im Wechsel von britischen und amerikanischen Sprecher(inne)n gelesen. Text 2 hören Sie zweimal – jeweils mit neutralem britischem Akzent und fiktiven Namen gesprochen: zuerst vom Bräutigam (= *bridegroom*), dann von der Braut (= *bride*).

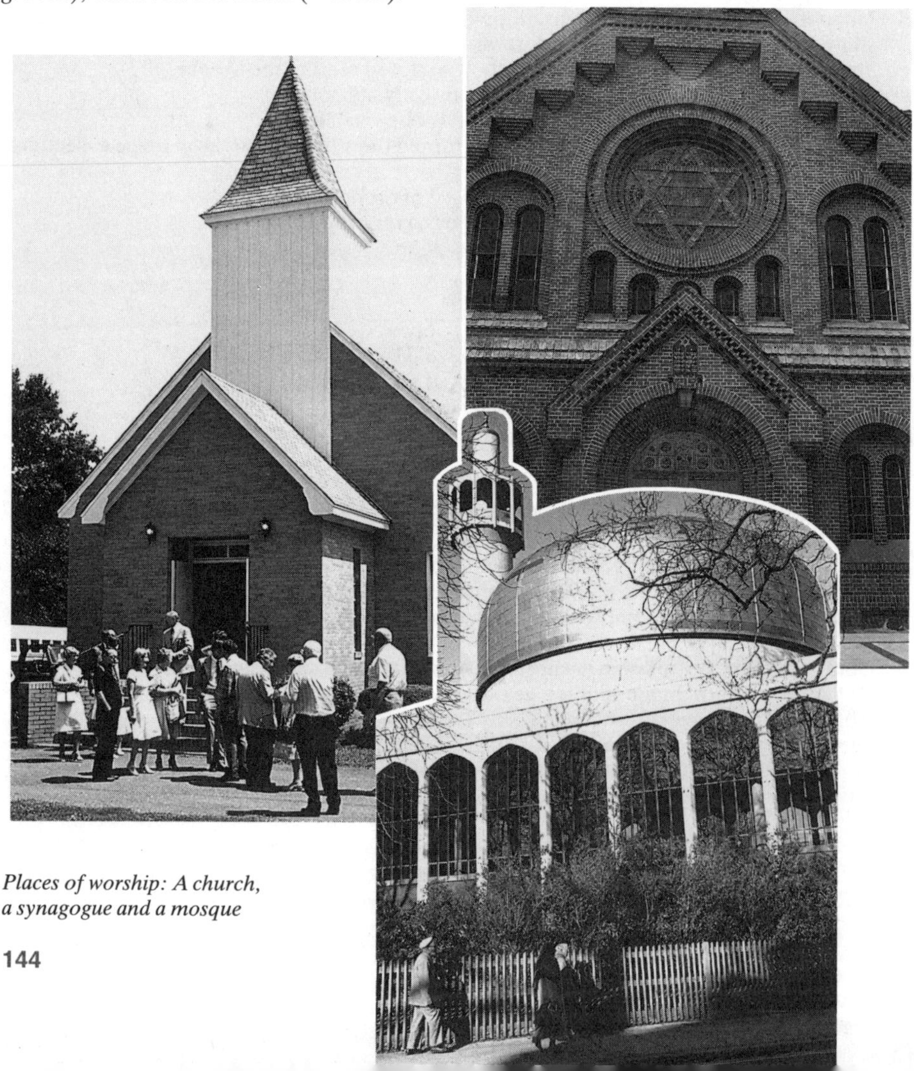

Places of worship: A church, a synagogue and a mosque

Religious groups in England and the United States

England's "established" church is the Church of England. Its head is the queen or king, and its religious leader is the Archbishop of Canterbury. Other major denominations are the Roman Catholics and the free churches such as the Presbyterians, Methodists and Baptists. Muslims, Jews, and Hindus are the largest non-Christian communities.
The United States does not have an established, or official, church. Protestant churches are in the majority, the largest groups being the Baptists, Methodists, and Lutherans. Roman Catholics are strongly represented too, and Jews are an important minority.

Wortschatz

religion	(die) Religion; (der) Glaube
religious groups	religiöse Gruppen; Glaubensgemeinschaften
the established church	die Staatskirche
the Church of England	die englische Staatskirche; die anglikanische Kirche (*ihre Mitglieder heißen* Anglicans)
its head is the queen or king	ihr Oberhaupt ist die Königin oder der König
religious leader	religiöser/geistlicher Führer
Archbishop of Canterbury	Erzbischof von Canterbury
major denominations	größere/bedeutende Konfessionen
free church	Freikirche (*Gegenteil:* established church)
Presbyterian	Presbyterianer(in)
Methodist	Methodist(in)
Baptist	Baptist(in)
Muslim(s)	Muslim(e); Moslem(s)
Jew	Jude; Jüdin
Hindu	Hindu
non-Christian communities	nichtchristliche Gemeinschaften
the United States does not have an established church	die Vereinigten Staaten haben keine Staatskirche (United States *ist Einzahl!*)
Protestant churches	protestantische Kirchen
Lutheran	Lutheraner(in)
strongly represented	stark/zahlreich vertreten
minority	Minorität; Minderheit

Verständnis- und Wortschatztest

a. What difference is there between England and the USA as far as religion is concerned? □ b. Who's the head, and who's the chief bishop, of the Church of England? □ c. Members of the Church of England are called ..... □ d. There are a number of *free* churches in England – what is the opposite of *free* in this context? □ e. Within the Christian church there are different ....., such as Anglicans, Roman Catholics, Presbyterians, Methodists, Baptists, etc. □ f. Another word for *established* in *established church*? □ g. While Christians are in the majority in Britain, there are also a number of important non-Christian minorities such as .....

From the Church of England marriage service

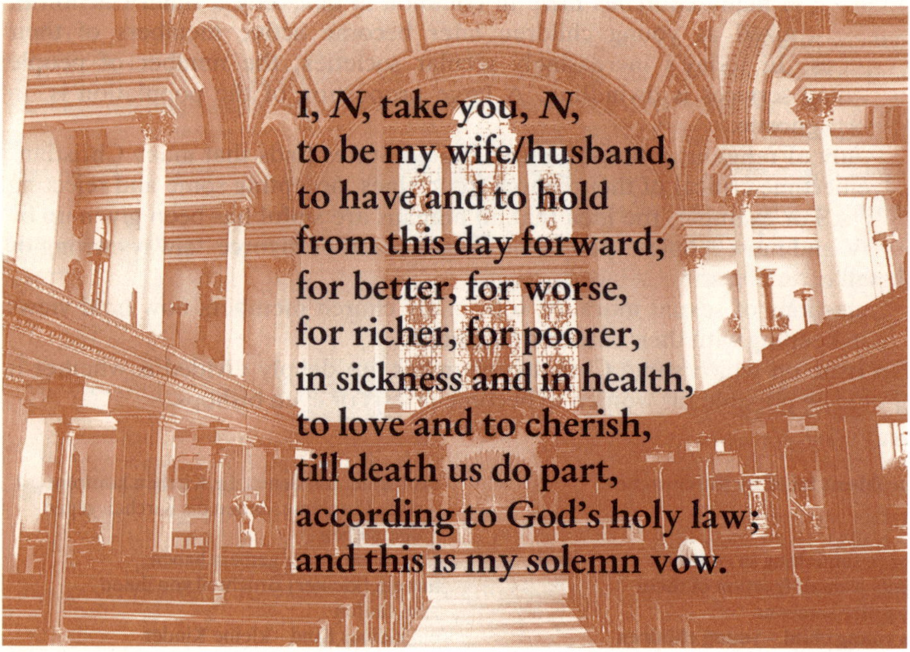

Wortschatz

marriage service	Traugottesdienst
N	(*Zeichen für den einzusetzenden Namen*)
my wife	meine (Ehe-)Frau
to have and to hold	(*traditionelle, ursprünglich rechtssprachliche Formel, mit der ein Inbesitznehmen ausgedrückt wird*)
from this day forward	von diesem / vom heutigen Tage an
for better, for worse	(*etwa:*) in guten und in schlechten Tagen
rich	reich
poor	arm
cherish someone	sich liebevoll um jem. kümmern
to love and to cherish	(*etwa:*) zu lieben und zu ehren
till death us do part	(*alte Ausdrucksweise für:* till death parts/separates us) bis daß der Tod uns scheidet
according to God's holy law	nach Gottes heiligem Gesetz
this is my solemn vow	„dies ist mein feierliches Gelübde“

Some problems faced by Christian churches

A problem many churches have in common is that only a small fraction of those baptized as young children later become active members of their churches. In today's increasingly secular societies, the number of people attending services is dwindling. A large proportion of the population is, in effect, agnostic.

A study of religious attitudes in the United States finds that many Christians have become critical of their church's doctrines, accepting some and rejecting others. For example, the idea that all humans are sinful has been given up by many, and most religious people no longer consider divorce "always wrong or sinful".

In questions of sexual morality, too, many church members now hold views not in keeping with their church's teachings.

An issue on which some Christian churches are deeply divided is whether it should be possible for women to become priests or even bishops.

Wortschatz

problems faced by the churches	Probleme, mit denen die Kirchen konfrontiert sind; Probleme, denen die Kirchen gegenüberstehen
have something in common	etw. miteinander gemein haben
only a small fraction of them	nur ein (kleiner) Bruchteil von ihnen
baptize someone	jem. taufen
a young child – young children	ein kleines Kind – kleine Kinder
an active member	ein aktives Mitglied
increasingly	zunehmend; immer mehr
secular	weltlich (orientiert); säkular
society	(die) Gesellschaft
attend a service	an einem Gottesdienst teilnehmen
the number is dwindling	die Zahl nimmt stetig ab
a large proportion of the population is, in effect, agnostic	ein großer Teil der Bevölkerung ist im Grunde agnostisch (Agnostiker bekennen sich dazu, daß der Mensch die letzten Gründe des Seins, insbesondere Gott, nicht erkennen kann)
a study of religious attitudes	eine Untersuchung über religiöse Einstellungen
they have become critical of their church's doctrines	sie stehen den Lehren ihrer Kirche kritisch gegenüber
accept or reject something	etw. annehmen oder ablehnen
all humans are sinful	alle Menschen sind sündhaft
give an idea up (– gave – given)	eine Idee / einen Gedanken aufgeben
consider divorce sinful	die Ehescheidung für eine Sünde halten
in questions of sexual morality	in Fragen der Sexualmoral/-ethik
views not in keeping with their church's teachings	Auffassungen, die nicht mit den Lehren ihrer Kirche in Einklang stehen
an issue on which they are deeply divided	eine Frage, die sie zutiefst entzweit
priests or even bishops	Priester(innen) oder gar Bischöfe

24 Erklärungen

1. Singular (Einzahl) oder Plural (Mehrzahl)?

Beachten Sie folgende Abweichungen vom deutschen Sprachgebrauch:

There have (*nicht:* has) been a number of accidents.
The number of accidents has (*nicht:* have) gone down.

A number steht in der Regel mit einem Pluralverb, *the number* mit einem Singularverb.

A hundred thousand pounds/dollars isn't enough.
Hunderttausend Pfund/Dollar sind nicht genug / genügen nicht.

Genau umgekehrt als im Deutschen! Beachten Sie die Pluralform *pounds/dollars* und das Singularverb *is*.

It's the children who suffer. *Es sind die Kinder, die leiden.*
Today it's not only the Scots who are fond of oats.
Heute sind es nicht nur die Schotten, die gern Hafer essen.

Eine Kombination von *it* (Singular!) und *are* (Plural!) entsprechend dem deutschen *es sind* gibt es im Englischen nicht.

This news comes to you in the World Service of the BBC.
Bad news travels fast. *Schlechte Nachrichten verbreiten sich schnell.*

The United States is the most powerful country in the world.
Die Vereinigten Staaten sind das mächtigste Land der Welt.
The United States does not have an established church.
Die Vereinigten Staaten haben keine Staatskirche.

The police were called. *Die Polizei wurde gerufen.*
The police believe it was to have been held late last night.
Die Polizei glaubt, daß es gestern abend hatte stattfinden sollen.

News und *the United States* sind immer Singular; *police* ist immer Plural.

2. Zum Gebrauch der Präposition *by*

a. Malta was occupied by the French. ... *von den / durch die Franzosen.*
b. The medicine was prescribed by the doctor. ... *wurde vom Arzt verschrieben.*

c. He shocked his employers by quitting. ... *indem er kündigte.*
d. You can learn a lot by listening to the radio. ... *indem man Radio hört.*

e. What do you mean by "sinful"? *Was meinen Sie mit „sündhaft"?*
f. What do you mean by that? *Was meinen Sie damit?*

g. Make sure you've checked out by three. ... *daß Sie bis drei abgereist sind.*
h. By 1956 the cinema had lost the battle against TV. *Spätestens 1956 ...*

i. Are you coming by Tube/taxi/train? ... *mit der U-Bahn / mit dem Taxi/Zug?*

1. Setzen Sie die folgenden Präpositionen ein.

at, by, for, in, of, off, on, to, with

a. Many Christians have become critical ..... their church's doctrines.
b. This is an issue ..... which Christian churches are deeply divided.
c. Fifty years ago people didn't give much thought ..... the garbage they produced.
d. Everybody can help to make recycling work ..... separating food, glass, metal, and paper when it is thrown away.
e. Everybody should take an interest ..... their community's waste management.
f. I'm not particularly fond ..... oats, I must say.
g. He's been ill ..... flu for the past week.
h. They have set up a new record ..... taking about five and a half hours ..... the previous fastest time.
i. Many patients are worried ..... the side effects of drugs.
j. Their main purpose ..... going to the doctor is to get a sick note.
k. Money could be saved ..... cutting down ..... the number of prescriptions.
l. We've been waiting ..... eleven hours now
m. ..... midday they said we'd be put ..... a bus ..... Luton, but nothing happened.
n. What do you mean ..... "nothing happened"?

2. Unregelmäßige Plurale. Setzen Sie die Mehrzahlform ein.

a. There are more (woman) working, and more (child) are being driven to day care.
b. There were two rough-looking (man) at the bottom of the stairs.
c. The cartons had been taken away – not by (thief) but by (dustman).
d. We still don't know why the two (aircraft) crashed.
e. Our supermarket (shelf) are stacked with health foods.
f. She has to buy (man's) shoes because she's got such large (foot).

3. Singular oder Plural? Setzen Sie die passende Verbform ein.

a. As far as I know, the police .....n't arrested anyone yet.
b. Here ..... the news, read by Brian Martin.
c. What ..... the United States going to do about this problem?
d. Three hundred pounds .....n't too much to pay for a taxi ride from Gatwick to the Scottish Highlands.
e. It..... these teenagers that need testing more often, not the elderly drivers.
f. There ..... a number of reasons why the number of people attending services ..... dwindling.

4. Übersetzen Sie.

a. Das Oberhaupt der Church of England ist der König oder die Königin, und ihr religiöser Führer ist der Erzbischof von Canterbury.
b. Die Vereinigten Staaten haben keine Staatskirche.
c. Die meisten Kirchen stehen vor dem Problem, daß die Zahl der Gottesdienstbesucher zurückgeht.
d. Viele Kirchenmitglieder haben Auffassungen, die mit den Lehren ihrer Kirche nicht in Einklang stehen.
e. Die Vorstellung, daß Ehescheidung immer eine Sünde sei, wird heute von vielen religiösen Menschen abgelehnt.

25 Tennis

Die Texte der letzten Lektion handeln vom Tennis. In Text 1, einem Dialog, geht es um ein verlorenes Spiel, das nicht hätte verloren werden dürfen. Text 2 erklärt, wie beim Tennis gezählt wird – wenn Sie nicht selber Tennis spielen, werden Sie sich das bei Fernsehübertragungen schon oft gefragt haben. Text 3 schließlich sagt Ihnen etwas über die Geschichte der Wimbledon-Turniere, der inoffiziellen Tennisweltmeisterschaften.
In der Tonaufnahme wird Text 1 mit amerikanischem, Text 2 und 3 mit britischem Akzent gesprochen.

"I've made less than fifty thousand so far this year – just can't get those first serves in."

A tennis match

A: Had a good workout?

B: A good workout? I played a tournament match.

A: Oh, did you? You're not looking too happy. Did you lose?

B: I went down 6–2, 4–6, 0–6.

A: H'm … well, it's not the end of the world, is it? You win some, you lose some.

B: Yes, I know. But I shouldn't have lost this one. He was an absolute nobody – I don't even remember his name. In the first set it looked like a walkaway for me. I played my usual game – you know, a good hard serve and then up to the net for the kill.

A: Primitive, but it works.

B: Yes, but somehow it didn't with this guy. In the second set he began feeding me really nasty lobs, and eventually he was up at the net most of the time and I was chasing round the court like crazy trying to return his shots.

A: He broke up your game.

B: He sure did, and I was dumb enough not to see how he was doing it. By the time we were into the third set I couldn't get my first serves in and my backhand had turned completely sour. I was swearing at myself and arguing with the umpire. Boy, was I frustrated …

Wortschatz

had a good workout?	hast du schön trainiert?
play a tournament match	ein Match/Spiel im Turnier spielen
go down (– went – gone)	untergehen
0–6 (love – six)	null zu sechs
an absolute nobody	ein absoluter Niemand
I don't even remember his name	ich weiß nicht mal mehr seinen Namen
in the first set	im ersten Satz
it looked like a walkaway *AE* / *BE* walkover	es sah wie ein Spaziergang/Kinderspiel aus
play a game	ein Spiel spielen/machen
a good hard serve	ein schöner harter Aufschlag
then up to the net	dann ans Netz
for the kill	um den Ball zu töten / den Punkt zu machen
primitive, but it works	primitiv, aber es funktioniert
somehow	irgendwie
with this guy	bei diesem Kerl/„Typ“
feed someone lobs (– fed – fed)	jem. Lobs / hohe Bälle geben
eventually	schließlich; am Ende
chase round the court like crazy	wie ein Irrer auf dem Platz (he)rumrennen
return his shots	seine Bälle zurückgeben/„kriegen“
he broke up your game	er hat dir dein Spiel kaputtgemacht
I was dumb enough not to see …	ich war zu blöd, um zu merken …
by the time we were into the third set	als wir schließlich im dritten Satz waren
I couldn't get my first serves in	meine ersten Aufschläge kamen nicht

turn sour	(*z. B. Milch:*) sauer werden
my backhand had turned sour	meine Rückhand war hin / zum Teufel
I was swearing at myself	ich fluchte/schimpfte mit mir selbst
argue with the umpire	sich mit dem Schiedsrichter streiten
boy, was I frustrated!	Mensch, war ich frustriert!

The rules of the game

A match lasts a maximum of three (for men sometimes five) sets, and the minimum number of games per set is six. A lead of two points is needed to win a game, and a lead of two games to win a set. If the score is "6–all", a tiebreak is often played to decide the set.

Points in a game are scored as "15", "30", "40", and "game". A score of "40–all" is called "deuce". The side that wins the next point then has the "advantage" and, with one further point, takes the game. If the opposing side equalizes, the score returns to "deuce".

In the tiebreak, points are scored as "one", "two" etc. up to "seven", at which score the set is decided if the leading side is at least two points ahead.

The score "0" is called "love" in tennis, except in the tiebreak, where it is called "zero".

If only one more point is needed to win a set, that point is called "set point". If only one more point is needed to win the match, that point is called "match point".

Wortschatz

rules of the game	Spielregeln
last a maximum of three sets	maximal/höchstens drei Sätze dauern
the minimum number of games	die Mindest(an)zahl an Spielen
a lead of two points	eine Führung von zwei Punkten; zwei Punkte Vorsprung
the score is "6–all"	der (Spiel-)Stand ist „6 beide"
tiebreak	(„Unentschieden-Brecher") Tie-Break
score points as "15", "30" etc.	Punkte als „15", „30" etc. zählen
deuce	Einstand
advantage	Vorteil
with one further point	mit einem weiteren Punkt
if the opposing side equalizes	wenn die Gegenseite gleichzieht
at least two points ahead	mindestens zwei Punkte voraus
zero	(*auch beim Thermometer:*) Null
set point	Satzball
match point	Matchball

Verständnis- und Wortschatztest

a. To win a match you must win at least two ..... ☐ b. To win a set you must win at least six ..... ☐ c. To win a game you must win at least four ..... ☐ d. A score of "40–all" is called ..... ☐ e. "0" is called ..... in a normal game, but ..... in a tiebreak.

Wimbledon

In 1877, the All England Croquet and Lawn Tennis Club at Wimbledon held its first tennis championship. There was only one event – the men's singles – with 22 amateurs competing for a silver Challenge Cup. The final attracted just about 200 spectators, and the total profit from the entire championship was £10.

Today, some 400,000 people pour into the grounds of Wimbledon's All England Club to watch the 443 matches in the five main championship events: the men's singles, women's singles, men's doubles, women's doubles, and mixed doubles. All the leading players are now professionals; tennis has become a multimillion-dollar industry.

Wortschatz

Wimbledon	(Teil d. Londoner Stadtteils Merton)
croquet	Krocket (*ein Rasenspiel*)
lawn tennis	Rasentennis
hold a championship (– held – held)	eine Meisterschaft abhalten
there was only one event	es gab nur einen Wettbewerb
the men's singles	das Herreneinzel
amateur	Amateur(sportler[in])
compete for a cup	um einen Pokal kämpfen
a silver challenge cup	ein silberner Wanderpokal
the final	das Endspiel
attract spectators	Zuschauer anziehen
just about 200 spectators	knappe 200 Zuschauer
total profit	Gesamterlös; Reingewinn
the entire championship	die gesamte Meisterschaft
some 400,000 people	ungefähr/etwa 400 000 Menschen
they pour into the grounds	sie strömen in die Anlagen
the women's singles	das Dameneinzel
the men's/women's doubles	das Herren-/Damendoppel
the mixed doubles	das gemischte Doppel / Mixed
the players are professionals	die Spieler(innen) sind Profis
a multimillion-dollar industry	(*etwa:*) ein Millionengeschäft

Verständnis- und Wortschatztest

a. When was the first tennis championship held in Wimbledon? ☐ b. Did women compete in that first championship? ☐ c. Was the player who won the first championship a professional? ☐ d. Before 1970 there was no tiebreak. Why do you think the tiebreak was introduced? ☐ e. Can you think of a word that means roughly the same as *championship*? ☐ f. You can't be a leading player if you haven't got a ..... serve. ☐ g. Another word for *leading* in *leading player*? ☐ h. *Had a good workout?* This sentence is good spoken English but it isn't complete grammatically. Can you complete it? ☐ i. I *should* have won. Another expression for *should*? ☐ j. "He broke up your game." – "He *sure* did." A more conventional word for *sure*? ☐ k. It didn't work with this *guy*. Another word for *guy*? ☐ l. That was a *dumb* thing to do. Another word for *dumb*?

Zur Aussprache und Schreibung von Zahlen und Ziffern

a. Some 400,000 people watch the 443 matches.
Some four hundred thousand people watch the four hundred and forty-three matches.
b. 107,000 vehicles cross the bridge every day.
one hundred / a hundred and seven thousand vehicles
c. His family has lived in the village for 170 years.
for a hundred / one hundred and seventy years

Die Gliederung größerer Tausenderzahlen erfolgt ggf. durch Kommas, nicht – wie im Deutschen – durch Punkte (a, b). Das *and* vor der Zehnerstelle (a–c) wird im AE manchmal weggelassen. Beachten Sie das *a* oder *one* in der Aussprache von *170* etc. (b, c): *a/one hundred and seventy* – nicht einfach *hundred and seventy*!

d. There are only 1.2 people in the average rush-hour car. *one point two*
e. Only 0.5 per cent of British engineers are female. *(nought/oh) point five*

Dezimalbrüche werden – anders als im Deutschen – mit einem Punkt geschrieben. Bei Dezimalbrüchen unter 1 wird die vor dem Dezimalpunkt stehende (sonst *nought* oder *oh* gesprochene) Null mitunter weggelassen.

f. Please ring Mr Terry Johnson on 01–327 4065 between 09–1600 hrs.
on oh–one three–two–seven four–oh–six–five between nine and sixteen hours
g. She called 911 (*Notruf in den USA*). She dialled 999 (*Notruf in Großbritannien*).
She called nine–one–one. She dialled nine–nine–nine.

Telefonnummern werden gruppenweise Ziffer für Ziffer gesprochen. *Null* wird in Telefonnummern stets *oh* gesprochen. Beachten Sie die Aussprache der Uhrzeit in (f). Alltäglicher als diese „bürokratische" Ausdrucksweise wäre natürlich: ... *between 9 a.m. and 4 p.m.*

h. I'm in room 4 / room 45 / room 405 / room 4216.
room four / room forty-five / room four oh five / room four two one six
i. The A4 / the A45 / the A405 / the A423 is still closed.
the A four / the A forty-five / the A four oh five / the A four twenty-three

Die Aussprache der Nummern von Hotelzimmern (h), Fernstraßen (i) u. dgl. variiert entsprechend der Ziffernzahl.

j. In 1798 Malta was occupied by the French, and in 1800 it was taken by the British.
in seventeen (hundred and) ninety-eight ... in eighteen hundred
k. Cary Grant was born in 1904 and died in 1986. *in nineteen hundred and four / in nineteen oh four ... in nineteen (hundred and) eighty-six*

Die umständlichere Form mit *hundred and* wird in der Alltagssprache beim Sprechen über aktuelle Jahreszahlen nur selten gebraucht.

l. The cab driver must be able to change a $10 bill. *a ten-dollar bill*
m. The fare was $10 / £10. *ten dollars / ten pounds*
n. He sold land worth more than £1 million at half price.
land worth more than one/a million pounds

Beachten Sie die Stellung des $- oder £-Zeichens: ohne Abstand direkt vor der Zahl.

1. Ausdrücke mit Zahlen. – Sprechen Sie die folgenden Sätze.

a. London Bed and Breakfast Services, 198 Cromwell Road, London SW5 0SW, telephone 01–373 3536.
b. Work on the A309 Kingston Bypass has been causing long delays.
c. I'm in room 409 and I'm due to check out today.
d. A recent survey of 1,000 homeless people found that 80 per cent were male, two-thirds were white, and 87 per cent had once held a job.
e. Malta has a population of about 350,000, 97 per cent of which are Roman Catholic.
f. The city will decide later whether to repair the bridge, at an estimated cost of $250 million, or replace it – for $500 million.
g. The dustmen carted away about £1000 worth of wedding presents.
h. The plan was for up to 25 owners of high-performance cars to race along the M25, the 117-mile motorway around the capital.
i. Malta's average temperatures are 27 °C in July and 14 °C in January.
j. In 1798 Malta was occupied by the French, and in 1800 it was taken by the British, who ruled until its independence in 1964.
k. Here's the weather forecast for 6 p.m. on Saturday the 25th of June.
l. You can take the subway to 42nd Street.
m. "Did you lose the match?" – "I went down 6–2, 4–6, 0–6."
n. The average British family has 0.8 children.

2. Infinitiv des Perfekts ohne und mit *to*.

Inf. des Perfekts ohne *to*: She should have won. *Sie hätte gewinnen müssen.*
Inf. des Perfekts mit *to*: She seems to have won. *Sie scheint gewonnen zu haben.*

Setzen Sie jeweils den Infinitiv des Perfekts ohne oder mit *to* ein, und übersetzen Sie den Satz.

a. I must (get) you wrong.
b. Don't mention any problems you may (have) with your previous employer.
c. He couldn't (do) it even if he had wanted to.
d. They hope (raise) more than £100,000 for the Royal National Lifeboat Institution.
e. It wouldn't even (cross) my mind to do that.
f. The cartons shouldn't (be) left near the dustbin.
g. The police ought (prevent) the race.
h. The police warnings appear (prevent) the race.
i. I wouldn't (hesitate) to help him.
j. The illegal car race on the M25 was (be) held last night.

3. Übersetzen Sie.

a. Ich hätte das Spiel gewinnen können.
b. Das Spiel hätte ein Spaziergang für mich sein müssen.
c. Dieses Spiel hätte ich nicht verlieren dürfen.
d. Wenn meine Rückhand besser gewesen wäre, hätte ich vielleicht gewonnen.
e. Du hättest dich nicht mit dem Schiedsrichter streiten sollen.
f. Ich scheine alles falsch gemacht zu haben.
g. Wenn ich ⟨doch⟩ nur nicht so blöd gewesen wäre!
h. Ich rannte wie verrückt auf dem Platz herum und versuchte, seine Bälle (*shots*) zurückzukriegen.
i. Er war so ein Niemand – ich weiß (*remember*) nicht mal mehr seinen Namen.

Schlüssel zu den Übungen

Bitte beachten Sie:

Bei Sätzen, in denen mehr als eine Lücke zu füllen ist, sind die einzelnen Lösungen durch Semikolons (;) getrennt.
Schrägstriche (/) bezeichnen alternative (d. h. weitere, ebenfalls richtige) Lösungen. Um Ihnen die Möglichkeit zu geben, Ihren Sprachschatz auch mit Hilfe des Lösungsschlüssels zu erweitern, werden möglichst viele, mitunter über den Stoff dieses Buches hinausgehende alternative Lösungen angegeben.
Auf Unterschiede zwischen britischem und amerikanischem Englisch wird durch die Abkürzungen *BE* und *AE* hingewiesen.
In den sehr häufigen Fällen, wo außer der Langform (z. B. *I would*) auch eine Kurzform (z.B. *I'd*) möglich ist, wird im Schlüssel meistens nur eine, nämlich die innerhalb des Kontexts wahrscheinlichere Form gegeben; selbstverständlich ist auch die jeweils andere Form in allen Fällen richtig. (Vgl. die Tabelle „Kurzformen" auf S. 197.)

Lektion 1

Verständnis- und Wortschatztest S. 7
a. supersonic / very fast. b. tyres *BE* / tires *AE*; Kennedy. c. bring; runway. d. narrowly. e. bumpy. f. pilot/captain.

Verständnis- und Wortschatztest S. 8
a. David and Cathy think flying is (reasonably) safe. b. did. c. far more people fly (these days). d. near disaster / near accident. e. air. f. road. g. anyone/anybody.

Verständnis- und Wortschatztest S. 9
a. flight attendant. b. emergency. c. exits/equipment / exits and equipment. d. happen/ occur; to. e. obey. f. enters / gets into; get.

Übungen

1. a. narrowly; as/when. b. hit; came/went; brought; been. c. gone; rather; got. d. pay; obey; get/be.

2. a. narrow. b. really quickly. c. lucky. d. Luckily. e. normally. f. normal. g. fantastically. h. seriously. i. usually. j. usually; carefully. k. important; exactly. l. exact.

3. a. A Concorde (jet) narrowly escaped disaster yesterday. b. The pilot managed to bring / succeeded in bringing the aircraft/plane to a halt. c. The passengers disembarked / got out / got off in the usual way. d. When we hit the runway there were five loud pops. e. Luckily/Fortunately no one / nobody was/got hurt/injured. f. We could have all been / We could all have been dead. g. In terms of percentages / Percentagewise the number of accidents/crashes has gone down / has dropped/decreased. h. "I'd / I would rather fly than drive." / "I'd rather go by plane than by car." – "Me too." / "So would I." / "Same here." i. I don't know exactly / I don't exactly know / I'm not quite/really sure how to use the oxygen mask. j. I always fasten my seat belt / put my seat belt on – just in case / you never know!

Lektion 2

Verständnis- und Wortschatztest S. 13

1. a. telephone. b. southeast. c. issued. d. There are likely to be <u>some showers</u> this evening and overnight, some of them quite <u>heavy</u>. Tomorrow it will be <u>mostly</u> cloudy, and again some showers are <u>likely</u>. Tomorrow's temperatures will be slightly <u>lower</u> than today's.

2. a. outlook. b. Some showers <u>are likely</u> tonight. c. remain. d. slightly / a bit.

Verständnis- und Wortschatztest S. 14
a. get/wake. b. cleared. c. is/comes. d. drought; sell. e. think. f. complain/talk.

Verständnis- und Wortschatztest S. 15

a. proclaimed/declared. b. drained/took. c. devastated/destroyed/ruined. d. replenish. e. relief/rain/change. f. forecast.

Übungen

1. a. It will remain. (It's going to remain *würde einen Grad an Gewißheit ausdrücken, der für eine Wettervorhersage in der Regel nicht angemessen ist.*) b. will be. c. I've had; I wish. d. it's / it has stopped raining and the sun's coming out / the sun is coming out / the sun's come out / the sun has come out. e. haven't had. f. shouldn't be complaining / shouldn't complain; are having to sell off / have to sell off; will see them through till the rain comes. g. had; have been devastated / were devastated / are being devastated.
2. a. the weather forecast issued by the Met. Office. b. A mild winter followed by a rainless spring. c. The weather (being) forecast. d. All the people injured. e. The prices paid for beef. f. no hay with which to replenish their rapidly diminishing stocks / no hay to replenish their rapidly diminishing stocks (with). g. the worst drought I've ever seen.
3. a. occur. b. be/remain/stay/continue. c. bound/expected/likely. d. complain. e. proclaimed/declared. f. devastated/destroyed/ruined/affected/damaged. g. are facing / are faced with. h. forecast.
4. a. There's a terrible drought in the United States. b. In some parts/areas they haven't had / there hasn't been any rain for months. c. Most of North Dakota has been proclaimed/ declared a disaster area. d. (Their) Hay stocks/reserves are rapidly/quickly diminishing / are diminishing rapidly, and there is nothing to replenish them. e. (The) Farmers are selling (off) their livestock/cattle in the hope that the extra/additional income will see them through until/till the rain comes. f. Many / A lot of farmers are facing (financial) ruin / are faced with (financial) ruin / are on the brink of (financial) ruin. g. Hot, dry weather with only scattered rainfall is (being) forecast for the next 30 days.

Lektion 3

Verständnis- und Wortschatztest S. 19

a. until/till. b. causing. c. heading / travelling *BE* / traveling *AE*. d. heavy / a lot of. e. due/scheduled/about; involve. f. unless.

Verständnis- und Wortschatztest S. 20

a. highway/road. b. driver's license *AE* / driving licence *BE*. c. speed limit. d. fast. e. ticket. f. hold. g. driving licence. h. motorway.

Verständnis- und Wortschatztest S. 21

a. congested/(over)crowded. b. gear. c. moved. d. transport *BE* / transit *AE* / transportation *AE*. e. environment.

Übungen

1. a. has been causing / has caused. b. heading. c. beginning. d. Avoiding. e. are getting / get. f. Driving . g. to drive. h. have moved / have been moving; putting. i. are being built.
2. a. travel. b. heading. c. till/until. d. no bad. e. unless you. f. Can; driver's license *AE*. g. roads / motorways *BE*. h. hold on. i. It takes me / I need. j. found (out); transit/ transportation *beide AE*. k. Improved mass-transport *BE* / mass-transportation *AE*.
3. a. into/for. b. because of. c. for. d. from the central city areas to the suburbs. e. at less cost and with less damage to the environment. f. for southeast England until/till dusk on Sunday, issued by the Met. Office for/at 6 p.m. on Saturday. g. on/from. h. with/on.
4. a. I need hardly remind you / I hardly need to remind you that there's heavy traffic in the Wimbledon area. b. You should avoid the Wimbledon area – unless you have / you've got semifinals tickets / tickets for the semifinals. c. You were doing almost/nearly 90 back

there. d. I didn't realize (that) I was going / I wasn't aware that I was going that fast. e. (The) Roads are getting more and more congested. f. A lot of new roads are being built (at the moment). g. I take/need an hour / It takes me an hour to drive the 18 miles to the/ my office.

Lektion 4

Verständnis- und Wortschatztest S. 25

a. Sandra is a computer programmer, and Steve is a steward (with a major airline) / an airline steward. b. Sandra works nine to five while Steve is often away for three weeks at a time on long-haul flights(, so he's often not at home when she is, and vice versa [= *und umgekehrt*]). c. It gives them a great opportunity / the opportunity to travel to places they couldn't afford otherwise. d. They would like a family and Sandra wants to be at home to bring up the children.

Verständnis- und Wortschatztest S. 26

a. cosmetics. b. haughty and unsympathetic. c. buying. d. sale. e. listen. f. salesclerk.

Verständnis- und Wortschatztest S. 27

a. newsreader/newscaster/presenter. b. quitting / leaving / handing in his notice / giving in his notice. c. stage / theatre *BE* / theater *AE*. d. becoming. e. adjust/adapt. f. blames. g. newscaster. h. interested in the theatre *BE* / theater *AE*.

Übungen

1. Steve started work as a steward two years ago shortly after he and Sandra got / had got married. He had been made redundant from his previous job. Steve's job gives / has given / gave them a great opportunity to travel / for travelling *BE* / traveling *AE* to places they couldn't afford / have afforded otherwise. So far they have been to Australia, New Zealand and the Far East. Both Sandra and Steve feel that flying is not the long-term answer for Steve. They would like a family and Sandra wants / would want to be at home to bring up the children, but she doubts they will/would be able to manage on Steve's salary alone, as they are now used to having two incomes.

2. Debbie Jenkins has just been voted Shop Assistant of the Year. Mrs Patterson, one of Debbie's regular customers, put her name up for the competition. Debbie, who sells cosmetics in a large store, is said to be so full of enthusiasm that you can't walk/go past her counter without buying something. But Debbie isn't the type/kind/sort of girl who'd sell/ recommend you something just to make a sale. She'll really listen to your problems and try to come up with what's best for you.

3. a. She has / She's been voted Shop Assistant of the Year. b. Your name has been put up for the competition. c. A lot of new roads have been built. d. Why has everything been changed? e. Haven't the children been taken to school? f. Why hasn't the state been proclaimed a disaster area? g. So much rain hadn't been expected. h. The spokesman said that the emergency equipment hadn't been used.

4. a. kids. b. been made redundant. c. salaries. d. wasn't planning. e. considering. f. keen on.

5. a. Travelling *BE* / Traveling *AE* is something I enjoy very much / I really enjoy. b. My job as a steward gives us an/the opportunity / the possibility to travel to places we couldn't afford otherwise / wouldn't be able to afford otherwise. c. The shop assistants *BE* / salesclerks *AE* / salesgirls/saleswomen/salesladies *BE&AE* working here / who work here are all very friendly and helpful. d. When I'm in the cosmetics department, I often buy things I wasn't planning / I didn't want / I didn't intend to buy at all. e. The drought we had five years ago was much worse. f. The new road that's / which is now being built / The new road now being built / The new road they're now building will probably solve the problem.

Lektion 5

Verständnis- und Wortschatztest S. 31
a. They're looking for sales people (to join their expanding sales force in West Germany). b. They should be aggressive and career-minded and have a lot of drive. c. Their job will be to sell personal tax-free (motor)cars to American, British and Canadian armed forces personnel. d. The advertisement mentions "high commission plus incentive bonuses" and it must be assumed there will be a (basic) salary as well / too. / If they work hard / do their job well, they'll have top earnings / they'll earn a lot of money. e. He can be reached in London (by phone) or in Frankfurt (by post/mail). f. It's 01 (*gesprochen:* oh one) for calls from within the UK / United Kingdom and 00441 (for calls) from West Germany.

Verständnis- und Wortschatztest S. 32
a. advertisements/adverts/ads/columns. b. (news)paper. c. experience/drive/aggressiveness. d. based. e. he would / he'd like to go back to Germany. f. off Oxford Street, between Oxford Circus and Tottenham Court Road. g. Oxford Circus and Tottenham Court Road.

Verständnis- und Wortschatztest S. 33
a. possible / you can / you possibly can. b. suitably/appropriately. c. relevant. d. ask. e. mention / discuss / talk about / bring up / touch on. f. being; sounding. g. fiddling / fidgeting / playing around.

Übungen
1. a. to join. b. asked. c. selling. d. to replenish. e. asked. f. coming. g. heading. h. to drive. i. flying; being. j. issued. k. changing.
2. a. We've been looking. b. joined. c. will join / is joining / is going to join / will be joining. d. sells. e. I've been trying. f. are you talking. g. I've been selling. h. were. i. I'm. j. will be / are going to be. k. I've been working. l. have had.
3. a. isn't it? b. isn't he? c. aren't they? d. don't you? e. wasn't it? f. haven't you? g. wouldn't I? h. aren't you? i. isn't she? j. doesn't it?
4. a. (*Am Telefon:*) Could I speak to / (*Persönlicher Besuch:*) Could I see / I wonder if I could see Mr Johnson, please? b. I'm looking forward to seeing you. c. I'm phoning / ringing up / *AE auch* calling about your advertisement in today's *Daily Mail*. d. I've been working in London for four years now. e. You should prepare yourself/yourselves carefully. f. She had prepared herself carefully. g. She gave the impression of being a very capable/competent woman.

Lektion 6

Verständnis- und Wortschatztest S. 37
a. Janet. b. 54. c. Bridport, Dorset. d. She doesn't like the loud music (that customers are bombarded with). e. It's a small notice/sign saying OUT OF ORDER, which she places on the jukebox. f. Everyone talks much more. g. pleasant/agreeable. h. puts. i. talk / chat / communicate / have a conversation.

Verständnis- und Wortschatztest S. 39 oben
a. Music, dogs, children, motorcycles, roadworks, and neighbours' TV or radio. b. She means she can hear practically every move her neighbours make, their TV, their radio and so on. c. great/huge/considerable. d. motorbike.

Verständnis- und Wortschatztest S. 39 unten
a. (More than / Over / About) 33 (per cent). b. Damage to hearing, lack of sleep / sleeplessness, irritability, heart trouble, indigestion, ulcers, high blood pressure, and mental illness. c. cause. d. lack. e. air/soil/river/sea/water/atmospheric/environmental pollution.

Übungen

1. When Mrs Moore is at the pub she ensures a quiet atmosphere by placing/putting a small notice on the jukebox that says/reads simply: out of order. The effect is that everyone talks much more. Mrs Moore believes/thinks/says she is part of a "silent majority" who would prefer to converse without shouting.
In the opinion of some experts we're getting/becoming more inconsiderate and selfish. They say we tend / we're tending/inclined/apt to do things for pleasure which cause annoyance to other people. We play loud music whenever we feel like it, even if it disturbs others.
It has been estimated/found/claimed that more than one in three Americans is affected by noise pollution. Noise-induced stress can create/cause severe tension in daily life and may even contribute/lead to mental illness.
2. a. secret. b. secretly. c. discreetly. d. discreetly. e. discreet. f. immediate. g. immediately. h. angrily. i. angry. j. Excessively amplified music (= „übermäßig verstärkte Musik") / Excessive amplified music (= „ein Übermaß an verstärkter Musik"). k. Excessive.
3. a. about; from. b. for; to. c. to. d. on *BE* / at *AE*. e. to. f. about. g. with/by. h. by. i. on. j. about.
4. a. I'd / I would prefer to be able to talk / to have a conversation / to converse without having to shout. b. Many of us tend / are tending to do things for pleasure/enjoyment which annoy other people / which cause annoyance to other people. c. I feel like / I wouldn't mind listening to some music. / I'd like to listen to some music. d. In these flats *BE* / apartments *AE* you can hear / you're able to hear practically every move a person / anyone / anybody makes / every move people make. e. More and more people / An increasing number of people / A growing number of people are (being) affected by noise pollution. f. I don't see why I should (have to / be forced to) listen to other people's music. g. "Excessive noise can lead to mental illness," says Professor Harrison.

Lektion 7

Verständnis- und Wortschatztest S. 43

a. In Wayford, Somerset. b. 69. c. For 170 years. d. Yes, he is. (I've been a school governor for over 30 years *schließt die Gegenwart mit ein;* I was a school governor for over 30 years *dagegen würde aussagen, daß er kein* school governor *mehr ist.*) e. He has seen the local youngsters / the young people (forced to) leave the area/village because of soaring house prices. f. He's decided to / He's going to sell part of his farm to the council at a special knockdown price on condition / provided it is used to build low-priced houses for young couples whose parents live in the village. g. soaring/rising. h. (special) knockdown / bargain / very low. i. low-priced/cheap/inexpensive. j. couples. k. yuppies.

Verständnis- und Wortschatztest S. 44

a. I don't know. b. I don't know. c. No(, they didn't). d. Yes(, they do). e. I don't know. f. Yes(, they did). g. No(, they didn't). h. No(, they don't).

Verständnis- und Wortschatztest S. 45

a. station. b. station. c. note. d. (tele)phone box / call box. e. lorry drivers. f. homeless. g. named.

Übungen

1. a. that/which. b. –. c. notice(,) which she. d. that/which/who. e. that/which. f. –. g. groups, which/who argue. h. –. i. morning(,) which will.
2. a. isn't it? b. don't they? c. do you? d. is there? e. wasn't he? f. did you? g. isn't there? h. are they? i. hasn't she? j. doesn't he? k. wouldn't you? l. would they?

3. a. sold. b. to build / to put up. c. be taken. d. (*Wenn er noch ein* school governor *ist:*) has been / (*wenn er kein* school governor *mehr ist:*) was. e. (*Da es um Familien geht, die noch immer hier leben:*) have lived / have been living; to leave.
4. a. My parents wouldn't have dreamed/dreamt of selling the land. b. My parents wouldn't have sold the land. c. I wouldn't have moved the television/TV into the kitchen. / I wouldn't have put the television/TV in the kitchen. d. She would never have moved the television/TV into the kitchen. / She would never have put the television/TV in the kitchen. e. I would(n't) have taken the job. f. I wouldn't have dreamed/dreamt of taking the job. g. His family would have helped him. h. His family could have helped him. i. He could have sold the land. j. We could have moved the television/TV into the kitchen. / We could have put the television/TV in the kitchen.

Lektion 8

Verständnis- und Wortschatztest S. 49
a. favourite *BE* / favorite *AE*; resort. b. the Maltese speak English, they cook the English way, and they drive on the left (like the English). c. Mediterranean. d. changing. e. improving/modernizing/upgrading; attract / bring in.

Verständnis- und Wortschatztest S. 50
a. consists / is made up. b. lies / is situated. c. Average. d. per cent *BE* / percent *AE*. e. official. f. publishes. g. doesn't have a king or queen / isn't ruled/governed by a king or queen. h. more. i. bilingual.

Verständnis- und Wortschatztest S. 51
a. history. b. importance/position/location; invaded/occupied. c. changed. d. occupied/ invaded/took; took/seized. e. withstood/sustained/suffered. f. awarded. g. became. h. followed / pursued / adhered to.

Übungen
1. a. are you driving; drive. b. being. c. has been moving / has moved; have been getting / have got / are getting. d. has been. e. is regarded; to avoid; relies; probably wouldn't be. f. come; we've made; we've been coming here; come. g. have you been; we'll be back. h. withstood. i. has followed / has been following.
2. a. In 870 Malta was invaded by the Arabs. / Malta was invaded by the Arabs in 870. b. The new shopping centre was designed by A. F. Richards. c. Tourists are attracted by a sunny climate. d. Tomorrow the President will be entertained by the Queen. e. Ulcers can be caused by excessive noise. f. Most crops have been devastated by the drought. g. A number of low-priced houses are being built by the council. h. Malta tends to be avoided by non-British tourists.
3. Malta has always been a favourite <u>among/with</u> British holidaymakers. It is often seen <u>as</u> an English-type resort. <u>Apart from</u> tourism, ship repair and shipbuilding are important industries. <u>Because of</u> its strategic importance, Malta frequently changed rulers <u>in/during</u> its long and turbulent history. The British ruled <u>for</u> over 160 years <u>until / till / up to</u> Malta's independence in 1964. <u>Since</u> 1974 Malta has been a republic <u>within</u> the Commonwealth.
4. a. Malta is a (particular) favourite *BE* / favorite *AE* among/with British holidaymakers *BE* / vacationers *AE*. b. It used to have a reputation for / the reputation of being particularly cheap. c. It has recently been trying / Recently it has been trying to attract tourists with more money. d. In the last few years / In recent years new hotels have been built and old ones have been improved / renovated / done up / given a face-lift. e. Malta lies / is (situated) about halfway between Gibraltar and Suez. f. Malta was under British rule / was ruled by the British for over 160 years. g. Since 1974 it has been a republic within the Commonwealth.

Lektion 9

Verständnis- und Wortschatztest S. 55
a. bed and breakfast. b. London Bed and Breakfast Services. c. No, it represents bed-and-breakfast places. d. They have the atmosphere of a real British home, they offer comforts and personal service that would cost a lot in a hotel, they are cheap/inexpensive. e. They are extremely/very expensive. f. 01 (*gesprochen:* oh one) is the dialling code *BE* / dialing code *AE* / area code *AE* for London.

Verständnis- und Wortschatztest S. 56
a. myself. b. possible. c. be. d. walk / (*by car:*) drive/ride / (*by bus:*) ride. e. isn't; after. f. mind. g. (right) next.

Verständnis- und Wortschatztest S. 57
a. landlady. b. looking. c. visit to. d. took; watching. e. alert/attentive. f. forward.

Übungen
1. a. Does it really only cost £10? b. Is he really a Londoner? c. The price is normally £10. / Normally the price is £10. d. Our guests normally stay at least a week. / Normally our guests stay at least a week. / Our guests stay at least a week normally. e. The rooms have been carefully selected by our staff. / The rooms have been selected carefully by our staff. f. Careful planning is important. g. Please contact us immediately. h. I'm not particularly keen to see the sights. i. Is there any particular area you'd prefer? j. It's difficult to find suitable accommodation. k. It certainly sounds very interesting.
2. a. That/This kind of service would cost a fortune in a hotel. b. You can come and go as you please/like. c. She often plays with our neighbours' dog. d. The daughter of our landlady in London is a stewardess / a flight attendant / an air hostess with British Airways. e. It's just/only a few minutes' walk to Buckingham Palace. f. Belgrave Road would be okay / OK / all right – Sloane Street would be okay / OK / all right / fine too. g. Is the bathroom next to my (bed)room also (being) used by other guests / used by other guests too / as well? h. We haven't got a dog, and we haven't got a cat either. / We don't have a dog, and we don't have a cat either. i. I don't mind dogs, and I don't mind cats either. / I have nothing against dogs, and I have nothing against cats either. j. We're looking forward to our next visit to / stay in London.

Anglophile's Crossword

1 B	R	2 E	A	3 K	4 F	A	5 S	6 T
A		V		I	R		7 M	E
8 T	H	E		T	E		A	R
H		9 N	I	C	E		L	M
R		I		H		10 A	L	I
O		11 N	E	E	D	S		N
O		12 G	O	N	E		13 B	A
14 M	Y		15 A	S		16 A	L	L

Lektion 10

Verständnis- und Wortschatztest S. 62 oben

a. customers. b. is cheap/inexpensive / offers excellent / particularly good value for money / offers comfort, cleanliness, an efficient switchboard and a friendly staff (all) at a reasonable price. c. budget hotels / cheap/inexpensive. d. sleazy places with smelly rooms, filthy floors and paper-thin walls. e. comfort, cleanliness, an efficient switchboard and a friendly staff (all) at a reasonable price / excellent value for money / a bright, clean room with comfortable beds, a remote-control colour TV and a perfectly adequate bathroom (all) at a reasonable price. f. very/extremely dirty. g. that smells / that has an unpleasant smell. h. you can hear a lot of noise / practically every move people in the other rooms / in adjoining rooms make. i. the coffee shop. j. included in the price of the room.

Verständnis- und Wortschatztest S. 62 unten

a. It has to be shown / It must be shown / You have to show it whenever you collect your key from the reception desk / from reception and if you wish/want to charge a(ny) bill / if you want a(ny) bill (to be) charged to your room account. b. No, it doesn't. / No, it wants / They want you to leave your key at the reception desk / at reception when(ever) you go out / leave the hotel. c. By midday / (12.00) noon / 12 (p.m.). d. You can ask/inquire at the reception desk / at reception / You can ask the receptionist (whether it's / it would be possible).

Verständnis- und Wortschatztest S. 63

a. due, extend. b. arranged. c. help; stay d. would. e. charge. f. indeed. g. sure; by; made. h. longer (than originally intended). i. give back one's key, pay one's bill and leave. j. keep it longer than originally intended. k. almost completely booked out/up / almost full up.

Übungen

1. a. The Royal used to be quite a good hotel. b. It seems to be a general trend. c. The farmers are having to sell / have to sell off their cattle. d. We're considering moving to Basingstoke. e. We're planning to buy a new car. f. I'm looking forward to seeing her next week. g. I'd prefer to stay at a budget hotel. h. She gave the impression of being very confident. i. Many young couples were forced to leave the area. j. I've always enjoyed travelling *BE* / traveling *AE* by train. k. Work is due to begin this morning. l. Malta used to have a reputation for being "cheap and cheerful". m. I'm used to having the dog around me all day. n. My parents would never have dreamed/dreamt of entertaining in the kitchen.

2. a. stayed. b. had/got/enjoyed. c. When I went to the reception desk to <u>get / fetch / pick up / collect</u> my key, I realized that I couldn't identify myself because I <u>had left</u> my key card in my room. d. I normally keep the card on me all the time because you also have to <u>show</u> it if you want to have a meal in the hotel restaurant <u>charged</u> to your room account. e. asked; keep. f. by keeping / by occupying / by staying in the room so long; to make it up. g. to avoid.

3. a. till / until / up to / up until. b. until/till. c. to. d. by.

4. a. As a salesperson / salesman / travelling salesman *BE* / traveling salesman *AE* / sales representative who is on the road something like 45 weeks a year, you want a hotel that offers a clean room with a comfortable bed, a colour *BE* / color *AE* TV and an adequate bathroom. b. I can't afford to stay at the Hilton or Sheraton – it's got to be / it has to be a budget hotel. c. Budget hotels used to be sleazy places/establishments with smelly rooms and paper-thin walls. d. Today's budget hotels offer comfort, cleanliness and friendly service at a reasonable price. e. They don't have restaurants / a restaurant or room service, but they do have / but there is a coffee shop where you can get a decent breakfast.

Lektion 11

Verständnis- und Wortschatztest S. 67
a. Ian Cummings is a doctor / physician / GP / general practitioner from Kilmorack in the Scottish Highlands. b. He found himself stranded by the rail strike. c. There was no one to take surgery at his practice. / He had to be back for the afternoon surgery. d. By taxi. / Taking a taxi. e. He had never been asked to drive to a place as far away as that / to drive that far. f. No, he hadn't. g. They arrived at about 12 noon. The fare was £300. h. Yes, he was.

Verständnis- und Wortschatztest S. 68
a. helicopters. b. East 34th Street. c. West Side. d. got you wrong / misunderstood you. e. make/catch. f. dollars. g. change.

Verständnis- und Wortschatztest S. 69
a. (taxi)cab. b. pavement. c. illegal/unlawful. d. bill. e. fare. f. toll.

Übungen
1. On his return from his holiday in Spain, Dr Ian Cummings found himself stranded at Gatwick Airport because of the rail strike. Knowing that his patients were waiting / would be waiting for him at his rural practice in Scotland, he did the only thing he could: he hailed a taxi. The cabby was flabbergasted when the doctor told him where he wanted to go: a little village in the Scottish Highlands 600 miles away. But after some haggling he agreed to make the trip for a bargain fare of £300, and eleven hours later they pulled up outside the doctor's house just in time for the afternoon surgery.
2. a. to take. Es war niemand da, der für ihn Sprechstunde halten konnte in seiner Landpraxis in Schottland. b. to do. In so einer Situation bleibt einem nichts anderes übrig, als ein Taxi zu nehmen. c. to spend / to go for. Wenn man eine englische Atmosphäre und auch viel Sonne will/sucht, dann sollte man seinen Urlaub in Malta verbringen. d. to ask / to go to / to talk to. Wenn du nicht weißt, wie du Karten bekommst, solltest du Judy fragen / zu Judy gehen / mit Judy sprechen. e. to stay / to spend the night at. Wenn man nicht viel Geld hat, sollte man in einem Privatquartier wohnen/übernachten. f. to leave. Wir hatten niemanden, bei dem wir den Hund hätten lassen können, und deshalb sind wir zu Hause geblieben. g. to ring/dial/phone/call. Wenn Sie ein Taxi wollen, rufen Sie die Nummer 565 5656 an. h. to read/take. Ich suche ein Buch, das man auf einer langen Bahnfahrt lesen kann / ein Buch für eine lange Bahnreise. i. to go to / to turn to. Viele von ihnen haben keine Familie, zu der sie gehen können / an die sie sich wenden können.
3. a. You can spend your holiday *bes. BE* / vacation *AE* here. b. We won't (= will not) / shan't (= shall not) be able to spend our holiday *bes. BE* / vacation *AE* here. c. He doesn't seem to be able to come. d. If I can't come / If I'm unable to come, I'll phone you (up) / ring you (up) / give you a ring / call you (up) *bes. AE* / give you a call *bes. AE*. e. We could solve this problem. f. We could have solved this problem. g. We should be able / ought to be able to solve this problem. h. Someone / Somebody / A (wo)man like you must be able / has to be able to solve such problems. i. She doesn't seem to be able to solve the problem. j. I wasn't able / was unable to solve the problem.
4. a. "Could you give me my (suit)case, please?" – "Which (one) is yours – this one here?" – "No, that one over there." b. Let's go to a restaurant. There's a good one in *BE* / on *AE* Dean Street. c. "There are a lot of / There are lots of restaurants here." – "But not many good ones. / Not many good ones, though." – "Yes, and the good ones are all pretty/fairly/ rather expensive." d. After a few minutes' haggling / After haggling for a few minutes we agreed on a fare of £300. e. Do you think you can make it in twenty minutes? f. (I'm) Sorry, I must have got you wrong / must have misunderstood you. g. This taxi / This cab was ordered by someone/somebody else. h. This taxi / This cab must have been ordered by

someone/somebody else. i. I've no idea how to get there. j. You'll have to pay a small extra charge for the suitcases / luggage *BE* / baggage *AE*.

Lektion 12

Verständnis- und Wortschatztest S. 74 oben
a. watching. b. heard; realized/suspected. c. bottom; removing / taking away. d. For a moment the boy didn't know what to do, but then he took/got/fetched the rifle he had got / been given for Christmas, loaded it, slid/crept/sneaked/went down the stairs and shot the two men. e. dialled *BE* / dialed *AE* / called *bes. AE* 911. f. learned / learnt / heard / was told / found out; wept/cried. g. had been.

Verständnis- und Wortschatztest S. 74 unten
a. blame. b. have been. c. have been given / have had / have owned. d. hadn't had a gun. e. hold.

Verständnis- und Wortschatztest S. 75
a. live. b. steals. c. rowing boat. d. boat; jacket/coat; wind. e. save.

Übungen
1. a. You'd be / You would be. b. took. c. wouldn't have hesitated. d. weren't. e. hadn't fastened. f. We'd have to / We would have to. g. I'd stay / I would stay. h. I would have stayed / I'd have stayed / I would've stayed. i. would have been able / would've been able. j. wasn't / weren't. k. would still be alive. l. hadn't taken.
2. a. who would. b. you would. c. He had. d. I would. e. we had. f. he had. g. I would. h. She would.
3. a. Noticing; jumped. b. Rowing; reached. c. making; gets. d. took; watching. e. consists; lying. f. In the old days, the kitchen was a small and stuffy place, the windows were steamed up, and there was always washing hanging from the clothesline.
4. a. Mike had seen the burglars at the bottom of the stairs. b. He had loaded his rifle/gun and shot the two men. c. The boy had got the rifle/gun for Christmas. d. He had been alone in the house. e. The burglars had been trying / had tried to steal a video (cassette) recorder. f. They had been unarmed. g. Mike told the police what had happened. h. Had the boy acted in self-defense *AE* / self-defence *BE*? i. According to the sheriff it had been self-defense *AE* / self-defence *BE*. j. Nobody / No one had noticed that the video (cassette) recorder was missing/gone.

Lektion 13

Verständnis- und Wortschatztest S. 79
a. It's used by people going from Brooklyn to Manhattan and vice versa. b. There was a danger that the bridge might collapse because of numerous defects – cracks, holes, and rust / because of erosion. c. Most took to / used other bridges, other subways, or even ferries, but some used the bridge's walkways, which were still open, to (bi)cycle or walk across the East River. d. (They had to decide) Whether to repair the bridge or (to) replace it.

Verständnis- und Wortschatztest S. 80
a. (She works) In an office in Manhattan. b. No, she doesn't. c. It was closed. d. They're still open. e. repair. f. faster/quicker. g. exercise. h. comfortable. i. He took the ferry. j. but who can afford the rents in Manhattan? / but rents in Manhattan are very/really/extremely/awfully/terribly expensive. k. transport. l. Underground train / Tube. m. flat.

Verständnis- und Wortschatztest S. 81

a. replaced. b. checked/investigated. c. vehicle; boat/ship/vessel; road / highway *bes. AE*. d. commuters. e. East River. f. ride/journey. g. dangerous. h. cracks, holes, and rust / erosion. i. drives a car. j. inspects bridges / checks bridges for safety / checks the safety of bridges. k. lasts/takes a year.

Übungen

1. a. He said he'd / he would probably walk. b. Jim said the Williamsburg Bridge was closed. c. He said it was an extremely busy bridge. d. Liz said it took her / it had taken her almost 90 minutes to get there/here. e. Her boss said he'd only just arrived himself / he had only just arrived himself. f. Someone said the walkways were still open. g. Janet said she was thinking of renting an apartment in Manhattan. h. I told her (that) people like us couldn't afford the rents in Manhattan. i. The press were told that failure to replace the boulders around the piers had led to erosion. j. City officials said they'd / they would decide later whether the bridge would be repaired or replaced. k. The boy said he'd been / he had been / he was alone in the house. l. The sheriff told me I had done / I'd done / I did the right thing. m. The coroner said (that) the boy had acted wisely. n. His mother said she'd / she would never forget that night. o. Janet said she knew what had happened.
2. a. latest. b. busiest / worst / longest / most important / most dangerous. c. most (of all). d. most common / worst. e. warmest / mildest / best / most agreeable. f. quickest/ fastest/shortest/best. g. most expensive / most luxurious / most elegant / most famous / most pleasant / best / nicest. h. greatest / worst / most serious / most pressing. i. fastest / most expensive / most exciting / most famous. j. worst / most dilapidated / most run down.
3. a. The bridge has been closed indefinitely / for an indefinite period of time. b. Experts feared the bridge might/could collapse. c. This is certainly/definitely/undoubtedly one of the worst bridges we have. d. For 80/eighty years the bridge hasn't been maintained. e. The city will decide later whether to repair or replace the bridge. f. Hundreds of thousands of commuters are having to find / have to find other ways to get / of getting from Brooklyn to Manhattan. g. I don't know what I'm going to do / what I'll do. Maybe/ Perhaps I'll walk. h. It's a nice ride by ferry / on the ferry. i. Or one could bicycle / cycle across the East River / go across the East River by bicycle. j. Maybe/Perhaps one should rent an apartment *AE* / a flat *BE* here in Manhattan after all. k. Could you afford the rents here? I (certainly) couldn't. / Would you be able to afford the rents here? I (certainly) wouldn't.

Lektion 14

Verständnis- und Wortschatztest S. 86 oben

a. He couldn't read properly. / He had trouble reading addresses on letters. b. He hid/kept them in his locker. c. He feared / was afraid he would be fired. d. (Because) It's a criminal offence *BE* / offense *AE* to delay the mail.

Verständnis- und Wortschatztest S. 86 unten

a. Popular national dailies in Britain: *Daily Express, Daily Mail, Daily Mirror, The Star, The Sun, Today*. The USA's only popular national daily is *USA Today*. b. They sign (them) with an "X". c. Reading, writing and arithmetic. d. He seems to be a (medical) doctor / a physician.

Verständnis- und Wortschatztest S. 87

a. 20 percent *AE* / per cent *BE*. b. They are ashamed of their disability and try to disguise it, so they don't seek help. c. They are offered adult-education classes or individual tutoring by volunteers. d. handicap. e. Job. f. where it's going (to). g. to make a call / to use it / the phone.

Übungen

1. For seven years a postman hid/kept hundreds of letters and cards in his locker because he could not read well enough to make out the addresses. He did not reveal/admit/disclose his problem / talk about his problem / tell anyone about his problem because he feared he would be fired/dismissed/sacked. His secret was discovered / found out in a routine clear-out at the sorting office when the undelivered mail fell out of his locker. Now he has resigned/ quit, leaving the Post Office to send on mail that's up to seven years old. Despite his disability/handicap, the man, who has not been named, managed to deliver 100,000 letters a year and was regarded as a good worker. "Strangely enough, we have had no complaints about him," said a Post Office spokesman. "None of the letters were opened. They hadn't even left the building." He added: "Delaying the mail is a criminal offence *BE* / offense *AE*, but no action will be taken." New postmen are now being given a written test to ensure / make sure they can read.

2. a. He was regarded as a good worker. b. No action was taken against the postman. c. The letters were hidden in his locker. d. The letters hadn't been opened. e. The statement hasn't been signed. f. It has been estimated that one out of five adults may be illiterate. g. He feared he would be fired. h. These people must be taught how to read and write properly.

3. a. simple; simply. b. successful; successfully. c. strange; Strangely. d. properly; proper. e. seriously; serious. f. individual; individually. g. deep; deeply.

4. a. I could hide / I'd be able to hide the letters for a while/time. b. I was able to hide the letters for a while/time. c. She knew that she couldn't be fired/sacked/dismissed / that they couldn't fire/sack/dismiss her. d. We suspected (that) he had stolen the letters, but he was able to explain everything. e. None of the letters had been opened. f. I'd be surprised if you were able to read / if you could read this/that. g. We need people who are able to teach / who can teach adults how to read and write. h. We're being taught/tutored/coached by a woman who was formerly illiterate herself.

Lektion 15

Verständnis- und Wortschatztest S. 91

a. About/Around/Roughly 700 million. b. French. c. There are between 500,000 and a million words in English, but to get along it's enough to know / you just need (to know) a few thousand of the words most frequently used. d. The English spoken by people from the south of England, from Wales, Scotland, Ireland, the United States, Australia and New Zealand. e. In Scotland. f. No, he was from Ireland / he was Irish. g. It indicates that there is a passage(way) for pedestrians under a busy road.

Verständnis- und Wortschatztest S. 92

a. listening to tapes and to the radio, by watching English and American films on TV and on video, by taking/grabbing every opportunity of talking with English-speaking people, by reading newspapers and books in English, by writing letters in English. b. Start (right) from the beginning. c. Start learning English. d. He/She told us again and again / time and again. e. Take/Grasp.

List of euphemisms

Adult = sex: adult book, adult film, adult entertainment, etc.

Bathroom = toilet. In an American restaurant you may ask: "Excuse me, where's the bathroom, please?", meaning the toilet/lavatory, of course.

Flight attendant = (air) steward/stewardess / air hostess.

Homemaker is often used in American English instead of *housewife*.

Industrial action is a British "official" or formal word for any kind of strike (go-slow, work to rule, etc.): "It is regretted that owing to industrial action this post office is closed today."

"*The Times* regrets that, in common with other national newspapers, it will probably be unable to publish tomorrow because of industrial action."
The loved one: A close relative who has died is often referred to euphemistically as one's loved one (sometimes capitalized Loved One): "We'll do it exactly as your loved one (= your [dead] husband) would have wished it."
Pass away = die: "I'm sorry to hear that your uncle passed away last week."
Previously owned = used/secondhand: "Our company specializes in previously owned Cadillacs."
Put to sleep / put down = kill (a pet so it doesn't have to suffer): "Sadly Mrs Clarke decided to have Blackie put to sleep / put down to save him further suffering."
Sunset years = old age: "She spent her sunset years in a sunset home (= home for the elderly) on the south coast."

Übungen

1. English is the closest/nearest thing to a world language. It has taken the place of / taken over from / replaced / succeeded / supplanted / superseded French as the language of diplomacy and German as the language of science. English is spoken by the most people / the greatest number of people and is also the language with the most words / the greatest number of words. Although / Though / Even though English has a vocabulary of over 500,000 words, you can get along / get on well if you know a few thousand of the words most frequently/commonly used. There are many different varieties of English, but on the whole English speakers from all over the world can all understand each other in spite of any regional differences/variations/peculiarities/characteristics their English may have. Learning English is very much a matter/question of practice. Listening to tapes and to the radio, watching English and American films, and talking/conversing/speaking with English-speaking visitors are all excellent ways of practising your English. In any language, people use euphemisms if they want to say something indirectly / in a roundabout way rather than call a spade a spade.

2. a. You know exactly what to do. b. Isn't it awful! c. There have been so/very many changes. d. She's such a nice girl. e. Other salesgirls could certainly learn a thing or two from her. f. Malta was a completely/very different place in those days. g. Inter Motors is a highly/very successful company. h. I thoroughly / very much enjoyed my recent stay at your house. i. Thank you very much indeed. j. I love you very much, Claire. k. I certainly / sure *AE* didn't realize I was going that fast. l. You did know that there was a speed limit of 55 on that highway.

3. a. must. b. have to. c. have to. d. have to. e. you only have to walk / you've only got to walk . f. must be / has to be. g. having to.

4. a. English, (which is) spoken by roughly/about/around/approximately / by some 700 million people, is the closest/nearest thing to a world language. b. English is the language with the most words. c. To get along in English, you have to know a few thousand of the words most frequently/commonly used / of the most frequently/commonly used words. d. We have / We've got a lot in common – except our language, of course. e. We understand each other, don't we? f. She keeps telling us (that) it's simply a matter/question of practice *BE* / practise *AE*.

Lektion 16

Verständnis- und Wortschatztest S. 97

a. Charter flights to Europe / to the Continent. b. Air-traffic controllers who are striking / on strike in several European countries. c. countries that have a lot of sunshine, such as Spain, Italy, Greece or Malta. d. holdups. e. overcrowded/packed. f. He must be crazy / mad / out of his mind / off his rocker/nut. / He must have a screw loose (somewhere).

Verständnis- und Wortschatztest S. 98
a. Because air-traffic controllers in several European countries are striking / on strike. b. No, they aren't. / No, they're all on time. c. In the departure lounges. d. (They've been waiting for) Anything up to 30 hours. e. They've been told to hang around / to wait / to stand by in the departure lounge so they can hear the announcements. / They've been told to stay "within call" so they can hear the announcements. f. (dead) on time. / (exactly) on schedule. g. more expensive. h. wait / stand by. i. noon. j. mess.

Verständnis- und Wortschatztest S. 99
a. sure; held. b. take out. c. due; conditions. d. arising/resulting; borne. e. circumstances/conditions; Cover. f. make sure = <u>ensure</u>; any <u>sort</u> of delay; <u>caused by</u> holdups / <u>arising from</u> holdups / <u>owing to</u> holdups; sickness = <u>illness</u>; strike(s) = <u>industrial action</u>.

Übungen
1. a. Some. b. any; some. c. any. d. any. e. any / (*als Bitte um etwas Kleingeld:*) some. f. any. g. any. h. Some. i. anything. j. something. k. anything. l. something. m. anything. n. anyone/anybody. o. someone/somebody.
2. a. If it hadn't been a package holiday, it would have cost a fortune. b. If we had taken a scheduled flight, we wouldn't have had to wait for 20 hours. c. If we had gone to Scotland, we wouldn't be sitting here. d. If you hadn't gone to have lunch, you would have heard the announcement. e. If we had taken out insurance, we would have got / we would get some sort of reimbursement. f. If the boy hadn't had a gun, those two unfortunate burglars would still be alive. g. If the film hadn't had German subtitles, I wouldn't have understood it. h. If you had walked, you would have got here faster. i. If the captain hadn't managed to bring the plane to a halt, we would all be dead / we would all have been dead now. j. If people had been told what was going on, they wouldn't be so angry / they wouldn't have been so angry.
3. a. We've been waiting for 20 hours (now). b. What are these enormous holdups/delays being caused by? / What's causing these enormous holdups/delays? c. If we had taken a scheduled flight, we wouldn't be in this mess. d. A scheduled flight would have cost a fortune. e. And we would have had to make all our own bookings / to make all the bookings ourselves. f. How long have we been waiting now? g. It would have been easier if they had told us / if we had been told what's going on / what was going on. h. We were supposed to fly / We were due to fly / We were scheduled to fly at 6.30 this morning. i. If we had taken out insurance, we might have got part/some of our money back. j. We should have read the small print.

Lektion 17

Verständnis- und Wortschatztest S. 103
a. (It happened) At the junction of Illinois Route 89 and Rutland Road in Marshall County. b. Two people were involved: (35-year-old) Terry Hufford from Toluca, Illinois, and (73-year-old) Byron Jenkins from Texas. c. No. (The injuries can't have been serious because both men were released after treatment.) d. Mr Jenkins was probably to blame because he realized too late that the car in front of him had stopped, lost control when he braked, and swerved from the southbound into the northbound lane. e. 73. f. accident/ collision. g. hospital. h. He was given a ticket / was fined / had to pay a fine.

Verständnis- und Wortschatztest S. 104
In the US, the percentage of older motorists is <u>rising / increasing / going up</u>. Drivers over 65 are <u>involved</u> in more accidents than those aged 25 to 65. Many people <u>think/believe/feel</u> that those who are no longer <u>fit</u> to drive should be <u>sifted</u> out. They want drivers over 65 to <u>take</u> periodic tests to <u>get</u> their licenses renewed.

Verständnis- und Wortschatztest S. 105
a. used. b. fit. c. slower / more slowly. d. aware. e. anything. f. do. g. older. h. old/elderly people. i. more slowly. j. very fast / a very fast car. k. a (traffic) policeman / traffic cop riding a motorcycle/motorbike. l. driver who drives very well. m. is neither young nor old / is between 40 and 60 years old.

Übungen
1. Two men were treated at St. Francis Medical Center Monday for injuries they suffered/ received/sustained in a collision at the junction of Illinois Route 89 and Rutland Road in Marshall County. Both were released/discharged after treatment. Terry Hufford, 35, of Toluca, was driving/heading north on Route 89 when his car was hit by a camper driven by Byron Jenkins, 73, of Texas. Jenkins, who was headed south, realized too late that a car in front of him had stopped to make a left turn. Jenkins lost control when he braked and swerved into the northbound lane, state police said. Hufford was ticketed for not wearing his seat belt. Jenkins was ticketed for failure to reduce speed and using / driving in the wrong lane, state police said.
2. a. does. b. do. c. did. d. did. e. done. f. so. g. So. h. Nor/Neither. i. nor/ neither. j. nor.
3. a. Charter flights aren't as expensive as / are less expensivc than scheduled flights. b. Flying isn't as dangerous as / is less dangerous than travelling *BE* / traveling *AE* by car. c. A pneumatic drill is noisier than a motorbike. d. A jukebox is worse than / is(n't) as bad as a barking dog. e. A senior citizen drives slower / more slowly than a young hot rodder. f. Watching TV is(n't) as interesting as / is more/less interesting than playing cards. g. At eighty you have slower reflexes than at eighteen. h. A friendly salesperson is usually more/less successful than an aggressive one. i. On the whole, old hotels are nicer than ultramodern ones.
4. a. Drivers over 65 are involved in considerably more accidents / are much/far more frequently involved in accidents. b. Drivers over 65 are required to take periodic tests. c. At seventy you don't see as well as you used to. d. I've been driving / I've driven for fifty years – I can't/couldn't possibly have done anything wrong. e. Older/Elderly drivers should be tested regularly/periodically, but so (too) should these young hot rodders. f. On the whole / All in all, elderly/older drivers/motorists drive more responsibly than young people.

Lektion 18

Verständnis- und Wortschatztest S. 109
a. She's looking after her baby and the house / and doing housework. b. She'd like to go out to work. c. stimulus. d. She'd use it to have a girl in to help out – an au pair perhaps. e. (Probably) A flat. f. She'd like to have a house because it'd give them more room. g. She'd keep her company / She'd be company for her, and she could look after the baby in the mornings. h. control. i. deadline. j. housework. k. salary. l. au pair. m. up.

Verständnis- und Wortschatztest S. 110
An Australian clergyman speaks on Mother's Day. What children desperately/urgently need are some old-fashioned mums with some unconditional love, some wholesome/good home cooking and some precious time set aside each day to read bedtime Bible stories, ending with a prayer and a kiss.
Mothers need/ought to start taking their children to Sunday school and church each Sunday, even if it means leaving Dad at home watching his rehashed/precious/beloved sport on TV or drinking and gambling with his mates at the club.

Verständnis- und Wortschatztest S. 111

a. group; discuss. b. money to buy it / money to pay for it. c. mother's or father's mother. d. content/happy. e. A full-time mother only works in the home / at home while a half-time one goes out to work part-time and so can't look after her child(ren) all day. f. mum *BE* / mom *AE*; kids.

Übungen

1. a. On Mother's Day Dad / (*auch:*) dad will read the children some stories from the Bible. b. Two men were treated at St. Francis Medical Center Monday for injuries they suffered in a collision at the junction of Illinois Route 89 and Rutland Road in Marshall County. c. On TV last night, Tourism Minister John Lee urged holidaymakers to forget the Continent and back British resorts instead. d. With the Williamsburg Bridge closed, commuters are having to find other ways of travelling across the East River from Brooklyn to Manhattan and vice versa. e. Family GP Dr Ian Cummings from Kilmorack in the Scottish Highlands faced a real emergency when he arrived back at Gatwick Airport and found himself stranded by the rail strike. f. In southwest London, work on the A309 Kingston Bypass at the Claygate Lane roundabout has been causing long delays for drivers heading into Central London, and in the West End Berkeley Square, Berkeley Street and Hay Hill are closed because of a fire.

2. a. Rowing as fast as he could, he reached the exhausted man just in time to save him from drowning. b. Throwing on his parka, he dashed out of the house to see what had happened. c. Facing financial ruin and unable to pay for extra animal feed, farmers were selling / farmers sold livestock in the hope that the extra income would/might help (to) see them through until the rain came. d. Realizing that there were strangers in the house, he took his rifle, loaded it and slid down the stairs. e. Fearing that the bridge might/would collapse, they immediately closed it to all traffic. f. Fearing that she might/would be fired, she didn't reveal her problem. g. Not knowing what to do, she sat down and wept. h. Yesterday he spent the afternoon drinking and gambling with his mates at the club. i. I enclose the photo I took of you and Bonnie watching TV in the evening. j. With thousands of people waiting at airports, the government finally decided to act. k. In the first year of our marriage, with my wife working nine to five and me working nights, we hardly ever had time for each other.

3. a. We'd / We would like to buy a house so that we've got / so we have more room. b. I think it would be a good idea for me to go (out) to work again / if I went (out) to work again. c. I don't think Sarah would suffer if I went (out) to work in the mornings. d. With both of us / With the two of us working, we'd have / we would have money for things we can't afford on one salary. e. You have a right to decide for yourself how you want to live your life, don't you? f. This clergyman wants all mothers to read their children stories from the Bible at bedtime. g. And on Sundays he wants them to take them (*klarer:* their children) to church / to go to church with them / with their children. / And on Sundays they're to take them to church / to go to church with them.

Lektion 19

Verständnis- und Wortschatztest S. 115

a. (About) 20 per cent *BE* / percent *AE*. b. Some patients go to the doctor just to get a sick note, some are not prepared to spend money on everything that is prescribed, and others are worried about/by the side effects of drugs. c. Antibiotics and the "mind drugs". d. medicine/medication. e. go easy on drugs / cut down on drugs. f. pick up. g. effect. h. prescribe these drugs / them less often.

Verständnis- und Wortschatztest S. 116

a. Mr Murray. b. He's been feeling terrible for some time. He's (been) sleeping badly, he's (been) tired and depressed, and he's had / he has difficulty concentrating. And he sometimes gets/has pains in his stomach. c. The company he works for has been taken over, and he's got a new boss who is constantly finding fault with his work. d. depressed / down (in the dumps) / blue.

Verständnis- und Wortschatztest S. 117

a. A certain amount of stress is normal / all right / necessary, but too much stress can lead to / cause illness / can be bad for your health / can be detrimental to one's health / can cause things like high blood pressure, stomach ulcers and heart disease. b. headaches, backache, high blood pressure, stomach ulcers or heart disease. c. reduce their / cut down on their work load or organize their time better, not to take things too seriously, to leave time for laughter, relaxation, meditation and regular exercise, to spend time with their family and friends, to eat sensibly, and to cut down on coffee, alcohol and cigarettes. d. go easy on coffee / drink less coffee.

Übungen

1. A British survey has revealed/found that 20 per cent of patients do not pick up medicine prescribed by the doctor. Asked why they didn't bother to collect / pick up their prescriptions, some people said their main purpose in going to the doctor was to get a sick note. Others cited cost as a reason for not collecting / picking up medicine, and a third group was worried by the side effects of drugs. Foremost among the drugs patients didn't pick up were antibiotics and the so-called mind drugs, which could mean they are prescribed too often and money could be saved by cutting down on the number of prescriptions.

2. a. bring up her three children / bring her three children up. b. put Debbie's name up / put up Debbie's name. c. make up the room / make the room up. d. woke him up. e. took up English / took English up. f. wrote everything down. g. points out the location of emergency exits in the aircraft. h. write out the ticket / write the ticket out. i. find out as much as possible about the company you're applying to. j. take out insurance. k. sell off their cattle / sell their cattle off. l. turn on the meter / turn the meter on. m. Throwing on his parka / Throwing his parka on. n. sift them out.

3. a. I've been feeling terrible for some time. b. The company I work for has been taken over, and my new boss is constantly finding fault with my work. c. The doctor doesn't want me to take any drugs/medicine/medication. d. He advised me to relax more / to leave more time for relaxation. e. He told me not to take things so seriously, to spend more time with my family and to cut down on alcohol. f. Of course we could save a lot of money by cutting down on alcohol, cigarettes and drugs.

Lektion 20

Verständnis- und Wortschatztest S. 122 oben

a. (Because) He had been suffering from chest pains. b. They sailed round Great Britain (= the largest island in the British Isles, consisting of England, Scotland, and Wales). c. It tells us that it's London's orbital motorway / that it's the 117-mile motorway around London.

Verständnis- und Wortschatztest S. 122 unten

a. dubbed. b. dubbing. c. voices / people / actors and actresses. d. sounds; announcer. e. shame/pity. f. amazing/surprising/incredible; watching/seeing.

Verständnis- und Wortschatztest S. 123

a. British Broadcasting Corporation. b. Four. (= Radio 1, Radio 2, Radio 3 and Radio 4.) c. No, it doesn't. / No, it concentrates on the spoken word. d. No, it can't. / No, unfortunately not. e. very high frequency. (Another English term corresponding to German UKW is FM = frequency modulation.) f. No, it can't. / No, only in the Greater Berlin area. g. Generally: the written word; in radio broadcasting: music.

Übungen

1. An attempt to stage an illegal car race on the M25, London's orbital motorway, has failed. The police believe it was to have been held / to be held late last night, but a Scotland Yard spokesman said the publicity, and advice that was issued / had been issued earlier, appeared to have prevented what he called an irresponsible race. Little is known about the organizers except that they placed / had placed an advertisement in a London newspaper with a box number for replies. The plan was for up to 25 owners of high-performance cars to race / to have raced along the 117-mile motorway around the capital.

2. a. "So do I." b. "So have I." c. "So did I." d. "So am I." e. "So do I." f. "So can I." g. "So am I." h. "So will I." i. "So would I." j. "So did I." k. "So have I." l. "So do I."

3. a. said. b. expected. c. been suffering. d. (*im vorhinein:*) to raise / (*im nachhinein:*) to have raised; breaking. e. had. f. (*im vorhinein:*) would tell / (*im nachhinein:*) had told. g. to have been held / to be held.

4. a. This is the worst drought I've ever seen. b. So far we've been to Australia, New Zealand and the Far East. c. I've had a headache all day. d. He's been living / He's lived in this village all his life. e. How long have you been learning English? f. She doesn't seem to have read it. g. She may not have read it. / It's possible that / Maybe she hasn't read it. h. I must have got you wrong / misunderstood you. i. We could have all been dead. / We could all have been dead. j. He shouldn't have been given a gun. / They shouldn't have given him a gun. k. I wouldn't have hesitated even if I had / I'd known.

Lektion 21

Verständnis- und Wortschatztest S. 127

a. There's too much sex and violence in them (for her liking). b. as it is. c. fighting and drugs. d. trouble. e. effects. f. a decade ago, young kids, the Hollywood oldies, pick a movie.

Verständnis- und Wortschatztest S. 128

a. films / motion pictures. b. cinema/pictures. c. is being shown / is on. d. What shall we do ...? e. A great film: very good / excellent / fantastic / terrific / outstanding / superb / brilliant / super / wonderful / marvellous *BE* / marvelous *AE*; good dialogue: great/excellent/tremendous; tremendous acting: terrific / great / brilliant / wonderful / excellent / exceptional / marvellous *BE* / marvelous *AE* / fantastic. f. Academy Awards. g. Let's get a move on. h. Shall we take the/a subway?

Verständnis- und Wortschatztest S. 129

a. In 1927. (Its title: *The Jazz Singer*. It was basically a silent picture but had several musical passages and a few sentences of spoken words, among them the famous phrase spoken by Al Jolson: "Wait a minute, wait a minute. You ain't (= haven't) heard nothing yet." Audiences stood up and cheered, and the film became a tremendous box-office hit [= *Kassenschlager*]. The first "100 per cent all-talking film", *Lights of New York*, came in 1928.) b. In the 1950s, because/when television became the new medium of mass entertainment (and the number of cinemas decreased dramatically). c. Today's movie audiences are much smaller but more sophisticated than the mass audiences of the 1940s.

Übungen

1. a. fighting; selling. b. watching; to get. c. had; watching. d. seeing. e. is showing / is being shown. f. came; seeing. g. (*Weil es sich um einen alten, „historischen" Film handelt:*) *Kramer vs. Kramer* won several Oscars, didn't it? (*Bei einem aktuellen Film dagegen, bei dem die Prämierung noch „news" ist:*) The film has won several Oscars, hasn't it? h. have been. i. had come; became. j. had lost; began producing / to produce.

2. a. regularly; easily available. b. tremendously; really excellent. c. dramatically. d. dramatic; violent; recent. e. illegal. f. irresponsibly; illegally. g. unnaturally. h. unnatural. i. amazing. j. amazingly quickly. k. main. l. mainly. m. terrible. n. terribly. o. completely; complete. p. serious; seriously.
3. a. He's one of New York's tens of thousands of homeless. b. I'm phoning / ringing (up) / calling *bes. AE* about your advertisement in today's *Daily Mail*. c. What are we going to do with the rest of the evening? d. Motion pictures have been around since the beginning of the twentieth/20th century. e. The number of accidents has gone up in the last few years / in recent years. f. The Republic of Malta is a member of the Commonwealth. g. Mr Burstock's family has lived / has been living in the village of Wayford in Somerset for 170 years. h. In/During the last twenty years the quality of life has improved dramatically. i. We've had a lot of problems in the last few weeks / in recent weeks.

Lektion 22

Verständnis- und Wortschatztest S. 134 oben
a. They're / Oats are believed to bring down the blood cholesterol level, thus reducing the risk of heart attacks and strokes. b. They prefer food which/that is high in fibre *BE* / fiber *AE*, low in fat, sugar and salt, additive-free and organically grown. c. creating / producing / coming up with.

Verständnis- und Wortschatztest S. 134 unten
a. reserve. b. dinner. c. Someone who doesn't eat meat or fish. (A vegan, incidentally, is someone who's not only a vegetarian but also doesn't eat animal products such as cheese, butter, milk or eggs.) d. menu. e. many different kinds of / a wide choice of. f. macaroni, spaghetti, vermicelli, ravioli, cannelloni, lasagna, rigatoni, etc., etc.

Verständnis- und Wortschatztest S. 135
a. added to it. b. residues/traces; soil. c. contaminated; pure/additive-free. d. grown; environment. e. stacked/filled. f. label. g. additive-free/uncontaminated/natural/ organic. h. full of / filled with. i. kinds. j. a customer.

Übungen
1. In the 1980s, oat bran was/became the darling of health-conscious Americans. "Oat bran sells itself," said the manager of a New York supermarket. The big cereal/food companies were quick to cash in on the oat-bran trend. Dozens of new oat-bran products were created/developed/introduced/marketed in a hurry and the TV commercials were full of people who smilingly told you oat bran had not only made them "happy, healthy and regular" but also brought down / lowered / reduced their cholesterol level. Thanks to oat bran they were going to live / would live to be a hundred and ten. For them, heart attacks and strokes had become a thing of the past. But food gurus warned that simply adding oat bran to one's diet was not enough. They advised/recommended/told/urged people generally to eat food that/which was high in fibre and low in fat, sugar and salt.
2. a. will remain; will be. b. will help; comes (in Nebensätzen, die mit *until, till, when, before, if, as soon as* eingeleitet werden, steht das Verb in der Regel nicht in einer Zukunftsform). c. will let. d. is going to be. e. don't get (*vgl. b*); I'll quit / I'm going to quit. f. There'll be / (*stärker, Gewißheit ausdrückend:*) There's going to be; close (*vgl. b*). g. It won't take; go (*vgl. b*). h. (*„Neutral":*) will begin / (*„ist so vorgesehen":*) is beginning (*oder:*) will be beginning / (*Terminplan:*) begins / (*Gewißheit:*) is going to begin. i. You won't mind the dog, will you? j. Will you need / (*sehr höflich, „Butler-Ton":*) Will you be needing / (*direkter, Frage nach der Absicht:*) Are you going to need. k. miss (*vgl. b*); I won't make (*klassischer Bedingungssatz vom Typ 1 – vgl. S. 76*) / I'm not going to make (*vgl. f*). l. (*Direkte Frage nach Absicht:*) are you going to pay / (*höfliche Frage nach Planung:*) will you be paying / (*unverblümte Frage nach Planung:*) are you paying. m. get (*vgl. b*).

n. we're going to be. o. I'll have to / I'm going to have to; don't fix (*vgl. b*). p. (*Terminplan:*) is / (*neutral:*) will be / (*Betonung der Gewißheit, hier nicht sehr wahrscheinlich:*) is going to be. q. (*Planung:*) I'm flying / I'll be flying.

3. a. The food companies are developing new products all the time. b. Oat bran is believed/thought/supposed to bring down the cholesterol level. c. Many people are dieting to lose weight. d. They have switched from butter to margarine and from white bread to wholemeal / whole-wheat *bes. AE* bread. e. The Piccadilly Restaurant has a great/large variety of vegetarian dishes on the/its menu. f. In the supermarkets there are all sorts of foods which/that are believed to be additive-free / free of additives. g. But experts have pointed out that today nearly/almost all foods have been contaminated with pesticides. h. There are nitrates / Nitrates are (to be) found / are contained even in organic(ally grown) foods. / Even in organic(ally grown) foods you find nitrates. i. But the nitrate level is much lower and the food itself is better – not only for the people who eat it but also for the environment.

Lektion 23

Verständnis- und Wortschatztest S. 139

a. In their/the yard. b. They were decorating it / their home. c. They were standing near the dustbin. / They had been left/placed/put near the dustbin. d. No, probably not. The insurers / insurance company said it was their own fault – they shouldn't have left the cartons near the dustbin. e. heartbroken / extremely upset f. took. g. gifts. h. refuse collectors. i. (cardboard) box.

Verständnis- und Wortschatztest S. 141 oben

a. Because (a lot of) hospital waste has been washed ashore / washed up on them. b. The waste came from hospitals, and it was illegally dumped offshore by disposal companies. c. The dumpers. d. By making it the hospitals' business to check where their medical waste goes. / The hospitals should make the disposal companies show/prove that they're disposing of the waste properly.

Verständnis- und Wortschatztest S. 141 unten

a. Industrialized countries have produced so much garbage over the years that they are running out / they have run out of landfills to dump it in / to dump the waste in. b. It's (being) dumped in landfills, shipped to faraway places, burned/burnt or recycled. c. Producing less garbage, using biodegradable and recyclable packaging, making recycling easier/work by separating food, glass, metal and paper when throwing it away. d. garbage: waste, refuse, rubbish, trash – garbage can: dustbin, (rubbish) bin, trash can.

Übungen

1. When Alison and Martin saw/found/discovered/realized that their wedding presents had been taken/carted away by the dustmen, they immediately phoned the council and told them what had happened. The council people said they would look/search for the missing presents, but the search turned out to be unsuccessful. When the couple put in a claim for compensation, they were told they had no one but themselves to blame because the cartons shouldn't have been left/placed/put near the dustbin. A council spokesman said later: "Our men had no reason to believe/assume that these materials were anything but rubbish." Yesterday, Alison was busy writing thank-you letters for the missing/lost/wedding gifts. Asked how she felt about the whole thing, she said/replied/answered: "It's terrible to think that all these lovely gifts have ended up at the rubbish dump without ever being used / having been used."

2. a. Our wedding presents have been taken away (by the dustmen). b. The gifts had been stored in cartons in the yard. c. A neighbour of ours saw them being taken away (by the refuse collectors). d. … told us we shouldn't have left the cartons near the dustbin.

e. … and most of the beaches have been closed. f. They shouldn't dump garbage of that sort directly offshore. g. There's no way the hospitals can be held responsible. h. Nobody knows what happens when the stuff has been turned over to the garbage collectors. i. The garbage collectors are paid to dispose of it. j. We don't know if they've disposed of the waste properly. k. In many cases, they have to ship our garbage to faraway places. l. The use of recyclable packing must be encouraged.
3. a. was/were. b. want. c. had. d. would. e. hadn't.
4. a. A neighbour saw the dustmen *BE* / refuse collectors *BE* / garbage men *AE* / garbage collectors *AE* taking the cartons away. b. The cartons shouldn't have been left near the dustbin *BE* / garbage can *AE*. / We/You/They shouldn't have left the cartons/boxes near the dustbin *BE* / garbage can *AE*. c. For weeks (now) we've been hearing of / we've had reports of hospital waste being washed ashore. d. There's no way the hospitals can be held responsible. e. They say / They're saying: "What the disposal companies do with the waste isn't our business." f. The hospitals ought to / should check what happens / what's happening to the waste. g. The disposal companies should be made/forced to show/prove that they're disposing of the waste properly. h. There should be / ought to be harsher/severer punishments for midnight dumpers. i. People who dump such waste / that kind/sort of waste into the sea should be treated as dangerous criminals.

Lektion 24

Verständnis- und Wortschatztest S. 145
a. England has an established church and/but/while the USA doesn't. b. The head of the Church of England is the queen or king / the monarch, its chief bishop is the Archbishop of Canterbury. c. Anglicans. d. established. e. denominations/groups. f. official. g. the Muslims, Jews, and Hindus.

Übungen
1. a. of. b. on. c. to. d. by. e. in. f. of. g. with. h. by; off. i. by/about. j. in. k. by; on. l. for. m. At; on; for/to. n. by.
2. a. women; children. b. men. c. thieves; dustmen. d. aircraft. e. shelves. f. men's; feet.
3. a. haven't. b. is. c. is. d. isn't. e. It's. f. are; is.
4. a. The head of the Church of England is the king or queen, and its religious leader is the Archbishop of Canterbury. b. The United States doesn't have an established church. c. Most churches face the problem / are faced with the problem / are facing the problem that the number of people attending services is dwindling / declining / falling / going down. d. Many church members hold views not in keeping / which aren't in keeping with their church's teachings/doctrines. e. The idea that divorce is always sinful / a sin is now (being) rejected by / has been given up by many religious people.

Lektion 25

Verständnis- und Wortschatztest S. 152
a. sets. b. games. c. points. d. deuce. e. love; zero.

Verständnis- und Wortschatztest S. 153
a. In 1877. b. No(, they didn't). c. No, he wasn't. / No, he was an amateur. d. It was introduced to prevent long sets. / They introduced the tiebreak to prevent matches (from) going on too long / to make sure matches didn't go on too long. e. tournament/competition/contest. f. good/hard. g. top. h. Did you have a good workout? i. ought to. j. certainly. k. chap/fellow/bloke. l. stupid/silly.

Übungen

1. a. London Bed and Breakfast Services, 198 (one hundred and ninety-eight / one nine eight) Cromwell Road, London SW5 0(= oh)SW, telephone 01–373 3536 (oh–one three–seven–three three–five–three–six). b. Work on the A309 (three oh nine) Kingston Bypass has been causing long delays. c. I'm in room 409 (four oh nine) and I'm due to check out today. d. A recent survey of 1,000 (one thousand) homeless people found that 80 (eighty) per cent were male, two-thirds were white, and 87 (eighty-seven) per cent had once held a job. e. Malta has a population of about 350,000 (three hundred and fifty thousand), 97 (ninety-seven) per cent of which are Roman Catholic. f. The city will decide later whether to repair the bridge, at an estimated cost of $250 million (two hundred and fifty million dollars), or replace it – for $500 million (five hundred million dollars). g. The dustmen carted away about £1000 (a thousand pounds) worth of wedding presents. h. The plan was for up to 25 (twenty-five) owners of high-performance cars to race along the M25 (twenty-five), the 117 ([one] hundred and seventeen)-mile motorway around the capital. i. Malta's average temperatures are 27 °C (twenty-seven degrees Celsius/centigrade) in July and 14 °C (fourteen degrees Celsius/centigrade) in January. j. In 1798 (seventeen [hundred and] ninety-eight) Malta was occupied by the French, and in 1800 (eighteen hundred) it was taken by the British, who ruled until its independence in 1964 (nineteen [hundred and] sixty-four). k. Here's the weather forecast for 6 (six) p.m. on Saturday the 25th (twenty-fifth) of June. l. You can take the subway to 42nd (forty-second) Street. m. "Did you lose the match?" – "I went down 6–2 (six–two), 4–6 (four–six), 0–6 (love–six)." n. The average British family has 0.8 (nought/oh point eight) children.

2. a. have got. Ich muß Sie falsch verstanden / mißverstanden haben. b. have had. Erwähnen Sie keine Probleme, die Sie vielleicht mit Ihrem früheren/bisherigen Arbeitgeber gehabt haben. c. have done. Er hätte es nicht tun können, auch wenn er (es) gewollt hätte. d. to have raised. Sie hoffen, über 100 000 Pfund für die Royal National Lifeboat Institution aufgebracht zu haben. / Sie hoffen, daß sie ... aufgebracht haben. e. have crossed. Ich wäre nie auf den Gedanken / die Idee gekommen, das zu tun. („Es wäre mir noch nicht einmal in den Sinn gekommen ...") f. have been. Die Kartons hätten nicht in der Nähe der Mülltonne abgestellt werden dürfen. g. to have prevented. Die Polizei hätte das Rennen verhindern müssen. h. to have prevented. Die Warnungen der Polizei scheinen das Rennen verhindert zu haben. i. have hesitated. Ich hätte nicht gezögert, ihm zu helfen. j. to have been. Das unerlaubte/illegale Autorennen auf der M25 hatte gestern abend („abgehalten werden sollen") stattfinden sollen.

3. a. I could have won the match/game. b. The match/game should have been / ought to have been a walkaway *AE* / walkover *BE* for me. c. I shouldn't have lost the/this/that match/game. d. I might have won if my backhand had been better. / If my backhand had been better, I might have won. e. You shouldn't have argued with the umpire. f. I seem to have done everything wrong. g. If only I hadn't been so dumb/stupid! h. I chased/ran round / I was chasing/running round the court like mad trying to return his shots. i. He was such a nobody – I don't/can't even remember his name.

Englische Aufbaugrammatik

1 Vorbemerkung zu den grammatischen Fachausdrücken

Lassen Sie sich durch die hier vorkommenden Fachwörter nicht abschrecken. Verstehen Sie sie lediglich als Namen, mit deren Hilfe die Informationen zum Sprachgebrauch gegliedert sind. In den meisten Fällen sind die Bezeichnungen verständlich; soweit es sich um nicht allgemein gebräuchliche Begriffe handelt, sind deutsche Erklärungen beigegeben.

Einige Fremdwörter lassen sich nicht vermeiden, da es manchmal keine gleichwertigen deutschen Entsprechungen gibt. So etwa der Ausdruck *Verb*, dem im Deutschen Bezeichnungen wie *Zeitwort, Tätigkeitswort, Tuwort* gegenüberstehen, die wir aber hier – auch mit Rücksicht auf den internationalen Sprachgebrauch – nicht verwenden.
Verben sind Wörter wie *go = gehen* und *follow = folgen. Follow* ist der *Infinitiv* (= *die Grundform*); *followed* ist entweder die Vergangenheitsform (= *folgte*) oder das *-ed*-Partizip (= *gefolgt*).

Der Begriff *-ed*-Partizip ist entsprechend der Bezeichnung *-ing*-Partizip (*following = folgend*) gebildet. (Wir nennen hier das *-ing*-Partizip der Einfachheit halber *-ing*-Form.) Der Name *-ed*-Partizip ist durchsichtiger als die ebenfalls gebräuchlichen Ausdrücke *Partizip Perfekt* oder *Perfektpartizip* (engl. *past participle*), ist aber insofern etwas unlogisch, als er sich auch auf Formen wie *gone* (= *gegangen*) oder *written* (= *geschrieben*) bezieht, die – weil „unregelmäßig" – keine *-ed*-Endung haben.

Bei den *Zeiten* des *Verbs* (z. B. *Präsens = Gegenwartsform*) ist besonders der Begriff *Perfekt* undurchsichtig. Es handelt sich dabei um die „*have*-Form", also z. B. *they have written = sie haben geschrieben* oder *she has arrived = sie ist angekommen.*

Um eine Stufe in die Vergangenheit „zurückversetzt", wird das *Perfekt* zum *Plusquamperfekt*, das man auch als *Vorvergangenheit* bezeichnen kann.

Eine recht schwierige Form ist der *Infinitiv des Perfekts* (= *perfect infinitive*), der Zusammensetzungen wie *she seems to have arrived = sie scheint angekommen zu sein* und *you could have helped = du hättest helfen können* ermöglicht.

Keine allzu großen Schwierigkeiten dürfte der Unterschied zwischen Aktiv (*they are going to sell it = sie werden es verkaufen*) und Passiv (*it is going to be sold = es wird verkauft [werden]*) bereiten.

Weniger leicht zu begreifen ist dagegen das für die Bildung englischer Sätze so wichtige Phänomen der *infiniten Verbformen*. Wir meinen damit *Infinitiv* (*[to] write = [zu] schreiben*), *-ing-Form* (*writing = schreibend, [das] Schreiben*) und *-ed-Partizip* (*written = geschrieben*).

Beim *Substantiv* (= *Nomen*, *Hauptwort*, engl. *noun*) gibt es neben *Singular – Plural* (= *Einzahl – Mehrzahl*) auch etwa den *Genitiv* (= *Wes[sen]-Fall*), der auf die Frage „Wessen?" antwortet und im Englischen entweder durch die Endung *-'s/-s'* oder eine Konstruktion mit *of* gebildet wird.

Häufig kommt schließlich der Ausdruck *Relativsatz* vor. *Relativsätze* dienen zur näheren Bestimmung eines Wortes oder einer Wortgruppe – in den folgenden Beispielen des vom Artikel *the* begleiteten Substantivs *people*: *the people <u>who came</u> were interested = die Leute, die kamen, waren interessiert, the people <u>he asked</u> were interested = die Leute, die er fragte, waren interessiert. Who came* und *he asked* sind hier Relativsätze, im ersten Beispiel eingeleitet durch das *Relativpronomen* (*bezügliche Fürwort*) *who* und im zweiten ohne *Relativpronomen* gebildet (*Kontaktkonstruktion*) – eine Möglichkeit, die es im Deutschen nicht gibt.

Noch einmal: Lassen Sie sich durch die grammatischen Fachausdrücke nicht abschrecken. In der Regel erklären sich die Grammatik-„Labels" durch die Beispiele und Erklärungen von selbst. Fachausdrücke sind ein nützliches Werkzeug zur Gliederung der Erklärungen; zum Erlernen der Sprache benötigt man sie nicht.

Substantiv (Nomen, Hauptwort, noun)

2 Singular (Einzahl) oder Plural (Mehrzahl)?

Beachten Sie folgende Abweichungen vom deutschen Sprachgebrauch:

There have (*nicht:* has) been a number of accidents.
The number of accidents has (*nicht:* have) gone down.

A number steht in der Regel mit einem Pluralverb, *the number* mit einem Singularverb.

A hundred thousand pounds/dollars isn't enough.
Hunderttausend Pfund/Dollar sind nicht genug / genügen nicht.

Genau umgekehrt als im Deutschen! Beachten Sie die Pluralform *pounds/dollars* und das Singularverb *is*.

It's the children who suffer. *Es sind die Kinder, die leiden.*
Today it's not only the Scots who are fond of oats.
Heute sind es nicht nur die Schotten, die gern Hafer essen.

Eine Kombination von *it* (Singular!) und *are* (Plural!) entsprechend dem deutschen *es sind* gibt es im Englischen nicht.

This news comes to you in the World Service of the BBC.
Diese Nachrichten „kommen zu Ihnen“ im World Service der BBC.
Bad news travels fast. *Schlechte Nachrichten verbreiten sich schnell.*

The United States is the most powerful country in the world.
Die Vereinigten Staaten sind das mächtigste Land der Welt.
The United States does not have an established church.
Die Vereinigten Staaten haben keine Staatskirche.

The police were called. *Die Polizei wurde gerufen.*
The police believe it was to have been held late last night.
Die Polizei glaubt, daß es gestern abend hatte stattfinden sollen.

News und *the United States* sind immer Singular; *police* ist immer Plural.

3 Fügungen mit dem -*'s*-Genitiv (vgl. 78, 79)

Steve's salary	*Steves Gehalt*
the doctor's house	*das Haus des Arztes*
the bridge's walkways	*die Gehwege der Brücke*
New York's tens of thousands of homeless	*New Yorks Zehntausende von Wohnungslosen*
New York's Williamsburg Bridge	*die New Yorker Williamsburg Bridge*
London's Regent's Park	*der Londoner Regent's Park*
Hollywood's powerful studios	*die mächtigen (Film-)Studios von Hollywood*
woman's fight against noise	*„Kampf einer Frau gegen den Lärm“*
Mother's Day	*(der) Muttertag*
driver's license *AE*	*Führerschein*

extending one's stay	*„Verlängerung des Aufenthalts"*
everybody's favourite room	*jedermanns Lieblingszimmer*
today's Daily Mail	*die heutige Daily Mail*
yesterday's prices	*die Preise von gestern*

Die deutschen Übersetzungen veranschaulichen die unterschiedlichen Beziehungen, die durch diese Konstruktion ausgedrückt werden. Die unter 4 dargestellte *of*-Fügung hat mitunter – aber keineswegs immer! – eine gleiche oder ähnliche Bedeutung. Soweit die beiden Konstruktionen in der Isolation austauschbar sind (z. B. *the doctor's house – the house of the doctor*), wird bei der Anwendung im Satz doch in der Regel die eine oder die andere Fügung eindeutig bevorzugt, wie etwa in folgendem Beispielpaar:

Eleven weary hours later they pulled up outside the doctor's house just as the first patients began to queue up for the afternoon surgery.

She pointed out the house of the doctor who had saved her mother's life.
Sie zeigte auf das Haus des Arztes, der ihrer Mutter das Leben gerettet hatte.

4 Fügungen mit *of*

the Prime Minister of New Zealand	*der Premierminister von Neuseeland*
owners of high-performance cars	*Besitzer von Hochleistungsautos*
this kind/type/sort of person	*diese Art von Mensch*
the movie capital of the United States	*die Filmhauptstadt der Vereinigten Staaten*
the beginning of the 20th century	*der Beginn des 20. Jahrhunderts*
the collapse of a bridge	*der Einsturz einer Brücke*
the south of England	*der Süden Englands*
the quality of life	*die Lebensqualität*
the 25th of June	*der 25. Juni*
a couple of / a lot of showers	*ein paar / viele Regenschauer*
a certain amount of stress	*ein gewisses Maß an Streß*
two sacks of letters	*zwei Säcke mit Briefen*
a cup of coffee	*eine Tasse Kaffee*
the village of Wayford	*das Dorf Wayford*
the Republic of Malta	*die Republik Malta*

Artikel (*a/an, the*)

5 Vom Deutschen abweichender Gebrauch des unbestimmten Artikels (*a/an*)

a hundred times a day	*hundertmal am/pro Tag*
the speed limit is 55 miles an hour	*55 Meilen in der / pro Stunde*
only £10 a night	*nur zehn Pfund die/pro Nacht*
Steve is a steward	*Steve ist Steward*
(*aber:* she's been voted Shop Assistant of the Year	*sie ist zur Verkäuferin des Jahres gewählt worden*)

I'm a school governor	*ich bin Mitglied des Schulbeirats*
he's become an actor	*er ist Schauspieler geworden*
stay here as a guest	*wohnen Sie hier als Gast*

I've got a headache	*ich habe Kopfschmerzen*
just a moment	*Moment mal*
he brought the plane to a halt	*er brachte die Maschine zum Stehen*
they have a reputation for being cheap	*sie stehen in dem Ruf, billig zu sein*
take an interest in the theatre	*Interesse am Theater haben*

6 Vom Deutschen abweichender Gebrauch des bestimmten Artikels (*the*)

drive on the left	*links fahren*
listen to the radio	*Radio hören*
by three at the latest	*spätestens bis drei (Uhr)*
half the programmes are in English	*die Hälfte der Programme …*

7 Ausdrücke ohne Artikel

it's in Oxford Street	*es ist in der Oxford Street*
a store on 42nd Street	*ein Geschäft in der 42. Straße*
I met her in Regent's Park	*ich traf sie im Regent's Park*
not far from Victoria Station	*nicht weit von der Victoria Station*
at Gatwick Airport	*am Flughafen Gatwick*
we saw Buckingham Palace	*wir sahen den Buckingham-Palast*
London Bridge (*aber AE* the Williamsburg Bridge) is closed	*die London Bridge / die Williamsburg Bridge ist gesperrt*

you can get there by Tube/taxi	*man kann da mit der U-Bahn / mit dem Taxi hinfahren*
television/TV is bilingual here	*das Fernsehen ist hier zweisprachig*
(*aber:* let's move the television / the TV into the kitchen	*laß uns den Fernseher in die Küche stellen)*
I learnt that at school	*das habe ich in der Schule gelernt*
she goes to church every Sunday	*sie geht jeden Sonntag in die Kirche*
can't we get together for lunch?	*können wir uns nicht zum Lunch treffen?*
we were there in July	*wir waren im Juli dort*
do you have the pain at night?	*haben Sie die Schmerzen nachts?*

life is hard	*das Leben ist schwer*
till death us do part	*bis daß der Tod uns scheidet*
people are scared	*die Leute/Menschen haben Angst*
waste has become a problem	*der Abfall ist zum Problem geworden*
I like today's movies	*mir gefallen die heutigen Filme*
I bought it at half price	*ich habe es zum halben Preis gekauft*
on condition that	*unter der Bedingung, daß*
drive in first gear	*im ersten Gang fahren*
take out insurance	*eine Versicherung abschließen*
please notify Reception	*benachrichtigen Sie bitte die Rezeption*

Pronomen (Fürwörter) und Substantivbegleiter (determiners)

8 Die *-self*-Pronomen (rückbezüglich)

I	might	hurt	myself	*ich könnte mich verletzen*
you	might	hurt	yourself	*du könntest dich / Sie könnten sich verletzen*
he	might	hurt	himself	*er könnte sich verletzen*
she	might	hurt	herself	*sie könnte sich verletzen*
it	might	hurt	itself	*es könnte sich verletzen*
we	might	hurt	ourselves	*wir könnten uns verletzen*
you	might	hurt	yourselves	*ihr könntet euch / Sie könnten sich verletzen*
they	might	hurt	themselves	*sie könnten sich verletzen*

9 Die *-self*-Pronomen (betonend)

I only just arrived myself. *Ich bin selber gerade erst gekommen.*
You'll have to decide that (for) yourself. *Das wirst du selbst entscheiden müssen.*
The President said so himself. *Der Präsident hat das selbst gesagt.*
The Prime Minister herself said so. *Die Premierministerin selbst hat das gesagt.*
The town itself has hardly changed. *Die Stadt selbst hat sich kaum verändert.*
We're looking for accommodation ourselves. *Wir suchen selber eine Unterkunft.*
Can't you eat them yourselves? *Könnt ihr sie nicht selber essen?*
The houses themselves aren't bad at all. *Die Häuser selbst sind gar nicht übel.*

10 Stützwort *one*

a. "You said the heliport, didn't you?" – "Yes, the one (= heliport) on East 34th Street." *Ja, der auf der 34. Straße, Ostseite.*
b. "I thought you said the one (= heliport) on the West Side."
Ich dachte, Sie meinten den auf der Westseite.
c. New roads are being built and existing ones (= roads) widened.
Neue Straßen werden gebaut und bestehende (werden) verbreitert.

Um die Wiederholung eines Substantivs (*heliport, roads*) zu vermeiden, ersetzt man es nach Adjektiven (c) und *the* (a, b) durch *one(s)*. Entsprechend auch nach Wörtern wie *this/that* und *which*:

Which one do you mean – this one or that one?
Welchen meinst du – diesen hier oder den da?

11 *Some – any*

a. Some people have been waiting for 30 hours.
Manche Leute warten nun schon seit dreißig Stunden.
b. There aren't any holidaymakers waiting at the airports at the moment.
Im Augenblick warten auf den Flughäfen keine Urlauber.
c. Are there any holidaymakers still waiting at the airports?
Warten noch Urlauber auf den Flughäfen?

d. There was something on TV about it. *Darüber war etwas im Fernsehen.*
e. There wasn't anything on TV about it. *Im Fernsehen war nichts darüber.*
f. Was there anything on TV about it? *War darüber was im Fernsehen?*

Some steht bei bejahtem Sinn (a, d); *any* steht bei verneintem (b, e) oder fragendem (c, f) Sinn. In bejahten, nichtfragenden Aussagen dagegen heißt *any* so etwas wie *jede (x-beliebige) / irgendeine / irgendwelche*:

Any such loss will have to be borne by the passenger.
Jeder solche Verlust muß durch den Reisenden getragen werden.
Anyone who pays to wait for 24 hours or more in an airport lounge needs their head testing. *Jeder/Jemand, der dafür bezahlt, daß ...*

Zahlen und Ziffern

12 Grundzahlen

a. Some 400,000 people watch the 443 matches.
Some four hundred thousand people watch the four hundred and forty-three matches.
b. 107,000 vehicles cross the bridge every day.
one hundred / a hundred and seven thousand vehicles
c. His family has lived in the village for 170 years.
for a hundred / one hundred and seventy years

Die Gliederung größerer Tausenderzahlen erfolgt ggf. durch Kommas, nicht – wie im Deutschen – durch Punkte (a, b). Das *and* vor der Zehnerstelle (a–c) wird im AE manchmal weggelassen. Beachten Sie das *a* oder *one* in der Aussprache von *170* etc. (b, c): *a/one hundred and seventy* – nicht einfach *hundred and seventy*!

13 Dezimalbrüche

There are only 1.2 people in the average rush-hour car. *one point two*
Only 0.5 per cent of British engineers are female. *(nought/oh) point five*

Dezimalbrüche werden – anders als im Deutschen – mit einem Punkt geschrieben. Bei Dezimalbrüchen unter 1 wird die vor dem Dezimalpunkt stehende Null *nought* oder *oh* gesprochen oder auch weggelassen.

14 Telefonnummern

a. Please ring Mr Terry Johnson on 01–327 4065 between 09–1600 hrs.
on oh–one three–two–seven four–oh–six–five between nine and sixteen hours
b. She called 911 (*Notruf in den USA*). She dialled 999 (*Notruf in Großbritannien*).
She called nine–one–one. She dialled nine–nine–nine.

Telefonnummern werden gruppenweise Ziffer für Ziffer gesprochen. *Null* wird in Telefonnummern stets *oh* gesprochen. – Beachten Sie auch die Aussprache der Uhrzeit in (a). Alltäglicher als diese „bürokratische" Ausdrucksweise wäre natürlich: ... *between 9 (a.m.) and 4 (p.m.).*

15 Andere Nummern

a. I'm in room 4 / room 45 / room 405 / room 4216.
room four / room forty-five / room four oh five / room four two one six
b. The A4 / the A45 / the A405 / the A423 is still closed.
the A four / the A forty-five / the A four oh five / the A four twenty-three

Die Aussprache der Nummern von Hotelzimmern (a), Fernstraßen (b) u. dgl. variiert entsprechend der Ziffernzahl.

16 Jahreszahlen

In 1798 Malta was occupied by the French, and in 1800 it was taken by the British.
in seventeen (hundred and) ninety-eight … in eighteen hundred
Cary Grant was born in 1904 and died in 1986. *in nineteen hundred and four / in nineteen oh four … in nineteen (hundred and) eighty-six*

Die umständlichere Form mit *hundred and* wird in der Alltagssprache beim Sprechen über aktuelle Jahreszahlen nur selten gebraucht.

17 Geldbeträge

The cab driver must be able to change a $10 bill. *a ten-dollar bill*
The fare was $10 / £10. *ten dollars / ten pounds*
He sold land worth more than £1 million at half price. *more than one/a million pounds*

Beachten Sie die Stellung des $- oder £-Zeichens: ohne Abstand direkt vor der Zahl.

Adjektiv und Adverb (Eigenschaftswort und Umstandswort)

18 Komparativ (Steigerungs-Höher- od. Mehrstufe)

Häufig steht der Komparativ in Verbindung mit *than*:

Is flying safer today than it used to be?
It involves no more than an eye test.
Roads are more congested than they were ten years ago.
They may drive slower than some of these young hot rodders.
I think they drive more responsibly than young people.
Testing them more often than other drivers wouldn't be fair.

Rufen Sie sich noch einmal die verschiedenen Arten der Bildung des Komparativs ins Gedächtnis zurück:

Bei kurzen Wörtern Anhängen von *-er*: *great – greater* etc.
Stummes End-*e* entfällt: *safe – safer* etc.
Verdopplung des Endkonsonanten in Fällen wie diesem: *hot – hotter*.
Bei zweisilbigen Wörtern wird *-y* zu *-i-*: *early – earlier* etc.

Bei längeren Wörtern mit *more*: *expensive – more expensive* etc.
-ly-Adverbien sind „längere Wörter": *deeply – more deeply* etc.

Unregelmäßig: *good – better* etc.

19 Superlativ (Steigerungs-Höchststufe)

Sehr häufig ist die Struktur Superlativ + Substantiv + Relativsatz:

This is certainly one of the worst bridges we have.
For me it's the most important book I've ever read.
Belgrave Road in Victoria is the best I can do.

Rufen Sie sich auch noch einmal die verschiedenen Arten der Bildung des Superlativs ins Gedächtnis zurück:

Bei kurzen Wörtern Anhängen von *-est*: *short – shortest* etc.
Stummes End-*e* entfällt: *late – latest* etc.
Verdopplung des Endkonsonanten in Fällen wie diesem: *big – biggest*.
Bei zweisilbigen Wörtern wird *-y* zu *-i-*: *busy – busiest* etc.

Bei längeren Wörtern mit *most*: *important – most important* etc.

Unregelmäßig: *bad – worst* etc.

20 Adjektiv (ohne *-ly*) oder Adverb (mit *-ly*)?

They had a narrow escape. They narrowly escaped disaster.	*Sie sind gerade noch einmal davongekommen.* *Sie entgingen knapp einer Katastrophe.*
I know their exact location. I know exactly where they are.	*Ich kenne ihren genauen Standort.* *Ich weiß genau, wo sie sind.*
Concorde is a supersonic plane. Concorde flies supersonically.	*Die Concorde ist ein Überschallflugzeug.* *Die C. fliegt mit Überschallgeschwindigkeit.*
The captain was fantastic. The captain reacted fantastically.	*Der Kapitän war phantastisch.* *Der Kapitän hat phantastisch reagiert.*

Die Wortform ohne *-ly* bezieht sich auf Substantive (*the captain was fantastic*) oder Pronomen (*he was fantastic*).
Die *-ly*-Endung wird angehängt, wenn das Wort sich nicht auf ein Substantiv oder Pronomen bezieht, sondern z. B. auf ein Verb (*he reacted fantastically*) oder ein Adjektiv (*the flight time is fantastically short*) oder ein Adverb (*he reacted fantastically fast*).
An Adjektive auf *-ic* wird in der Regel nicht einfach *-ly*, sondern *-ally* angehängt: *supersonic – supersonically, fantastic – fantastically* (Ausnahme z. B. *public – publicly*).

21 *Auch*

Positiv: Sandra gets discounted tickets too.
Sandra bekommt auch/ebenfalls verbilligte Flugscheine.
Negativ: Sandra doesn't get discounted tickets either.
Sandra bekommt auch/ebenfalls keine verbilligten Flugscheine.

Verneintes *auch/ebenfalls* heißt also *either*. Weitere Beispiele:

Positiv:
The newsreader also blamed the increasing pressure of the job for his decision.
... gab auch dem zunehmenden Arbeitsdruck die Schuld ...
Television is also bilingual. / Television is bilingual too.
Das Fernsehen ist ebenfalls zweisprachig.

Negativ:
Buckingham Palace isn't very far either. *B. P. ist auch nicht weit (entfernt).*
"My parents would never have dreamed of entertaining in the kitchen." – "Mine wouldn't have either." ... *„Meine auch nicht."*

Verb

22 Unregelmäßige Verben

Die Liste nennt bei jedem Verb drei Formen:
1. den Infinitiv (Grundform, z. B. *write = schreiben*)
2. die Vergangenheitsform (past, z. B. *wrote = schrieb*)
3. das „*-ed*-Partizip" (Perfektpartizip, past participle, z. B. *written = geschrieben*)

Der Zusatz (R) bedeutet, daß neben der unregelmäßigen auch die regelmäßige (*-ed-*)Form gebräuchlich ist.

arise – arose – arisen
beat – beat – beaten
become – became – become
begin – began – begun
bind – bound – bound
bite – bit – bitten
bleed – bled – bled
blow – blew – blown
break – broke – broken
bring – brought – brought
broadcast – broadcast – broadcast
build – built – built
burn – burnt (R) – burnt (R)
burst – burst – burst
buy – bought – bought
catch – caught – caught
choose – chose – chosen
come – came – come
cost – cost – cost
cut – cut – cut
deal – dealt [e] – dealt [e]
dig – dug – dug
do – did – done
draw – drew – drawn
dream – dreamt (R) – dreamt (R)
drink – drank – drunk
drive – drove – driven
eat – ate – eaten
fall – fell – fallen
feed – fed – fed
feel – felt – felt
fight – fought – fought
find – found – found
fly – flew – flown
forecast – forecast – forecast
forget – forgot – forgotten
freeze – froze – frozen
get – got – got / *AE auch* gotten
give – gave – given
go – went – gone [gɒn]
grow – grew – grown
hang – hung (R) – hung (R)
have – had – had
hear – heard – heard
hide – hid – hidden
hit – hit – hit
hold – held – held
hurt – hurt – hurt
keep – kept – kept
know – knew – known
lay – laid – laid
lead – led – led
learn – learnt (R) – learnt (R)
leave – left – left
lend – lent – lent
let – let – let

lie – lay – lain
lose – lost – lost
make – made – made
mean – meant [e] – meant [e]
meet – met – met
pay – paid – paid
put – put – put
read – read [e] – read [e]
ride – rode – ridden
ring – rang – rung
rise – rose – risen
run – ran – run
say – said [e] – said [e]
see – saw – seen
seek – sought – sought
sell – sold – sold
send – sent – sent
set – set – set
shake – shook – shaken
shoot – shot – shot
show – showed – shown
shut – shut – shut
sing – sang – sung
sink – sank – sunk
sit – sat – sat
sleep – slept – slept
slide – slid – slid
smell – smelt (R) – smelt (R)
speak – spoke – spoken
spell – spelt (R) – spelt (R)
spend – spent – spent
spread – spread – spread
stand – stood – stood
steal – stole – stolen
stick – stuck – stuck
strike – struck – struck
swear – swore – sworn
swim – swam – swum
take – took – taken
teach – taught – taught
tell – told – told
think – thought – thought
throw – threw – thrown
understand – understood – understood
upset – upset – upset
wake – woke – woken
wear – wore – worn
win – won – won
withstand – withstood – withstood
write – wrote – written

23 Gebrauch der Perfektformen

a. They have broken the record for circumnavigating Britain by boat.
Sie haben den Rekord für die Umseglung Großbritanniens gebrochen.
b. Mr Lange has been ill with flu for the past week.
Mr Lange ist seit einer Woche grippekrank.
c. He has been admitted to hospital with a heart condition.
Er ist wegen Herzbeschwerden in ein Krankenhaus eingeliefert worden.
d. He had been suffering from chest pains.
Er hatte an Schmerzen in der Brust gelitten.
e. They hope to have raised more than a hundred thousand pounds.
Sie hoffen über hunderttausend Pfund aufgebracht zu haben.
f. The race was to have been held late last night.
Das Rennen hatte gestern am späten Abend „abgehalten werden sollen".

a. Gebrauch des Perfekts (present perfect simple) für abgeschlossene, aber nicht „datierte" Handlungen. Wäre die Handlung „datiert", so müßte die Vergangenheitsform (past tense) stehen: *They broke the record only last week. (= Sie haben den Rekord erst vergangene Woche gebrochen.)*
b. Gebrauch des Perfekts (present perfect simple) für aus der Vergangenheit in die Gegenwart dauernde Handlungen. Ein Verb wie *suffer* (anstelle von *be*) würde in der Verlaufsform (present perfect progressive) stehen: *He has been suffering from chest pains for the past week. (= Er leidet seit einer Woche an Schmerzen in der Brust.)*

c. Gebrauch des Perfekts wie in (a), aber im Passiv.
d. Gebrauch des Perfekts wie in (b), aber um eine Zeitstufe in die Vergangenheit versetzt (Verlaufsform des Plusquamperfekts, past perfect progressive) – die Handlung erstreckt sich also aus der Vorvergangenheit in die Vergangenheit.
e. Infinitiv des Perfekts (perfect infinitive).
f. Wie (e), aber im Passiv.

Weiteres Beispiel zu (b):

I've had a headache since I got up this morning.
Ich habe Kopfschmerzen, seitdem ich heute morgen aufgestanden bin.

Gebrauch des Perfekts (*I've had*) für eine aus der Vergangenheit in die Gegenwart reichende Handlung; Gebrauch der Vergangenheit (*got up*) für eine durch eine Zeitbestimmung der Vergangenheit (*this morning*) „datierte" Vergangenheitshandlung.

24 Perfekt oder Vergangenheit?

a. Malta was invaded many times. *Malta ist häufig überfallen worden.*
b. Malta has been invaded many times. *Malta ist häufig überfallen worden.*

(a) und (b) unterscheiden sich durch den Zeitraum, in dem Invasionen stattfanden oder hätten stattfinden können. In (a) schließt dieser Zeitraum die Gegenwart *nicht* ein, während der Gebrauch des Perfekts in (b) den gedachten Zusatz „bis heute" bedingt.
In den beiden folgenden Beispielen ist der Gebrauch der Vergangenheit (c) durch die Zeitbestimmungen der Vergangenheit (*in 1798, in 1800, until 1964*) und der Gebrauch des Perfekts (d) durch den Bezug zur Gegenwart („bis heute") geboten:

c. In 1798 it was occupied by the French, and in 1800 it was taken by the British, who ruled until 1964.
d. Since the early 1970s, Malta has followed a policy of strict nonalignment.

25 Verlaufsform oder einfache Form?

The farmers are having to sell off their cattle. *Die Bauern müssen ihr Vieh abstoßen.*

Die einfache Form *have to sell off* wäre hier ebenfalls möglich, aber die Verlaufsform *are having to sell off* betont, daß diese Notwendigkeit jetzt gerade im Augenblick besteht. Die Verlaufsform verrät auch eine stärkere innere Teilnahme der sprechenden Person.
Dagegen wird mit der einfachen Form *we complain* im folgenden Beispiel ausgedrückt, daß die Leute allgemein über das Wetter klagen, nicht gerade jetzt im Augenblick:

And we complain about the rain here. *Und wir klagen über den Regen hier.*

26 Verlaufsform und einfache Form des Perfekts

a. Work on the Kingston Bypass has been causing long delays.

Vergleichen Sie Satz (a) mit den Sätzen (b) und (c):

b. Work on the Kingston Bypass is causing long delays.
c. Work on the Kingston Bypass has caused long delays.

a. Verlaufsform des Perfekts: Die Handlung hat in der Vergangenheit begonnen und dauert noch an. Mögliche Übersetzung:
(Bau-)Arbeiten … verursachen (seit einiger Zeit) erhebliche Verkehrsstockungen.
b. Verlaufsform des Präsens: Die Handlung läuft zur Zeit gerade ab. Übersetzung:
(Bau-)Arbeiten … verursachen (zur Zeit) erhebliche Verkehrsstockungen.
c. Einfache Form des Perfekts: Die Handlung ist abgeschlossen. Übersetzung:
(Bau-)Arbeiten … haben erhebliche Verkehrsstockungen verursacht.

Weitere Beispiele für den Unterschied zwischen Verlaufsform und einfacher Form des Perfekts:

d. That has been changing.	*(Etwa:) Das ändert sich in letzter Zeit.*
e. That has changed.	*Das hat sich geändert.*

d. Der „Vorgang des Sichänderns“ hat in der Vergangenheit begonnen und dauert zur Zeit noch an.
e. Der „Vorgang des Sichänderns“ ist abgeschlossen.

f. Thousands of people have been spending another night at airports.
Tausende von Menschen haben eine weitere Nacht auf Flughäfen verbracht.
g. Thousands of people have spent another night at airports.
Tausende von Menschen haben eine weitere Nacht auf Flughäfen verbracht.

Satz (f) stellt die Handlung (*have been spending*) als sich aus der Vergangenheit in die Gegenwart erstreckend – also noch andauernd – dar, wird also etwa an dem auf die Nacht folgenden Morgen gesprochen (Nachrichten!), während die Reisenden immer noch auf den Flughäfen warten.
Satz (g) berichtet einfach die Tatsache (*have spent*), ohne etwas darüber auszusagen, ob die Reisenden immer noch warten oder nicht.

27 Plusquamperfekt (Vorvergangenheit)

a. They hailed Mike as a brave little boy who had done the right thing.
Sie lobten Mike als einen tapferen kleinen Jungen, der das Richtige getan hatte.
b. Later he learned that the man he saved had earlier stolen his canoe.
Später erfuhr er, daß der von ihm gerettete Mann zuvor sein Kanu gestohlen hatte.
c. He took the rifle he had got for Christmas.
Er nahm das Gewehr, das er zu Weihnachten bekommen hatte.

Wie im Deutschen gebraucht man diese „*had*-Form“ für Handlungen, die zeitlich vor der „Erzählebene Vergangenheit“ liegen: *had done* liegt vor *hailed* (a), *had stolen* vor *learned* (b) und *had got* vor *took* (c).
In (b) liegt allerdings nicht nur *had stolen*, sondern auch *saved* vor *learned*. „Logisch“ richtig wäre also eigentlich: *Later he learned that the man he had saved had earlier stolen his canoe.* Auf ein solches stilistisch schwerfälliges Plusquamperfekt wird aber in der Regel dann verzichtet, wenn – wie hier – die Zeitverhältnisse auch ohne den Gebrauch der *had*-Form nicht mißzuverstehen sind. (Vgl. 68.)

28 Futur (Zukunft)

Will (bzw. die Kurzform *'ll*) ist die am häufigsten vorkommende und „neutralste" Ausdrucksform für die Zukunft. Wie die Übersetzungen (b, d, e) zeigen, entspricht der englischen *will*-Zukunft im Deutschen oft die Gegenwart:

a. We'll have to wait and see. *Wir werden abwarten müssen.*
b. It will stay mostly cloudy tomorrow. *Morgen bleibt es überwiegend bewölkt.*
c. I'll see if it can be arranged. *Ich will mal sehen, ob es sich machen läßt.*
d. Maybe I'll walk. *Vielleicht gehe ich zu Fuß.*
e. I'm sure / I think / I hope you'll like it.
Ich bin sicher / Ich glaube / Ich hoffe, daß es dir gefällt.
f. She doubts whether they'll be able to manage.
Sie bezweifelt, daß sie zurechtkommen werden.

Eine Zukunftsaussage mit *be going to* betont gegenwärtige Absicht (a–c) oder Gewißheit (d):

a. We're going to have lunch at the Piccadilly Restaurant.
Wir werden im Piccadilly Restaurant (zu Mittag) essen.
b. I'm not going to carry something as heavy as that.
Ich habe nicht die Absicht, so was Schweres zu tragen.
c. What are we going to do with the rest of the evening?
Was machen wir mit dem angebrochenen Abend?
d. There's going to be a delay of 45 minutes.
Es wird eine Verspätung von 45 Minuten geben.

Die Verlaufsform der Gegenwart als Ausdruck einer zukünftigen Handlung betont das Element der Planung:

I'm taking my family to Scotland. *Ich fahre mit meiner Familie nach Schottland.*
Are you coming by Tube? *Kommst du mit der U-Bahn?*

Auch die Konstruktion *will be -ing* wird in der Nichtfrageform (a–b) für Aussagen über geplante Zukunftshandlungen gebraucht; als Frageform (c–d) wirkt sie distanzierter, unaufdringlicher und damit höflicher als *be going to* oder die Verlaufsform der Gegenwart:

a. We'll be arriving at about half past twelve.
Wir werden so gegen halb eins ankommen.
b. I'll be taking my family to Scotland.
Ich werde mit meiner Familie nach Schottland fahren.
c. Will you be coming by Tube? *Werden Sie mit der U-Bahn kommen?*
d. About what time d'you think you'll be arriving?
Um welche Zeit werden Sie etwa ankommen?

Für Handlungen oder Ereignisse, die aufgrund eines Fahrplans, Terminplans, Programms usw. eintreten werden, steht oft die einfache Form der Gegenwart:

The movie starts at 8.30. *Der Film fängt um halb neun an.*
My plane leaves at 10.15 from Heathrow.
Mein Flugzeug geht um 10.15 Uhr von Heathrow.
My driving test is tomorrow. *Meine Fahrprüfung ist morgen.*

In Nebensätzen mit *if, unless, when, before, as soon as* etc. steht das Verb auch bei Zukunftsbezug in der Gegenwart:

If I miss the helicopter, I won't make my flight to Berlin.
Wenn ich den Hubschrauber verpasse, schaffe ich nicht meinen Flug nach Berlin.
Unless we get extra money, we'll have to close.
Wenn wir nicht zusätzliche Geldmittel bekommen, müssen wir zumachen.
You can tell her when / as soon as she gets back.
Du kannst es ihr sagen, wenn / sobald sie zurückkommt.
We must discuss it before you go.
Wir müssen das bereden, bevor du gehst.

Das folgende Beispiel ist keine Ausnahme von der vorstehenden Regel, da *will* hier nicht Zukunft, sondern eine Bitte ausdrückt:

If you'll just hold on for a minute, I'll look it up in the phone book.
Wenn Sie einen Augenblick warten wollen (= Warten Sie doch bitte einen Augenblick), dann schaue ich im Telefonbuch nach.

Passiv (Leideform)

29 Einfache Form und Verlaufsform des Passivs

(Einfache Form:)	New roads are built (every year). *Es werden (jedes Jahr) neue Straßen gebaut.*
(Verlaufsform:)	New roads are being built (at the moment). *Es werden (zur Zeit) neue Straßen gebaut.*

Das Passiv wird im Englischen mit einer Form von *be* gebildet. Beispiele:

is built = wird gebaut	*has been built = ist gebaut worden*
are built = werden gebaut	*have been built = sind gebaut worden*
was built = wurde gebaut	*had been built = war(en) gebaut worden*
were built = wurden gebaut	*can be built = kann/können gebaut werden*

Um auszudrücken, daß es sich um etwas gerade Geschehendes, Vorübergehendes u. dgl. handelt, kann auch im Passiv – hier durch Einschieben von *being* – die Verlaufsform gebildet werden:

A new road is/was being built. *Eine neue Straße wird/wurde gerade gebaut.*

Die Verlaufsform kommt im Passiv vor allem nach *am/is/are* und *was/were* vor. Nach *has/have/had been* und Hilfsverben wie *can* ist sie sehr selten. Dagegen findet man sie durchaus gelegentlich nach dem *to*-Infinitiv:

A new road seems to be being built.
Es scheint gerade eine neue Straße gebaut zu werden.

Gefälliger klingt hier allerdings die Aktivform:
They seem to be building a new road. *Sie scheinen eine neue Straße zu bauen.*

30 Passiv der Perfektformen

Aktiv: They have voted her Shop Assistant of the Year.
Passiv: She has been voted Shop Assistant of the Year.
Sie ist zur Verkäuferin des Jahres gewählt worden.
Man hat sie zur Verkäuferin des Jahres gewählt.

Aktiv: They had made him redundant.
Passiv: He had been made redundant. *„Er war redundant gemacht worden."*

31 Nennung des „Handlungsurhebers" im Passivsatz

Passiv: In 1798 Malta was occupied by the French.
Aktiv: In 1798 the French occupied Malta.

Der „Handlungsurheber" wird im Passivsatz mit *by* angeschlossen. Diese Nennung des Urhebers ist allerdings die Ausnahme, nicht die Regel, denn die Passivform wird ja gerade dann bevorzugt, wenn der Urheber nicht bekannt oder in dem gegebenen Zusammenhang nicht von Bedeutung ist.

32 *Have* als Vollverb und Hilfsverb

a. Do you have the pain at night? *Haben Sie die Schmerzen nachts?*
b. I don't have the pain at night. *Nachts habe ich die Schmerzen nicht.*

c. Have you got any worries? *Haben Sie irgendwelche Sorgen?*
d. She hasn't got any sales experience. *Sie hat keine Verkaufserfahrung.*

In (c) wäre genausogut *Do you have any worries?* möglich und in (d) *She doesn't have any sales experience.*
Umgekehrt läßt sich aber in (a) *Do you have* nicht durch *Have you got* ersetzen, und in (b) kann es statt *I don't have* nicht *I haven't got* heißen, da die *have got*-Konstruktion weitgehend auf die Bedeutung *have = besitzen* beschränkt ist, *have* in (a) und (b) aber so etwas wie *get/feel* heißt: *Do you get/feel the pain at night? I don't get/feel the pain at night.*
Im Zweifel sollten Sie also bei *have* der *do*-Konstruktion den Vorzug geben – Sie können dann nichts falsch machen: *Does she have a car?, What time do you have breakfast?, I don't have enough money, Budget hotels don't have restaurants* etc.

Modalverben (*can, may, must* etc.)

33 *Can – could – may* in Fragesätzen

Can I see your driver's license, please? *Kann ich bitte mal Ihren Führerschein sehen?*
Could I speak to Mr Johnson, please? *Könnte ich bitte mal Herrn Johnson sprechen?*
May I use your phone? *Darf/Kann ich Ihr Telefon benutzen?*

Could ist höflicher als *can*. *May* ist förmlicher als *can*.

34 *Can* und *may* in Aussagesätzen

It can make all the difference whether you know exactly what to do.
Es kann viel ausmachen, ob Sie wissen, wie Sie sich verhalten müssen.
Bring with you any documents that may be relevant to your application.
Bringen Sie alle Unterlagen mit, die für Ihre Bewerbung von Bedeutung sein könnten.

Can drückt Fähigkeit oder eine durch die Umstände gegebene Möglichkeit aus.
May drückt eine durch ein gewisses Maß an Wahrscheinlichkeit gegebene Möglichkeit aus („vielleicht"). Vergleichen Sie:

There can be problems.
(Durch die Umstände gegebene Möglichkeit:) *Es kann (durchaus) Probleme geben.*

There may be problems.
(Es besteht eine gewisse Wahrscheinlichkeit – „möglicherweise":)
Es könnte Probleme geben. / Es kann sein, daß es Probleme gibt. / Möglicherweise gibt es Probleme.

35 *Can – be able to*

a. The driver can change a $10 bill.
Eine Zehndollarnote kann der Fahrer wechseln.
b. The driver must/should/will be able to change a $10 bill.
Eine Zehndollarnote muß/müßte/wird der Fahrer wechseln können.
c. The driver doesn't seem to be able to change a $10 bill.
Eine Zehndollarnote scheint der Fahrer nicht wechseln zu können.
d. Being able to change a $10 bill – I mean, that's the least you can expect, isn't it?
Eine Zehndollarnote wechseln zu können – ich meine, das ist doch das Wenigste, was man erwarten kann, oder?

Can ist ein „unvollständiges" Verb – z. B. kann man es nicht im Infinitiv (mit oder ohne *to*) oder in der *-ing*-Form gebrauchen. Die Beispiele b–d zeigen, wie *can* in solchen Fällen durch eine Konstruktion mit *be able to* ersetzt wird.

36 *Could = könnte/konnte*

A Tyneside postman hid sacks of letters for seven years because he could not read properly. ... *weil er nicht richtig lesen konnte.*
He could manage simple addresses, but the more difficult family and place names baffled him. *„Einfache Adressen konnte er bewältigen ..."*

Bei diesen Sätzen aus einer Zeitungsstory kann kein Zweifel darüber aufkommen, daß *could* sich auf die Vergangenheit bezieht, also dem deutschen *konnte* entspricht. Aber wie wäre es mit folgendem Satz?

I could help her.

So wie es in diesem Satz steht, könnte *could* nur als „Möglichkeit in der Gegenwart" verstanden werden: *Ich könnte ihr helfen.* Die Vergangenheit müßte man dagegen mit Hilfe von *be able to* (vgl. 35) ausdrücken:

I was able to help her. *Ich konnte ihr helfen.*

37 *Must – have to*

Gegenwart: You must / have to start from scratch. *Du mußt von vorn anfangen.*
Vergangenheit: I had to start from scratch. *Ich mußte von vorn anfangen.*
Nach *will/would*: I'll/I'd have to start from scratch.
Ich werde/würde von vorn anfangen müssen.
To-Infinitiv/-*ing*-Form: I don't like to have to / having to start from scratch.
Ich habe es nicht gern, von vorn anfangen zu müssen.

Der Gebrauch von *must* ist im wesentlichen auf die Gegenwart beschränkt. In anderen Zeiten oder Formen wird es u. a. durch *have to* ersetzt.

38 *Could* + einfacher Infinitiv und *could* + Infinitiv des Perfekts

Beachten Sie den Unterschied zwischen den beiden Konstruktionen und auch die Stellungsmöglichkeiten für *all*:

We could (all) be dead.	*Wir könnten (alle) tot sein.*
We could (all) have (all) been dead.	*Wir hätten (alle) tot sein können.*

39 *May* + Infinitiv des Perfekts

Don't mention any problems you may have had with him.
... Probleme, die Sie mit ihm gehabt haben mögen / vielleicht mit ihm gehabt haben.

Während *may have had* sich also auf die Vergangenheit bezieht, würde *may be having* die Gegenwart bezeichnen:

Don't mention any problems you may be having with him.
... Probleme, die Sie mit ihm haben mögen / vielleicht mit ihm haben.

40 *Should – ought to – must*

You should pay / ought to pay careful attention. *Sie sollten genau aufpassen.*
There should be / ought to be harsher punishments. *Es müßte strengere Strafen geben.*
Midnight dumpers should be / ought to be treated as dangerous criminals.
Leute, die Abfälle illegal beseitigen, müßten/sollten als gefährliche Verbrecher behandelt werden.
I don't see why I should have to listen to other people's music.
Ich sehe nicht ein, warum ich gezwungen sein sollte, mir die Musik anderer Leute anzuhören.
The hospitals ought to check where their medical waste goes.
Die Krankenhäuser müßten (eigentlich) überprüfen, wo ihre Abfälle hinkommen.

The driver must be able to change a $10 bill.
Der Fahrer muß einen Zehndollarschein wechseln können.
The driver should be able to change a $10 bill.
Der Fahrer müßte/sollte einen Zehndollarschein wechseln können.
The driver ought to be able to change a $10 bill.
Der Fahrer müßte eigentlich einen Zehndollarschein wechseln können.

Should und *ought to* sind in der Bedeutung *müßte/sollte* häufig austauschbar, aber *ought to* klingt stärker, nachdrücklicher als *should*.

41 *Would* + einfacher Infinitiv

I wish the weather would clear up. *Ich wünschte, das Wetter würde sich bessern.*
She'd (= She would) prefer to be able to converse without shouting.
Sie würde es vorziehen, wenn sie sich unterhalten könnte, ohne zu schreien.

They'd (= They would) like a family. *Sie hätten gern Kinder.*
I'd (= I would) like to go back to Germany.
Ich würde gern nach Deutschland zurückgehen.

42 *Would* + Infinitiv des Perfekts

My parents would never have dreamed of entertaining in the kitchen.
Meine Eltern „würden nie davon geträumt haben", in der Küche zu „unterhalten".
Meine Eltern hätten nicht im Traum daran gedacht, Gäste in der Küche zu empfangen.

Die folgende, auf die Gegenwart bezogene Version könnte als Hinführung zu dieser schwierigen Konstruktion hilfreich sein:
My parents would never dream of entertaining in the kitchen.
Meine Eltern würden nicht im Traum daran denken, Gäste in der Küche zu empfangen.

43 *Would rather*

I'd (= I would) rather fly than drive.
Ich würde lieber fliegen als (mit dem Auto) fahren.

44 *Use(d) to*

Is flying safer today than it used to be?
Ist das Fliegen heute sicherer, als es „zu sein pflegte" / als es früher war?
Malta used to have a reputation for being "cheap and cheerful".
M. pflegte den Ruf zu haben / hatte früher den Ruf, billig und vergnügt zu sein.
Budget hotels used to be sleazy places.
Billighotels pflegten verkommene Etablissements zu sein / waren früher ...

Frageform und verneinte Form werden meistens wie folgt gebildet:

She used to live here, didn't she? *Sie hat (doch) früher hier gewohnt, nicht wahr?*
Did(n't) she use to live here? *Hat sie (nicht) früher hier gewohnt?*
She didn't use to live here. *Sie hat hier früher nicht gewohnt.*

Das Hilfsverb *used (to)* darf nicht mit dem Adjektiv *used (to)* verwechselt werden:
They're now used to having two incomes.
Sie sind jetzt daran gewöhnt, zwei Einkommen zu haben.

Frageanhängsel (Bestätigungsfragen, question tags)

45 Positiv – negativ und umgekehrt

It was a completely different kind of room then, wasn't it?
Damals war es eine völlig andere Art von Raum, nicht wahr?
It wasn't the same kind of room then, was it?
Damals war es nicht die gleiche Art von Raum, oder?

You think we should move the TV into the kitchen, don't you?
Du meinst, wir sollten den Fernseher in die Küche stellen, nicht wahr?
You don't think we should move the TV into the kitchen, do you?
Du meinst (doch) nicht, daß wir den Fernseher in die Küche stellen sollten, oder?

Sie erkennen die Regel: Einem positiven Vorderteil folgt ein negatives Anhängsel und umgekehrt.

46 Positiv – positiv

a. It's getting more expensive, is it? *Es wird also teurer(, was/hm)?*

---

b. It's getting more expensive, isn't it? *Es wird teurer, nicht wahr?*
c. It isn't getting more expensive, is it? *Es wird doch nicht teurer, oder?*

Satz (a) „positiv – positiv“ entspricht nicht der in 45 beobachteten Regel, daß auf ein positives Vorderteil ein negatives Anhängsel und auf ein negatives Vorderteil ein positives Anhängsel folgt.
Diese Variante (a) „positiv – positiv“ ist seltener als die Konstruktionen „positiv – negativ“ (b) und „negativ – positiv“ (c). Sie drückt hier aus, daß der Sprecher das Ausgesagte aus dem vorher Gesagten schließt und eine Bestätigung seiner Aussage erwartet. Die Form „positiv – negativ“ (b) dagegen wäre gebraucht worden, wenn der Sprecher das Ausgesagte bereits gewußt, also nicht aus dem vorher Gesagten geschlossen hätte.

47 *Do* und *so/nor/neither* als Stellvertreter

Accidents happen, and when they do (= when they “happen”), it can make all the difference whether you know exactly what to do.
Unfälle passieren nun einmal, und wenn sie es tun ...

I wish we'd given as much thought to the sitting room as we did (= as we “gave”) to planning the kitchen. *Ich wünschte, wir hätten uns beim Wohnzimmer soviel Gedanken gemacht wie bei der Planung der Küche.*

I suppose I got ahead faster than I would have done (= than I would have “got ahead”) without my school English.
Ich bin wohl schneller vorangekommen, als ich es ohne mein Schulenglisch wäre.

Die Beispiele zeigen, wie ein verbaler Ausdruck durch eine Form von *do* wieder aufgenommen werden kann. Die eingeklammerten Umschreibungen deuten jeweils an, wofür *do* stellvertretend steht; sie sind keine idiomatisch gleichwertigen Alternativen.

In dem folgenden Satz steht stellvertretendes *do* in Verbindung mit rückweisendem *so*:

Of course some older drivers have problems, but so do individuals in the other age groups (= inviduals in the other age groups have problems too).
Natürlich haben manche älteren Fahrer Probleme, aber Angehörige der anderen Altersgruppen haben sie auch.

Wird statt auf einen bejahten auf einen verneinten Sachverhalt bestätigend zurückverwiesen, so steht statt *so* entweder *nor* oder *neither*:

Of course the older drivers don't have this problem, but nor/neither do individuals in the other age groups (= individuals in the other age groups don't have this problem either). *Natürlich haben die älteren Fahrer dieses Problem nicht, aber Angehörige der anderen Altersgruppen haben es auch nicht.*

48 Gebräuchliche Kurzformen

aren't = are not
can't = cannot
couldn't = could not
didn't = did not
doesn't = does not
don't = do not
hadn't = had not
hasn't = has not
haven't = have not
he'd = he would/had
he'll = he will
here's = here is
he's = he is/has
I'd = I would/had
I'll = I will/shall
I'm = I am
isn't = is not
it'd = it would/had
it'll = it will
it's = it is/has
I've = I have
let's = let us
mightn't = might not
mustn't = must not
needn't = need not
oughtn't = ought not
shan't = shall not
she'd = she would/had
she'll = she will
she's = she is/has
shouldn't = should not
that's = that is/has
there's = there is/has
they'd = they would/had
they'll = they will
they're = they are
they've = they have
use(d)n't = used not
wasn't = was not
we'd = we would/had
we'll = we will/shall
we're = we are
weren't = were not
we've = we have
what's = what is/has
where's = where is/has
who's = who is/has
won't = will not
wouldn't = would not
you'd = you would/had
you'll = you will
you're = you are
you've = you have

Infinite Verbformen (*to*-Infinitiv, -*ing*-Form und -*ed*-Partizip)

49 *To*-Infinitiv und -*ing*-Form nach Kettenausdrücken

Als Kettenausdrücke bezeichnen wir Wörter, an die ein Verb angehängt werden kann. Der Kettenausdruck kann ein Verb (a, d, e), ein Substantiv (b, f) oder ein Adjektiv (c, g) sein. Das angehängte Verb ist in den meisten Fällen ein *to*-Infinitiv (a–c) oder eine -*ing*-Form (d–g); ist es eine -*ing*-Form, so steht sie entweder allein (d) oder nach einer Präposition (e–g).

a. Kettenverb + *to*-Infinitiv:

He had/helped/managed/tried/wanted to bring the car to a halt.

b. Kettensubstantiv + *to*-Infinitiv:

There was no chance/opportunity to do it. It's the only way to do it.

c. Kettenadjektiv + *to*-Infinitiv:

They're bound/due/forced/unable to leave the area.

d. Kettenverb + -*ing*-Form:

I'd consider/enjoy/miss seeing her.

e. Kettenverb + Präposition + -*ing*-Form:

I wouldn't look forward to / dream of / feel like going there.

f. Kettensubstantiv + Präposition + -*ing*-Form:

He gave the impression of / He had a reputation for being very selfish.

g. Kettenadjektiv + Präposition + -*ing*-Form:

She says she's bad at / good at / sick of / used to saying no.

50 *To*-Infinitiv nach Fragewort (*what, who, when, how* etc.)

We didn't know what to expect.
Wir wußten nicht, „was wir erwarten sollten" / was auf uns zukam.

She demonstrated how to use the oxygen masks.
Sie zeigte, wie man die Sauerstoffmasken benutzt.

51 *To*-Infinitiv nach *for*-Konstruktion

The plan was for up to 25 cars to race along the motorway.
Der Plan sah vor, daß bis zu 25 Wagen die Autobahn entlangrasen sollten.
I could arrange for you to stay on till three o'clock free of charge.
Ich könnte es einrichten, daß Sie das Zimmer bis drei Uhr kostenlos behalten.

I think it's a very good idea for mothers to work.
Ich finde es sehr gut, wenn Mütter arbeiten (gehen).
In the US it's nothing unusual for a boy around the age of twelve to get his first shotgun and learn how to handle it.
In den USA ist es keineswegs ungewöhnlich, wenn ein Junge mit etwa zwölf Jahren seine erste Schrotflinte bekommt und lernt, wie man damit umgeht.

52 *To*-Infinitiv nach Verb + Objekt

a. Anything that forces a person to react is stress.
Alles, was einen Menschen zwingt zu reagieren, ist Streß.
b. They require drivers over 65 to take periodic tests.
Sie verlangen von Autofahrern über 65, daß sie sich regelmäßig testen lassen.
c. They just tell you to hang around and listen to the announcements.
Die sagen einem bloß, man soll warten und auf die Ansagen achten.
d. Many Americans want all older motorists to be tested regularly.
Viele Amerikaner wollen, daß sich alle älteren Kraftfahrer regelmäßig testen lassen.

Für diese im Englischen häufige Konstruktion gibt es im Deutschen nur selten – etwa wie in (a) – eine direkte Entsprechung. Besonders ungewöhnlich klingt sie für das deutsche Sprachempfinden bei einem Verb wie *want* (d), ist aber gerade hier im Englischen sehr häufig: What do you want me to do? *„Was willst du, daß ich tue?" / Was soll ich tun?* You don't want me to tell her that, do you? *Du willst doch nicht, daß ich ihr das sage, oder?*

53 *To*-Infinitiv nach passiven Verben

He is expected to be back in about a fortnight.
Er wird in etwa vierzehn Tagen zurück erwartet.
He is said to be comfortable. *Es soll ihm (den Umständen entsprechend) gut gehen.*
People over 65 are required to take periodic tests.
Von Personen über 65 wird verlangt, daß sie sich regelmäßig testen lassen.

54 -*ing*-Form nach Präpositionen

They're used to having two incomes. *Sie sind gewöhnt, zwei Einkommen zu haben.*
He has shocked the BBC by quitting. *„Er hat die BBC durch sein Kündigen geschockt."*
Thank you for calling. *„Danke fürs Anrufen."*

Ein auf eine Präposition folgendes Verb kann nur in der -*ing*-Form (nicht – wie im Deutschen – im Infinitiv) stehen. Vergleichen Sie: *He left without paying. = Er ging, ohne zu zahlen.*

55 -*ing*-Form als Subjekt und Objekt

Als Subjekt:
Flying is not the long-term answer for Steve.
Das Fliegen ist für Steve keine langfristige Lösung.
Avoiding the Wimbledon area is no bad thing.
„Ein Vermeiden der Gegend um Wimbledon ist kein Fehler."

Als Objekt:
I enjoy flying. *„Ich genieße das Fliegen."*
I miss being at home. *„Ich vermisse das Zuhausesein."*
He's considering changing his role. *„Er erwägt ein Verändern seiner Rolle."*

56 *To*-Infinitiv in relativsatzähnlicher Funktion

We are seeking aggressive, career-minded salespeople to join (≈ who could/would join) our expanding sales force in West Germany…
Wir suchen … Vertreter für unseren expandierenden Außendienst …

With no one to take (≈ who could take) surgery at his rural practice in Scotland, the doctor did the only thing he could … *Da er niemanden hatte, der in seiner schottischen Landpraxis die Sprechstunde übernehmen konnte …*

There is nothing to replenish (≈ with which one can/could replenish) the rapidly diminishing stocks.
Es ist nichts da, womit man die sich rasch vermindernden Vorräte ergänzen könnte.
The only thing left to do (≈ that one can do) is pray.
Das einzige, was man noch tun kann, ist beten.

Dieser eigentümliche Gebrauch des *to*-Infinitivs läßt sich nur unvollkommen durch eine andere Form ersetzen (daher das ≈) und hat auch keine direkte deutsche Entsprechung.

57 *-ing*-Form in relativsatzähnlicher Funktion

The number of people attending services (= who attend / are attending services) is dwindling. *Die Zahl der (Menschen, die an den Gottesdiensten teilnehmen) Gottesdienstbesucher geht zurück.*
People suffering from stress (= who suffer / are suffering from stress) must learn not to take things too seriously.
Menschen, die unter Streß leiden, müssen lernen, die Dinge nicht so ernst zu nehmen.

58 *-ed*-Partizip in relativsatzähnlicher Funktion

One patient in five does not pick up medicine prescribed by the doctor (= which is / has been / was prescribed by the doctor).
Jeder fünfte Patient holt vom Arzt verschriebene Medikamente nicht ab.

A mild winter followed (= which was followed) by a rainless spring drained the moisture from the soil. *Ein milder Winter, auf den ein regenloser Frühling folgte …*

59 *To*-Infinitiv in adverbialer Funktion

They went out to bring the boxes back in.
Sie gingen raus, um die Kartons wieder reinzubringen.
The car in front of him had stopped to make a left turn.
Der Wagen vor ihm hatte angehalten, um links abzubiegen.
A tiebreak is often played to decide the set.
Oft spielt man einen Tie-Break, um den Satz zu entscheiden.

I always take my umbrella – just to be on the safe side.
... um sicherzugehen / um auf Nummer Sicher zu gehen / für alle Fälle.
I was dumb enough not to see how he was doing it.
Ich war „blöd genug, nicht zu sehen, wie er es machte".
To think of those poor people, and the animals ...
Wenn man an die armen Menschen denkt und die Tiere ...

60 *-ing*-Form in adverbialer Funktion

Facing financial ruin, farmers are selling livestock ...
Vor dem Ruin stehend / Dem Ruin nahe, verkaufen die Bauern Vieh ...

Being at home you've got no deadlines any more.
Dadurch, daß man zu Hause ist, hat man keine Termine mehr.
Noticing that his canoe was missing, he jumped into an old, leaky rowboat.
Da/Als er sah, daß sein Kanu nicht da war, sprang er in ein altes, leckes Ruderboot.

Mike Bratton was alone in the house watching TV.
Mike Bratton war allein zu Hause und sah fern.
They drive up and down through country villages making this horrible noise.
Sie fahren durch kleine Dörfer und machen dabei diesen scheußlichen Lärm.
I feel very safe flying. *Ich fühle mich vollkommen sicher, wenn ich fliege.*

... even if it means leaving Dad at home watching his rehashed sport on TV.
... auch wenn das bedeutet, daß man Papi zu Hause läßt, wo er sich im Fernsehen seinen wiederaufgewärmten Sport ansehen kann.

With the US population getting older, the percentage of older motorists is rising.
Da die US-Bevölkerung älter wird, nimmt auch die Zahl der älteren Autofahrer prozentual zu. / Das Durchschnittsalter der amerikanischen Bevölkerung steigt, und mit ihm nimmt auch der Anteil älterer Kraftfahrer zu.

61 *-ed*-Partizip in adverbialer Funktion

When asked why you're leaving your present job, don't mention any problems you may have had with your previous employer.
Wenn Sie gefragt werden, warum Sie Ihren jetzigen Arbeitsplatz verlassen ...
Asked the main reason for their plight, 21 per cent cited family conflicts, while half named economic factors. *Nach dem Hauptgrund für ihre Notlage gefragt, führten 21 Prozent familiäre Probleme an ...*

Relativsätze

62 Relativsatz ohne Relativpronomen (Kontaktkonstruktion)

She knows a lot about the things (which/that) she sells.
Sie weiß eine Menge über die Dinge, die sie verkauft.
The stage is something (which/that) I've been keen on for a long time.
Die Bühne ist etwas, wofür ich mich schon lange begeistere.

Das Relativpronomen kann wegfallen, wenn es in Objektposition steht. Besser als diese recht abstrakte Regel sagt Ihnen bei hinreichender Spracherfahrung Ihr Gefühl, wann Sie das Relativpronomen weglassen können und wann nicht. Bei den folgenden Relativsätzen zum Beispiel ist die Kontaktkonstruktion nicht möglich:

You find a lot of salesgirls who are haughty and unsympathetic.
Even in places which escape the showers it will remain rather cloudy.
We never hear about the flights that go well.

63 Definierende und nichtdefinierende Relativsätze

a. Mr Burstock's land will be used to build low-priced houses for young couples whose parents live in the village.
... für junge Ehepaare, deren Eltern im Dorf wohnen.

b. Mr Burstock, whose family has lived in the village for 170 years, is sad to see young people being forced to leave the area.
Mr Burstock, dessen Familie seit 170 Jahren in dem Dorf ansässig ist ...

In Satz (a) kann auf den Relativsatz nicht verzichtet werden, wenn deutlich werden soll, um was für *young couples* es sich handelt. (Ohne den Relativsatz könnte man z. B. meinen, daß die *low-priced houses* auch ortsfremden Yuppie-Ehepaaren zur Verfügung stehen.) Der Relativsatz hat also eine definierende Funktion, er ist zum Verständnis der von ihm näher bestimmten Substantivphrase *young couples* unentbehrlich.
In Satz (b) wird der Relativsatz nicht zum Definieren von *Mr Burstock* benötigt, er könnte wegfallen, ist entbehrlich. Die in ihm enthaltene Information könnte genausogut in einem getrennten Satz gegeben werden.

Der Relativsatz in (a) ist definierend; er wird nicht durch Sprechpause(n) bzw. Komma(s) abgesetzt.
Der Relativsatz in (b) ist nichtdefinierend; er wird beim Sprechen durch Pause(n) und beim Schreiben durch Komma(s) abgetrennt.
Nichtdefinierende Relativsätze (b) sind fast ganz auf die Schriftsprache beschränkt; definierende (a) finden sich außer im geschriebenen auch häufig im gesprochenen Englisch.

Bedingungssätze

64 Grundtypen 1–3

Typ 1: If I miss the helicopter, I won't make my flight.
Wenn ich den Hubschrauber verpasse, schaffe ich meinen Flug nicht.

Typ 2: If I missed the helicopter, I wouldn't make my flight.
Wenn ich den Hubschrauber verpaßte, würde ich meinen Flug nicht schaffen.

Typ 3: If I had missed the helicopter, I wouldn't have made my flight.
Wenn ich den Hubschrauber verpaßt hätte, („würde ich meinen Flug nicht geschafft haben") hätte ich meinen Flug nicht geschafft.

65 Typ 3

Für Englischlernende besonders schwierig ist Typ 3. Weitere Beispiele für diesen Typ:

The boy would have been in danger if he hadn't had the gun.
Der Junge wäre in Gefahr gewesen, wenn er das Gewehr nicht gehabt hätte.
Peters wouldn't have hesitated even if he'd (= he had) known that the man had taken his canoe. *Peters hätte auch dann nicht gezögert, wenn er gewußt hätte, daß der Mann sein Kanu gestohlen hatte.*

Auch der nächste Satz folgt diesem Muster, allerdings nicht mit *would*, sondern mit *might*:

The boy might have been in greater danger if he hadn't had the gun.
Der Junge wäre vielleicht in größerer Gefahr gewesen, wenn er das Gewehr nicht gehabt hätte.

66 Mischtypen

Die folgenden Beispiele illustrieren die häufig vorkommende Mischung von Typ 3 (*if*-Satz) und 2 (Hauptsatz):

(Typ 3:) If we hadn't gone charter, (Typ 2:) we wouldn't be in this mess.
Wenn wir nicht Charter gebucht hätten, wären wir nicht in diesem Schlamassel
(Typ 2:) The burglars would still be alive (Typ 3:) if the boy hadn't had a gun.
Die Einbrecher wären noch am Leben, wenn der Junge kein Gewehr gehabt hätte.

Indirekte Rede

67 Normalfall: Mit Zeitverschiebung

Direkte Rede:
"Thousands of bridges have a design similar to the one that collapsed."
Indirekte Rede:
The expert said (that) thousands of bridges had a design similar to the one that collapsed. *Der Experte sagte, Tausende von Brücken hätten eine ähnliche Konstruktion wie die eingestürzte.*

Direkte Rede:
"The bridge will collapse."
Indirekte Rede:
Inspectors feared (that) the bridge would collapse.
Prüfer befürchteten, daß die Brücke einstürzen würde.

Beachten Sie in der indirekten Rede die Zeitverschiebung gegenüber der direkten Rede. Steht das Berichtsverb wie hier in der Vergangenheit (*said*, *feared*), so „rutscht" das Verb des berichteten Satzes um eine Zeitstufe in die Vergangenheit: *have* → *had*, *will* → *would* etc. Weitere Beispiele:

"The men are dead." – Later he learned that the men were dead.
"87 per cent (have) once held a job." – A survey of 1,000 homeless people found that 87 per cent had once held a job.

68 Sonderfall: Ohne Zeitverschiebung

Steht das Verb der direkten Rede in der Vergangenheit, so kann die Zeitverschiebung unterbleiben, sofern ein Mißverstehen der zeitlichen Beziehungen ausgeschlossen ist (vgl. 27):

Direkte Rede: "It was a nice ride."
Indirekte Rede nach der „Verschiebungsregel" eigentlich:
He said it had been a nice ride.
Die Aussage ist im Textzusammenhang aber auch ohne Zeitverschiebung nicht mißzuverstehen:
He said it was a nice ride.

Betonung, Verstärkung, Hervorhebung bewirkende Wörter und Strukturen

69 Betonendes *do*

Accidents do happen. *Unfälle passieren nun einmal.*
He does seem to know about it. *Er scheint tatsächlich/wirklich davon zu wissen.*
Well, I did start from the beginning, actually.
(Etwa:) Na ja, an sich habe ich tatsächlich von vorne angefangen.

70 Betonende *-self*-Pronomen (vgl. 9)

I only just arrived myself. *Ich bin selber gerade erst gekommen.*
Can't you do it yourself? *Kannst du es nicht selber machen?*

71 Verstärkende Adverbien

It was a completely different kind of place then. ... *ein völlig anderer Ort.*
It really gets to me. *Das nervt/wurmt mich vielleicht.*
I thoroughly enjoyed my stay. *Ich habe meinen Aufenthalt sehr genossen.*
I sure didn't realize it. *(AE) Ich habe es wirklich nicht gemerkt.*
You know damn well what I mean. *Du weißt doch ganz genau, was ich meine.*
Thank you very much indeed. *Vielen herzlichen Dank.*

72 *So* oder *such*

She's so friendly and helpful. *Sie ist (ja) so freundlich und hilfsbereit.*
She's got such enthusiasm. *Sie ist so voller Begeisterung.*

73 Besondere Wortstellung

(Normal betont:) We must really get together one of these days.
(Stärker betont:) We really must get together one of these days.

74 Einleitendes *it is / it was* und Relativsatz

It was you who told me that. *Du warst es doch, der mir das gesagt hat.*
It was you who put Debbie's name up for the competition.
Sie waren es doch, die Debbie für den Wettbewerb vorgeschlagen hat.

75 Ausrufesatz

Isn't it awful! *Ist das nicht furchtbar!*
What a nightmare! *Was für ein Alptraum!*

Wortstellung

76 Stellung des Objekts bei zusammengesetzten Verben (phrasal verbs)

a. Why didn't you pick up the medicine?
b. Why didn't you pick up the medicine Dr Day prescribed for your cough?

---

c. Why didn't you pick the medicine up?
d. Why didn't you pick it up?

Zusammengesetzte Verben sind z. B. *bring up, point out, sell off, take over, write down.* Haben sie – wie *pick up (= abholen)* in den Beispielen a–d – ein Objekt, so kann dieses grundsätzlich auf das Verb folgen (a–b) oder vom Verb „eingerahmt" sein (c–d). Dabei sind folgende Gesetzmäßigkeiten zu beobachten:
Ist das Objekt sehr lang (b), so verbietet sich die „Einrahmung".
Ist das Objekt ein Personalpronomen (d), so wird es immer „eingerahmt".
Ein kurzes Objekt wie *the medicine* erlaubt beide Stellungen (a und c), je nachdem ob das Objekt *the medicine* (a) oder das Verb *pick up* (c) betont werden soll:
a. = *Warum hast du die Arznei nicht abgeholt?*
c. = *Warum hast du die Arznei nicht abgeholt?*

77 Wortstellung im Zwischen- oder Nachsatz zu direkter Rede

"The effect on the place is immediate," she says.
"The effect on the place is immediate," says Mrs Moore.

"This is the worst drought I've ever seen," he says.
"This is the worst drought I've ever seen," says a farmer.

Grundregel für die Stellung:
Subjekt – Verb, wenn das Subjekt ein Pronomen (hier: *she, he*) ist.
Verb – Subjekt, wenn das Subjekt substantivisch (hier: *Mrs Moore, a farmer*) ist.

Schreibung

78 Bedeutungen der Endung *-'s*

-'s = Genitiv-Endung:	The landlady's dog is very friendly.
-'s = *is*:	The landlady's very friendly.
-'s = *has*:	The landlady's got a very friendly dog.
-'s = *us*:	Let's go to Buckingham Palace first.

79 Genitivendung: *-'s* oder *-s'*?

Singular:	the youngster's friends	*die Freunde des Jugendlichen*
Plural:	the youngsters' friends	*die Freunde der Jugendlichen*
Singular:	our neighbour's house	*das Haus unseres Nachbarn*
Plural:	our neighbours' house	*das Haus unserer Nachbarn*
Singular:	it's a minute's walk	*es ist eine Minute zu Fuß*
Plural:	it's a few minutes' walk	*es ist ein paar Minuten zu Fuß*

80 Großschreibung

an airline spokesman – a British Airways spokesman
the southern states – the (United) States (of America)
a post office (= *ein Postamt*) – the Post Office (= *die Postbehörde/„Bundespost“*)
there have been two world wars – the Second World War
she's a shop assistant – she's Shop Assistant of the Year
a day in (the) summer – a Saturday in June
a local cinema owner – a British cinema owner

Namen und namenähnliche Bezeichnungen im weitesten Sinn werden im Englischen groß geschrieben. Abweichend vom Deutschen werden auch von Namen abgeleitete Adjektive (*Britain – British, Europe – European* etc.) groß geschrieben.
Bei Grenzfällen schwankt die Schreibweise, je nachdem ob die Vorstellung „Name“ oder „normales Substantiv“ überwiegt: *Are you coming by Tube/tube? He doesn't like Yuppies/yuppies. It's somewhere in the South/south of England. Where's Dad/dad?*
Gern wird Großschreibung auch zur Heraushebung bzw. zur Betonung des „Institutionscharakters“ benutzt:

We are seeking aggressive, career-minded Sales People to join our expanding sales force in West Germany.
The Management and the Staff of the Royal Hotel welcome you and hope you will enjoy your stay.
If you wish to extend your stay, please give our Reception as much notice as possible.
Any loss will have to be borne by the passenger, with possible reimbursement under certain circumstances because of Delay Insurance Cover.

81 Gebrauch des Bindestrichs

adult-education classes	*aber:* classes in adult education
a remote–control TV	*aber:* a TV with remote control

a limited-service hotel	*aber:* a hotel with limited service
a lake-shore home	*aber:* a house on a/the lake shore
clay-pigeon shooting	*aber:* shooting at clay pigeons
a one-church town	*aber:* a town with one church
an eleven-year-old boy	*aber:* a boy of eleven years

Werden Wortzusammensetzungen wie *adult education* oder *clay pigeon* gleich einem Adjektiv vor ein Substantiv gestellt, so werden sie bei sorgfältiger Schreibweise durch einen Bindestrich verbunden.

Auch zusammengesetzte Adjektive wie die folgenden werden in aller Regel mit Bindestrich geschrieben:

long-haul long-term low-priced paper-thin tax-free

Bei vielen Wortzusammensetzungen schwankt auch der sorgfältige Sprachgebrauch zwischen Bindestrichsetzung und Zusammenschreibung:

a clear-out / a clearout
car-pooling / carpooling (car pooling *wäre ebenfalls richtig*)
non-alignment / nonalignment
over-confident / overconfident
a thank-you letter / a thankyou letter

Bei ausgeschriebenen Bruchzahlen ist die Schreibung mit Bindestrich üblich (beachten Sie allerdings die Ausnahme):

two-thirds three-quarters one-sixth one-twentieth
(*Aber wenn eine der beiden Zahlen bereits einen Bindestrich enthält, entfällt der Bindestrich zwischen Zähler und Nenner:*)
one twenty-third two twenty-fifths twenty-one forty-eighths

82 Abkürzungen

Abkürzungen wie die folgenden werden im britischen Englisch in der Regel ohne und im amerikanischen Englisch in der Regel mit Punkt geschrieben:

BE:	Mr	Mrs	Ms	Dr	St	Rd
AE:	Mr.	Mrs.	Ms.	Dr.	St.	Rd.

Großer Abschlußtest

Anhand der folgenden 64 Testaufgaben können Sie überprüfen, inwieweit Sie knifflige Details aus den Texten dieses Lehrbuches im Gedächtnis behalten haben. Eine Aussage über Ihre praktische Sprachbeherrschung macht das Testergebnis nicht. Mit anderen Worten: Es kann sein, daß Sie gut Englisch verstehen und sich wirksam auf englisch ausdrücken können und trotzdem im Test viele Fehler machen. Sehen Sie den Test also als eine sportliche Herausforderung an, bei deren Bewältigung Sie „Aha-Erlebnisse" haben, durch die Sie Ihr Englisch in einigen Feinheiten noch weiter verbessern können.
Wenn Sie die Lösung zu wissen glauben, kreuzen Sie bitte (a) oder (b) an. Durch die Antwortmöglichkeit (c) soll verhindert werden, daß Sie die Aussagekraft des Tests durch Raten ungewollt verfälschen.
Der Schlüssel ist auf Seite 218. Bei den Lösungen finden Sie Hinweise auf die Stellen im Buch, wo die betreffende Spracherscheinung vorkommt bzw. erklärt ist.

1. The police . . . . . there within five minutes.

- ☐ a. was
- ☐ b. were
- ☐ c. *Don't know.*

2. The United States . . . . . have an established church.

- ☐ a. doesn't
- ☐ b. don't
- ☐ c. *Don't know.*

3. The number of people attending services . . . . . dwindling.

- ☐ a. are
- ☐ b. is
- ☐ c. *Don't know.*

4. It . . . . . usually the children who suffer.

- ☐ a. are
- ☐ b. is
- ☐ c. *Don't know.*

5. The fare was five . . . . . ten.

- ☐ a. dollar
- ☐ b. dollars
- ☐ c. *Don't know.*

6. It'll cost about 250 . . . . . dollars to repair the bridge.

- ☐ a. million
- ☐ b. millions of
- ☐ c. *Don't know.*

7. Hensley, a former trucker, is one of New York's . . . . . thousands of homeless.

- ☐ a. ten
- ☐ b. tens of
- ☐ c. *Don't know.*

8. She didn't play in the . . . . . doubles this year.

- ☐ a. woman's
- ☐ b. women's
- ☐ c. *Don't know.*

9. The M25 is the . . . . . motorway around London.

- ☐ a. 117-mile
- ☐ b. 117 miles
- ☐ c. *Don't know.*

10. He wants to become . . . . .

- ☐ a. actor
- ☐ b. an actor
- ☐ c. *Don't know.*

11. You don't think we should move . . . . . into the kitchen, do you?

- ☐ a. television
- ☐ b. the television
- ☐ c. *Don't know.*

12. Traffic was so slow – I had to drive in . . . . . gear most of the time.
- ☐ a. first
- ☐ b. the first
- ☐ c. *Don't know.*

13. If you don't take out . . . . . , you'll be completely unprotected.
- ☐ a. an insurance
- ☐ b. insurance
- ☐ c. *Don't know.*

14. The pilot managed to bring the plane to . . . . . halt.
- ☐ a. a
- ☐ b. the
- ☐ c. *Don't know.*

15. I hope there weren't . . . . . problems.
- ☐ a. any
- ☐ b. some
- ☐ c. *Don't know.*

16. Gatwick is Britain's . . . . . holiday airport.
- ☐ a. busiest
- ☐ b. most busy
- ☐ c. *Don't know.*

17. On the whole, I think older drivers drive more . . . . . than young people.
- ☐ a. responsible
- ☐ b. responsibly
- ☐ c. *Don't know.*

18. You can't hold the tour operator . . . . . if there's a delay.
- ☐ a. responsible
- ☐ b. responsibly
- ☐ c. *Don't know.*

19. I suspect there are millions who can't read . . . . .

- ☐ a. proper
- ☐ b. properly
- ☐ c. *Don't know.*

20. Don't you think the recording sounds rather . . . . . ?

- ☐ a. unnatural
- ☐ b. unnaturally
- ☐ c. *Don't know.*

21. The scheduled flights are all . . . . . on time.

- ☐ a. dead
- ☐ b. deadly
- ☐ c. *Don't know.*

22. Try not to take things too . . . . .

- ☐ a. serious
- ☐ b. seriously
- ☐ c. *Don't know.*

23. The first Wimbledon championship . . . . . held in 1877.

- ☐ a. has been
- ☐ b. was
- ☐ c. *Don't know.*

24. He's . . . . . for years – he's a very competent driver.

- ☐ a. driven
- ☐ b. driving
- ☐ c. *Don't know.*

25. . . . . . feeling terrible for some time.

- ☐ a. I'm
- ☐ b. I've been
- ☐ c. *Don't know.*

26. How long . . . . . waiting now?
- ☐ a. are we
- ☐ b. have we been
- ☐ c. *Don't know.*

27. . . . . . working here in London for the last couple of years.
- ☐ a. I'm
- ☐ b. I've been
- ☐ c. *Don't know.*

28. She . . . . . ill with flu for the past week.
- ☐ a. has been
- ☐ b. was
- ☐ c. *Don't know.*

29. Farmers are selling livestock in the hope that the extra income will help to see them through until the rain . . . . .
- ☐ a. comes
- ☐ b. will come
- ☐ c. *Don't know.*

30. I wish the weather . . . . . clear up.
- ☐ a. will
- ☐ b. would
- ☐ c. *Don't know.*

31. I don't think the child . . . . . if we had that sort of arrangement.
- ☐ a. suffered
- ☐ b. would suffer
- ☐ c. *Don't know.*

32. If I had the choice, ... to the theatre.
- ☐ a. I'd go
- ☐ b. I went
- ☐ c. *Don't know.*

33. I wouldn't have hesitated even if . . . . . known that.

- ☐ a. I'd
- ☐ b. I would've
- ☐ c. *Don't know.*

34. People wouldn't go on the beaches even if . . . . . open.

- ☐ a. they were
- ☐ b. they'd be
- ☐ c. *Don't know.*

35. If we hadn't gone charter, we . . . . . in this mess.

- ☐ a. weren't
- ☐ b. wouldn't be
- ☐ c. *Don't know.*

36. At midday they said . . . . . fly at three.

- ☐ a. we'd
- ☐ b. we'll
- ☐ c. *Don't know.*

37. He realized too late that the car in front of him . . . . . stopped.

- ☐ a. had
- ☐ b. has
- ☐ c. *Don't know.*

38. The police suspected that theft . . . . . the motive.

- ☐ a. is
- ☐ b. was
- ☐ c. *Don't know.*

39. Is there anything worth . . . . . ?

- ☐ a. seeing
- ☐ b. to be seen
- ☐ c. *Don't know.*

40. She usually avoids . . . . . a spade a spade.
- ☐ a. calling
- ☐ b. to call
- ☐ c. *Don't know.*

41. I wasn't actually planning . . . . . anything.
- ☐ a. buying
- ☐ b. to buy
- ☐ c. *Don't know.*

42. He's considering . . . . . his job.
- ☐ a. changing
- ☐ b. to change
- ☐ c. *Don't know.*

43. Instead . . . . . "no", she said "I'll think about it".
- ☐ a. of saying
- ☐ b. to say
- ☐ c. *Don't know.*

44. They're used to . . . . . two incomes.
- ☐ a. have
- ☐ b. having
- ☐ c. *Don't know.*

45. How did you manage . . . . . English so well?
- ☐ a. learning
- ☐ b. to learn
- ☐ c. *Don't know.*

46. I'm looking forward to . . . . . you tomorrow.
- ☐ a. see
- ☐ b. seeing
- ☐ c. *Don't know.*

47. I wish we'd given as much thought to the sitting room as we did to . . . . . the kitchen.

- ☐ a. plan
- ☐ b. planning
- ☐ c. *Don't know.*

48. My parents would never have dreamed . . . . . in the kitchen.

- ☐ a. of entertaining
- ☐ b. to entertain
- ☐ c. *Don't know.*

49. The enormous holdups are . . . . . caused by air controllers striking in several countries.

- ☐ a. been
- ☐ b. being
- ☐ c. *Don't know.*

50. They want . . . . . tested regularly.

- ☐ a. all older motorists to be
- ☐ b. that all older motorists are
- ☐ c. *Don't know.*

51. About what time d'you think . . . . . arriving?

- ☐ a. will you be
- ☐ b. you'll be
- ☐ c. *Don't know.*

52. . . . . . the pain at night?

- ☐ a. Do you have
- ☐ b. Have you got
- ☐ c. *Don't know.*

53. Where . . . . . lunch today?

- ☐ a. did you have
- ☐ b. had you
- ☐ c. *Don't know.*

54. That would be illegal and almost certainly . . . . . your disadvantage.
- ☐ a. at
- ☐ b. to
- ☐ c. *Don't know.*

55. You can ring me . . . . . 327 4065 at any time between nine and five.
- ☐ a. on
- ☐ b. under
- ☐ c. *Don't know.*

56. Mr Burstock's been a school governor . . . . . over 30 years.
- ☐ a. for
- ☐ b. since
- ☐ c. *Don't know.*

57. Please make sure that you've checked out . . . . . three at the latest.
- ☐ a. by
- ☐ b. till
- ☐ c. *Don't know.*

58. You have to take a test to . . . . . your licence renewed.
- ☐ a. get
- ☐ b. let
- ☐ c. *Don't know.*

59. Any such loss will have to be . . . . . by the passenger.
- ☐ a. born
- ☐ b. borne
- ☐ c. *Don't know.*

60. Public *transit* would be called public . . . . . in British English.
- ☐ a. transport
- ☐ b. transportation
- ☐ c. *Don't know.*

61. If the doctor tells you to *cut down on coffee*, he wants you to . . . . .

☐ a. drink less coffee
☐ b. give coffee up completely
☐ c. *Don't know*.

62. When we talk about *wholesome* food, we mean it's . . . . .

☐ a. good for you
☐ b. organically grown
☐ c. *Don't know*.

63. The agnostic says: . . . . .

☐ a. "I don't know if there is a God."
☐ b. "There is no God."
☐ c. *Don't know*.

64. In the photo below, the word *subway* refers to . . . . .

☐ a. a passageway for pedestrians
☐ b. the London Tube
☐ c. *Don't know*.

Schlüssel zum Großen Abschlußtest

Die Zahlen ohne vorangestelltes G verweisen auf einen Lektionstext, in dem das betreffende Sprachproblem vorkommt. (Beispiel: 20/1 = Lektion 20, Text 1.)
Die Zahlen mit vorangestelltem G beziehen sich auf die Englische Aufbaugrammatik (Seite 178–207). (Beispiel: G2 = Englische Aufbaugrammatik, Abschnitt 2.)

1. b. → 20/1, G2.
2. a. → 24/1, G2.
3. b. → 24/3, G2.
4. b. → 18/3, G2.
5. b. → 11/2, G17.
6. a. → 13/1.
7. b. → 7/3.
8. b. → 25/3, G79.
9. a. → 20/1, G81.
10. b. → 4/3, G5.
11. b. → 7/2, G7.
12. a. → 3/3, G7.
13. b. → 16/3, G7.
14. a. → 1/1, G5.
15. a. → G11.
16. a. → 16/1, G19.
17. b. → 17/3, G20.
18. a. → 16/3, G20.
19. b. → 14/2, G20.
20. a. → 20/2, G20.
21. a. → 16/2.
22. b. → 19/3, G20.
23. b. → 25/3, G24.
24. a. → 17/3, G23.
25. b. → 19/2, G23, G26.
26. b. → 16/2, G23, G26.
27. b. → 5/2, G23, G26.
28. a. → 20/1, G23.
29. a. → 2/3, G28.
30. b. → 2/2, G41.
31. b. → 18/1, G64.
32. a. → 21/1, G64.
33. a. → 12/3, G64, G65.
34. a. → 23/2, G64.
35. b. → 16/2, G66.
36. a. → 16/2, G67.
37. a. → 17/1, G67.
38. b. → 14/1, G67.
39. a. → 21/2, G54.
40. a. → 15/3, G49d.
41. b. → 4/2, G49a.
42. a. → 4/3, G49d.
43. a. → 15/3, G54.
44. b. → 4/1, G54.
45. b. → 15/2, G49a.
46. b. → 5/2, G49e, G54.
47. b. → 7/2, G54.
48. a. → 7/2, G54.
49. b. → 16/1, G29.
50. a. → 17/2, G52.
51. b. → 22/2.
52. a. → 19/2, G32.
53. a. → G32.
54. b. → 11/3.
55. a. → 5/1.
56. a. → 7/1.
57. a. → 10/3.
58. a. → 17/2.
59. b. → 16/3.
60. a. → 3/3.
61. a. → 19/3.
62. a. → 18/2.
63. a. → 24/3.
64. a. → 15/1.

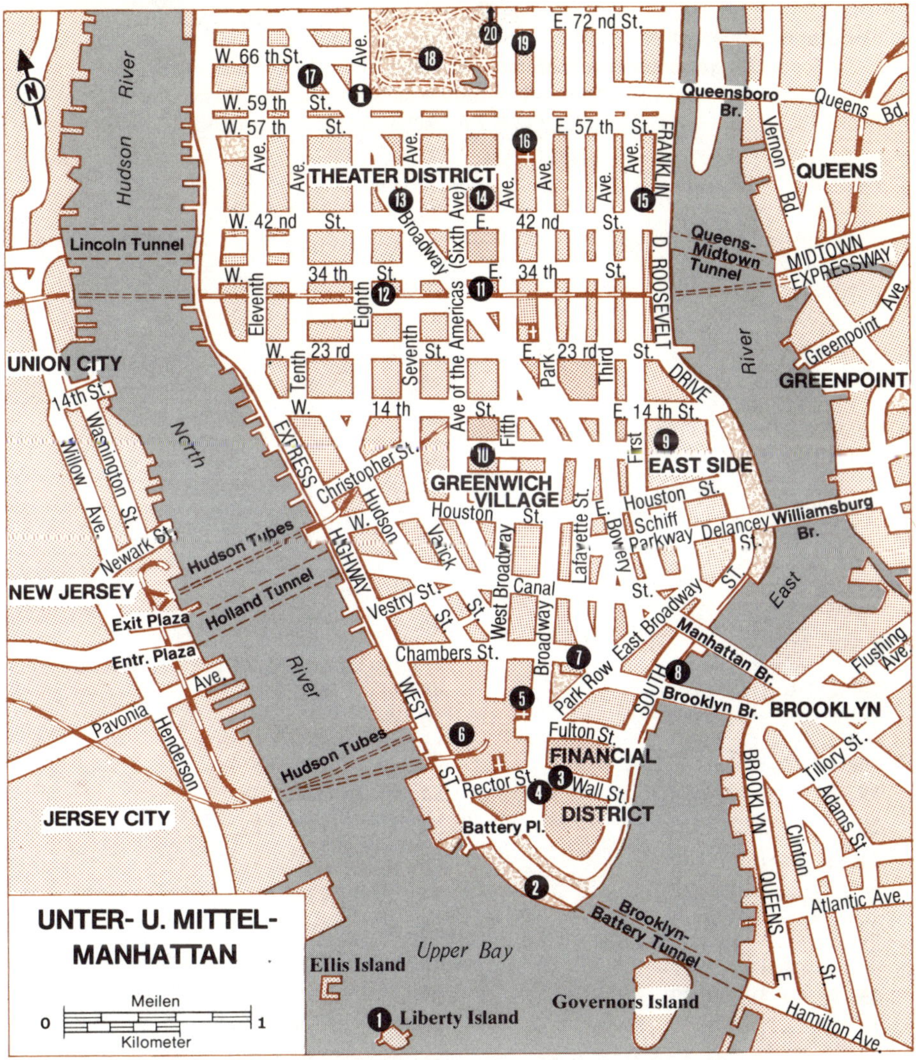

Die einzelnen Positionen auf dieser Karte aus dem Polyglott Welt-Reiseführer (Seite 285):

1 Liberty Island, **2** Battery Park, **3** Wall Street, **4** New York Stock Exchange, **5** St. Paul's Chapel, **6** World Trade Center, **7** City Hall, der Sitz des Bürgermeisters, **8** Brooklyn Bridge, **9** Lower East Side, **10** Washington Square, **11** Empire State Building, **12** Madison Square Garden Center, **13** Times Square, **14** Rockefeller Center, **15** United Nations Headquarters, **16** St. Patrick's Cathedral, **17** Lincoln Center, **18** Central Park, **19** The Frick Collection, **20** Metropolitan Museum of Art.

Grammatikregister

Die Verweise ohne vorangestelltes G beziehen sich jeweils auf den Abschnitt *Erklärungen* der betreffenden Lektion.
Die Verweise mit vorangestelltem G beziehen sich auf den betreffenden Abschnitt der *Englischen Aufbaugrammatik* (Seite 178–207). Beispiele:

9.1 = Lektion 9, Abschnitt 1 der *Erklärungen* (Seite 58).
22 = Lektion 22, *Erklärungen* (Seite 136).
G5 = Englische Aufbaugrammatik, Abschnitt 5 (Seite 180).

Zum Problem der grammatischen Fachausdrücke beachten Sie bitte die Erläuterungen in G1 (Seite 178).

Wortschatzregister

Die Zahlen verweisen auf die Wörterverzeichnisse nach den Texten der Lektionen. Beispiel:

> 9/2 = Lektion 9, Text 2 (Seite 56)

Nach den Stichwörtern steht in eckigen Klammern die Ausspracheangabe in der allgemein gebräuchlichen Internationalen Lautschrift.
Die Zeichen der Lautschrift sind auf der Innenseite des hinteren Buchdeckels erklärt.
Während die Tonaufnahme zur Übung des Hörverstehens auch amerikanische Stimmen und bestimmte regionale Akzente berücksichtigt, beruhen die Lautschriftangaben ausschließlich auf der britischen Standardaussprache.
Durch das Betonungszeichen [ˈ] wird bei mehrsilbigen Ausdrücken die Hauptbetonung angegeben. In der Regel entsprechen die Betonungsangaben den Betonungsverhältnissen in den betreffenden Textstellen. Häufig sind allerdings statt der angegebenen Betonung auch andere Akzentsetzungen denkbar – erstens weil die Betonungsgewohnheiten verschiedener Sprecher voneinander abweichen und zweitens weil je nach Aussageabsicht verschiedene Wörter oder Silben besonders hervorgehoben werden können.
Beispiele für unterschiedliche Betonungsmöglichkeiten:

> *ˈtelevision – teleˈvision*
> *ˈsyringe – syˈringe*
> *the ˈmen's singles and the ˈwomen's singles – the men's ˈsingles and the men's ˈdoubles*
> *he was watching TV in his ˈupstairs room – he went upˈstairs*
> *ˈthank you* – (in der Bedeutung „ich habe zu danken" dagegen:) *thank ˈyou*
> *selling ˈtax-free cars to soldiers – soldiers can get them tax-ˈfree*

Wortschatzregister

ahead [ə'hed] 15/2, 25/2
air [eə] 16/3
air-traffic controller ['eə-træfɪk kən'trəʊlə] 16/1
aircraft ['eəkrɑ:ft] 1/3
airline ['eəlaɪn] 1/1, 4/1
airport ['eəpɔ:t] 11/1, 16/1
airspace ['eəspeɪs] 16/1
alcohol ['ælkəhɒl] 19/3
alcoholism ['ælkəhɒlɪzm] 14/3
alert [ə'lɜ:t] 5/3
alive [ə'laɪv] 12/2
all [ɔ:l] 21/1, 25/2
all over [ɔ:l 'əʊvə] 1/2, 2/2
almost ['ɔ:lməʊst] 3/2, 13/2
although [ɔ:l'ðəʊ] 14/1
always ['ɔ:lweɪz] 4/3
amateur ['æmətə] 25/3
amazing [ə'meɪzɪŋ] 20/2
amount [ə'maʊnt] 19/3
amplifier ['æmplɪfaɪə] 6/2
amplify ['æmplɪfaɪ] 6/2
anchor(wo)man ['æŋkə-] 4/3
anchorperson ['æŋkəpɜ:sn] 4/3
and so on [ænd 'səʊ ɒn] 1/3
angina (pectoris) [æn'dʒaɪnə ('pektərɪs)] 20/1
Anglophile ['æŋgləʊfaɪl] 8/1
angry ['æŋgrɪ] 6/1
animal ['ænɪməl] 2/3
announcement [ə'naʊnsmənt] 16/2
announcer [ə'naʊnsə] 20/2
annoy [ə'nɔɪ] 6/2
annoyance [ə'nɔɪəns] 6/2
answer ['ɑ:nsə] 4/1
antibiotic(s) [æntɪbaɪ'ɒtɪk(s)] 19/1
any good [enɪ 'gʊd] 4/3
any more [enɪ 'mɔ:] 18/1
any time [enɪ 'taɪm] 1/2
anyone ['enɪwʌn] 1/2, 16/1
anything ['enɪθɪŋ] 21/2
apart from [ə'pɑ:t frəm] 6/3, 8/2, 14/1
apartment [ə'pɑ:tmənt] 6/2, 13/2
appear [ə'pɪə] 20/1
appetite ['æpətaɪt] 19/2
applicable ['æplɪkəbl/ə'plɪkəbl] 10/2
application [æplɪ'keɪʃn] 5/3
apply [ə'plaɪ] 5/3
approve [ə'pru:v] 9/1
archbishop ['ɑ:tʃbɪʃəp] 24/1
area ['eərɪə] 3/1, 3/3, 7/1, 9/2, 16/1
argue ['ɑ:gju:] 3/3
arise from [ə'raɪz] 16/3
arithmetic [ə'rɪθmətɪk] 14/2
arm [ɑ:m] 11/3
armed forces [ɑ:md 'fɔ:sɪz] 5/1
around [ə'raʊnd] 11/3, 16/2, 18/3, 21/3
arrange [ə'reɪndʒ] 10/3
arrangement [ə'reɪndʒmənt] 18/1
arrive [ə'raɪv] 13/2, 22/2
artificial [ɑ:tɪ'fɪʃl] 22/3
as [æz/əz] 9/1, 16/1, 21/1
as a matter of fact [æz ə mætər əv 'fækt] 5/2, 21/2
as a result [æz ə rɪ'zʌlt] 21/3
as … as [æz … æz] 10/2
as far as [əz 'fɑ:r əz] 21/2
as well as [əz 'wel əz] 14/2, 20/3
as you please [æz jʊ 'pli:z] 9/1
ashamed [ə'ʃeɪmd] 14/3
Asia ['eɪʃə] 15/1
ask [ɑ:sk] 5/3
assistant [ə'sɪstənt] 4/2
at home [ət 'həʊm] 4/1, 18/2
at last [ət 'lɑ:st] 13/2
at least [ət 'li:st] 17/3, 21/1, 25/2
at the latest [æt ðə 'leɪtɪst] 10/3
at work [ət 'wɜ:k] 19/2
atmosphere ['ætməsfɪə] 6/1, 9/1
attack [ə'tæk] 22/1
attempt [ə'temt] 20/1
attend [ə'tənd] 24/3
attendant [ə'tendənt] 1/3
attention [ə'tenʃn] 1/3
attitude ['ætɪtju:d] 6/2, 24/3
attract [ə'trækt] 8/1, 25/3
audience ['ɔ:djəns] 21/3
au pair [əʊ 'peə] 18/1
Australian [ɒ'streɪljən] 18/2
authorities [ɔ:'θɒrətɪz] 16/1
available [ə'veɪləbl] 11/3, 12/3, 14/2, 21/3
average ['ævərɪdʒ] 7/3, 8/2, 21/3
avoid [ə'vɔɪd] 3/1, 15/3
award [ə'wɔ:d] 8/3, 21/2
aware [ə'weə] 17/3
awful ['ɔ:fl] 1/2, 7/2

B & B ['bi: ən 'bi:] 9/1
baby ['beɪbɪ] 18/1
back [bæk] 5/2, 14/2, 15/2, 16/1
back there [bæk 'ðeə] 3/2
backache ['bækeɪk] 19/3
backhand ['bækhænd] 25/1
bad [bæd] 2/2
badly ['bædlɪ] 19/2
baffle ['bæfl] 14/1
bag [bæg] 11/2
banknote ['bæŋknəʊt] 7/3
banquet hall ['bæŋkwɪt hɔ:l] 10/1
Baptist ['bæptɪst] 24/1
baptize [bæp'taɪz] 24/3
based [beɪst] 5/2
bathroom ['bɑ:θrʊm] 9/1
battle ['bætl] 21/3
BBC [bi:bi:'si:] 20/3
be able to ['eɪbl] 4/1, 6/1, 6/2, 18/3
be afraid [ə'freɪd] 10/3
be around [ə'raʊnd] 18/3, 21/3
be ashamed of [ə'ʃeɪmd] 14/3
be aware [ə'weə] 17/3
be bound to [baʊnd] 2/2
be comfortable ['kʌmftəbl] 20/1
be due [dju:] 3/1, 10/3
be fond of [fɒnd] 22/1
be forced to [fɔ:st] 7/1
be headed ['hedɪd] 17/1
be ill with [ɪl] 20/1
be into ['ɪntʊ/'ɪntə] 25/1
be late [leɪt] 13/2
be lucky ['lʌkɪ] 3/1, 18/3

important [ɪmˈpɔ:tnt] 7/2
impression [ɪmˈpreʃn] 5/3, 11/3
improve [ɪmˈpru:v] 8/1
in a way [ɪn ə ˈweɪ] 8/1
in common [ɪn ˈkɒmən] 24/3
in effect [ɪn ɪˈfekt] 24/3
in fact [ɪn ˈfækt] 1/2, 13/2
in flight [flaɪt] 1/3
in front of [frʌnt] 17/1
in general [ˈdʒenrəl] 6/2
in good time [ɪn gʊd ˈtaɪm] 9/3
in keeping with [ˈki:pɪŋ] 24/3
in order to [ˈɔ:də] 8/1
in spite of [spaɪt] 15/1
in terms of [tɜ:mz] 1/2
in the first place [ɪn ðə ˈfɜ:st pleɪs] 12/2
in time [ɪn ˈtaɪm] 10/3, 11/2
incentive bonus [ɪnˈsentɪv ˈbəʊnəs] 5/1
included [ɪnˈklu:dɪd] 10/1
including [ɪnˈklu:dɪŋ] 10/2
income [ˈɪŋkʌm] 4/1, 18/3
inconsiderate [ɪnkənˈsɪdrət] 6/2
increasing [ɪnˈkri:sɪŋ] 4/3
increasingly [ɪnˈkri:sɪŋlɪ] 24/3
indeed [ɪnˈdi:d] 10/3, 19/3, 22/2
indefinitely [ɪnˈdefnətlɪ] 13/1
independence [ɪndɪˈpendəns] 8/3
indigestion [ɪndɪˈdʒestʃən] 6/3
indirect(ly) [ɪndɪˈrekt(lɪ)] 15/3
individual [ɪndɪˈvɪdʒʊəl] 14/3, 17/3
individually [ɪndɪˈvɪdʒʊəlɪ] 4/2
induce [ɪnˈdju:s] 6/3
industrial action [ɪnˈdʌstrɪəl ˈækʃn] 15/3
industrialized [ɪnˈdʌstrɪəlaɪzd] 23/3
industry [ˈɪndəstrɪ] 8/1, 8/2, 21/3, 25/3
information [ɪnfəˈmeɪʃn] 16/2, 20/3
injured [ˈɪnʒəd] 1/1
injury [ˈɪnʒərɪ] 17/1
inspector [ɪnˈspektə] 13/1
instead [ɪnˈsted] 16/1
institution [ɪnstɪˈtju:ʃn] 20/1
instructions [ɪnˈstrʌkʃnz] 14/3
insurance [ɪnˈʃʊərəns] 16/3
insurance cover [ɪnˈʃʊərəns kʌvə] 16/3
insurer [ɪnˈʃʊərə] 23/1
intake [ˈɪnteɪk] 22/1
interesting [ˈɪntrəstɪŋ] 5/2
international [ɪntəˈnæʃnəl] 15/1
interstate [ˈɪntəsteɪt] 3/2
interview [ˈɪntəvju:] 5/3
into [ˈɪntʊ/ˈɪntə] 13/3, 17/1, 21/1, 25/1, 25/3
intruder [ɪnˈtru:də] 12/1
invade [ɪnˈveɪd] 8/3
investigation [ɪnvestɪˈgeɪʃn] 13/3
involve [ɪnˈvɒlv] 3/1, 17/2
involved [ɪnˈvɒlvd] 17/2
Irishman [ˈaɪrɪʃmən] 20/2
irresponsible [ɪrɪˈspɒnsəbl] 20/1
irritability [ɪrɪtəˈbɪlətɪ] 6/3
irritable [ˈɪrɪtəbl] 6/3
island [ˈaɪlənd] 8/2, 20/1
issue [ˈɪʃu:] 2/1, 20/1, 24/3
Italian [ɪˈtæljən] 8/3
Italy [ˈɪtəlɪ] 8/2

jacket [ˈdʒækɪt] 1/3
jet [dʒet] 1/1
Jew [dʒu:] 24/1
job [dʒɒb] 3/3, 4/1, 4/3, 5/1, 7/3, 18/3
job ad(vertisement) [æd/ədˈvɜ:tɪsmənt] 5/1
Johnson [ˈdʒɒnsn] 22/1
join [dʒɔɪn] 5/1
juice [dʒu:s] 10/1
jukebox [ˈdʒu:kbɒks] 6/1
jump [dʒʌmp] 12/3
junction [ˈdʒʌŋkʃn] 17/1
just [dʒʌst] 2/2, 9/2, 12/3, 13/2, 18/1
just about [ˈdʒʌst əbaʊt] 22/1, 25/3
just for [ˈdʒʌst fə] 18/1
just in case [dʒʌst ɪn ˈkeɪs] 1/3
just like that [dʒʌst laɪk ˈðæt] 23/2
justified [ˈdʒʌstɪfaɪd] 12/1

keen on [ki:n] 4/3
keep [ki:p] 10/2, 10/3
keep doing something [ki:p ˈdu:ɪŋ] 15/2
keep the change [tʃeɪndʒ] 11/2
keeping [ˈki:pɪŋ] 24/3
key [ki:] 9/1, 10/2
key card [ˈki: kɑ:d] 10/2
kid [kɪd] 4/1, 21/1
kill [kɪl] 13/3, 25/1
king [kɪŋ] 24/1
kiss [kɪs] 18/2
kitchen [ˈkɪtʃən] 7/2
knock [nɒk] 1/3
knockdown price [ˈnɒkdaʊn praɪs] 7/1
know [nəʊ] 1/2, 1/3, 9/3, 11/3, 16/2, 21/2
Kramer [ˈkreɪmə] 21/2

label [ˈleɪbl] 14/2, 22/3
laboratory rat [ləˈbɒrətrɪ ˈræt] 23/2
lack [læk] 6/3
lake [leɪk] 12/3
lake shore [ˈleɪk ʃɔ:] 12/3
land [lænd] 7/1
landfill [ˈlændfɪl] 23/3
landing [ˈlændɪŋ] 1/1
landlady [ˈlændleɪdɪ] 9/2
lane [leɪn] 3/1, 17/1
language [ˈlæŋgwɪdʒ] 8/2, 15/1, 15/3
lapse [læps] 14/1
large [lɑ:dʒ] 24/3
last [lɑ:st] 5/2, 25/2
late [leɪt] 11/2, 13/2, 21/2
latest [ˈleɪtɪst] 10/3
laughter [ˈlɑ:ftə] 19/3
law [lɔ:] 17/3, 24/2
lawn tennis [lɔ:n ˈtenɪs] 25/3
lead [li:d] 13/3, 25/2

midday [ˈmɪddeɪ] 10/2
middle-aged [ˈmɪdl-eɪdʒd] 17/3
midnight [ˈmɪdnaɪt] 12/3
midnight dumpers [ˈmɪdnaɪt ˈdʌmpəz] 23/2
might [maɪt] 12/2, 15/3, 22/3
mild [maɪld] 2/1
mile [maɪl] 3/2, 8/2, 17/2
milk [mɪlk] 22/1
million [ˈmɪljən] 7/1, 13/1, 15/1
mind [maɪnd] 9/2, 12/3, 13/2, 21/2
mind drug [ˈmaɪnd drʌg] 19/1
mine [maɪn] 7/2
minimum [ˈmɪnɪməm] 25/2
minister [ˈmɪnɪstə] 20/1
minority [maɪˈnɒrətɪ] 24/1
minute [ˈmɪnɪt] 9/2, 13/2
miss [mɪs] 1/2, 4/1, 11/2
missing [ˈmɪsɪŋ] 12/3
mixed [mɪkst] 25/3
moisture [ˈmɔɪstʃə] 2/3
mom [mɒm] 18/2
money [ˈmʌnɪ] 10/1, 19/1, 20/1
morality [məˈrælətɪ] 24/3
more than [ˈmɔː ðən] 19/3
morning [ˈmɔːnɪŋ] 13/2, 18/1
most of [məʊst] 2/3
mostly [ˈməʊstlɪ] 2/1, 20/3
Mother's Day [ˈmʌðəz deɪ] 18/2
motion picture [məʊʃn ˈpɪktʃə] 21/3
motive [ˈməʊtɪv] 14/1
motorbike [ˈməʊtəbaɪk] 6/2
motorcycle [ˈməʊtəsaɪkl] 6/2
motorcycle officer [ˈɒfɪsə] 17/3
motorist [ˈməʊtərɪst] 13/3
motorway [ˈməʊtəweɪ] 3/2, 20/1
move [muːv] 3/3, 4/3, 6/2, 11/2
move upmarket [ʌpˈmɑːkɪt] 8/1
movie [ˈmuːvɪ] 21/1
movie buff [ˈmuːvɪ bʌf] 21/3
movies [ˈmuːvɪz] 21/2
much [mʌtʃ] 9/2, 10/3
multimillion [mʌltɪˈmɪljən] 25/3
mum [mʌm] 18/2
music [ˈmjuːzɪk] 6/1, 6/2, 20/3
Muslim [ˈmʊzlɪm] 24/1
must [mʌst/məst] 10/2, 11/2

N [en] 24/2
name [neɪm] 14/2, 25/1
narrowly [ˈnærəʊlɪ] 1/1
nasty [ˈnɑːstɪ] 1/3
national [ˈnæʃnəl] 20/1
near [nɪə] 16/1
near miss [nɪə ˈmɪs] 1/2
nearby [nɪəˈbaɪ] 9/2
necessary [ˈnesəsərɪ] 19/3
need [niːd] 3/1, 7/2, 13/2, 16/1, 17/3, 18/2
net [net] 25/1
network [ˈnetwɜːk] 20/3
never [ˈnevə] 11/2
never mind [nevə ˈmaɪnd] 13/2
new [njuː] 4/3
New York [njuː ˈjɔːk] 23/2
New York City [njuː jɔːk ˈsɪtɪ] 13/1
New Zealand [njuː ˈziːlənd] 15/1, 20/1
Newcastle [ˈnjuːkɑːsl] 14/1
news [njuːz] 3/1, 20/3
newscaster [ˈnjuːzkɑːstə] 4/3
newspaper [ˈnjuːspeɪpə] 20/1
newsreader [ˈnjuːzriːdə] 4/3
next [nekst] 9/3
nice [naɪs] 13/2
night [naɪt] 2/1
nightmare [ˈnaɪtmeə] 3/3
nitrate [ˈnaɪtreɪt] 22/3
no one [ˈnəʊ wʌn] 1/1
nobody [ˈnəʊbədɪ] 25/1
noise [nɔɪz] 6/1, 6/2, 6/3
noise pollution [ˈnɔɪz pəluːʃn] 6/3
noise-induced [ˈnɔɪz-ɪndjuːst] 6/3
noisy [ˈnɔɪzɪ] 6/2
non-Christian [nɒn-ˈkrɪstʃən] 24/1
nonalignment [nɒnəˈlaɪnmənt] 8/3
none [nʌn] 14/1
noon [nuːn] 10/2
normal [ˈnɔːməl] 19/3
North Dakota [nɔːθ dəˈkəʊtə] 2/3
northbound [ˈnɔːθbaʊnd] 17/1
northeasterly [nɔːθˈiːstəlɪ] 2/1
note [nəʊt] 7/3, 11/3, 19/1
nothing [ˈnʌθɪŋ] 21/2
notice [ˈnəʊtɪs] 6/1, 10/2
notify [ˈnəʊtɪfaɪ] 10/2
nowadays [ˈnaʊədeɪz] 21/3
number [ˈnʌmbə] 1/2, 20/1, 20/3, 21/3, 24/3, 25/2
numerous [ˈnjuːmərəs] 13/1
N.Y. [njuː ˈjɔːk] 23/2
NYC [njuː jɔːk ˈsɪtɪ] 13/1

o'clock [əˈklɒk] 10/3, 16/2
oat bran [ˈəʊt bræn] 22/1
oat-based [ˈəʊt-beɪst] 22/1
oatmeal [ˈəʊtmiːl] 10/1, 22/1
oats [əʊts] 22/1
obey [əˈbeɪ] 1/3
occasional [əˈkeɪʒnəl] 7/3
occupy [ˈɒkjʊpaɪ] 8/3
occur [əˈkɜː] 2/1
off [ɒf] 5/2
off duty [ɒf ˈdjuːtɪ] 11/3
offence/offense [əˈfens] 14/1
offer [ˈɒfə] 10/1
office [ˈɒfɪs] 13/2
officer [ˈɒfɪsə] 3/2, 14/2, 17/3
official [əˈfɪʃl] 8/2, 13/1, 13/3
offshore [ɒfˈʃɔː] 23/2
often [ˈɒfn] 17/2
Okanagan Lake [əʊkəˈnɑːgən ˈleɪk] 12/3
old age [əʊld ˈeɪdʒ] 15/3
old-fashioned [əʊld-ˈfæʃnd] 18/2
oldie [ˈəʊldɪ] 21/1
on (+ phone number) [ɒn] 5/1
on average [ɒn ˈævərɪdʒ] 21/3
on condition (that) [kənˈdɪʃn] 7/1
on the left [left] 11/2
on the whole [həʊl] 17/3

prescription [prɪ'skrɪpʃn] 19/1
present ['preznt] 21/3, 23/1
presenter [prɪ'zentə] 4/3
press [pres] 8/2
pressure ['preʃə] 4/3, 6/3
prevent [prɪ'vent] 20/1
previous ['pri:vɪəs] 4/1, 5/3
previously owned [pri:vɪəslɪ 'əʊnd] 15/3
price [praɪs] 7/1, 8/1, 10/1
priest [pri:st] 24/3
Prime Minister [praɪm 'mɪnɪstə] 20/1
primitive ['prɪmɪtɪv] 25/1
print [prɪnt] 16/3
privacy ['prɪvəsɪ] 6/2
private ['praɪvət] 9/2
probable ['prɒbəbl] 13/3
problem ['prɒbləm] 4/2, 5/3, 14/2, 19/3, 24/3
proclaim [prə'kleɪm] 2/3, 22/3
produce [prə'dju:s] 8/2, 21/3
product ['prɒdʌkt] 22/1, 22/3
professional [prə'feʃnəl] 25/3
profit ['prɒfɪt] 25/3
program(me) ['prəʊgræm] 8/2, 14/2, 20/3
properly ['prɒpəlɪ] 7/2, 14/1, 23/2
proportion [prə'pɔ:ʃn] 24/3
prospects ['prɒspekts] 14/3
protest ['prəʊtest] 3/3
Protestant ['prɒtəstənt] 24/1
provide [prə'vaɪd] 16/1
pub [pʌb] 6/1
public transit [pʌblɪk 'trænsɪt] 3/3
public transport [pʌblɪk 'trænspɔ:t] 3/3
public transport(ation) ['trænspɔ:t/trænspɔ:-'teɪʃn] 17/2
publicity [pʌb'lɪsətɪ] 20/1
publish ['pʌblɪʃ] 8/2
pull down [pʊl 'daʊn] 10/1
pull up [pʊl 'ʌp] 11/1
punctual ['pʌŋktʃʊəl] 5/3
punishment ['pʌnɪʃmənt] 23/2
pure [pjʊə] 22/3
purpose ['pɜ:pəs] 19/1
put [pʊt] 4/3, 16/2, 23/3
put in a claim [kleɪm] 23/1
put it ['pʊt ɪt] 16/1
put to sleep [sli:p] 15/3
put up [pʊt 'ʌp] 4/2
put up with [pʊt 'ʌp wɪð] 16/2

quality ['kwɒlətɪ] 20/3
quality of life [kwɒlətɪ əv 'laɪf] 17/2
quarantine ['kwɒrənti:n] 16/3
quarrel ['kwɒrəl] 18/3
queen [kwi:n] 24/1
question ['kwestʃən] 5/3, 24/3
queue up [kju: 'ʌp] 11/1
quiche [ki:ʃ] 22/2
quiet ['kwaɪət] 6/1
quit [kwɪt] 4/3
quite [kwaɪt] 4/2, 22/2

race [reɪs] 20/1
rack [ræk] 12/2
radio ['reɪdɪəʊ] 20/2
radio announcer [ə'naʊnsə] 20/2
radio call ['reɪdɪəʊ kɔ:l] 11/3
radio network ['reɪdɪəʊ netwɜ:k] 20/3
radio play ['reɪdɪəʊ pleɪ] 20/3
rail [reɪl] 16/3
rail strike ['reɪl straɪk] 11/1
rain [reɪn] 2/2, 21/2
rainfall ['reɪnfɔ:l] 2/3
raise [reɪz] 20/1
rapidly ['ræpɪdlɪ] 2/3
rat [ræt] 23/2
rather ['rɑ:ðə] 1/2, 2/1, 10/3
react [rɪ'ækt] 19/3
read [ri:d] 14/1
read back [ri:d 'bæk] 14/2
reader ['ri:də] 15/2
reading ['ri:dɪŋ] 14/2, 15/2, 20/3
real [rɪəl] 2/2, 9/1
realize ['rɪəlaɪz] 3/2, 12/1
really ['rɪəlɪ] 4/2, 6/2, 20/2
reason ['ri:zn] 7/3
reasonable ['ri:znəbl] 10/1
receive [rɪ'si:v] 20/3
recent ['ri:snt] 7/3, 9/3
reception desk [rɪ'sepʃn desk] 10/2
recorder [rɪ'kɔ:də] 12/1
recyclable [ri:'saɪkləbl] 23/3
recycle [ri:'saɪkl] 23/3
recycling [ri:'saɪklɪŋ] 23/3
reduce [rɪ'dju:s] 17/1, 19/3, 22/1
redundant [rɪ'dʌndənt] 4/1
reflex ['ri:fleks] 17/3
refuse ['refju:s] 23/2
refuse collectors ['refju:s kəlektəz] 23/1
regard [rɪ'gɑ:d] 14/1
regatta [rɪ'gætə] 3/1
region ['ri:dʒən] 2/1
regional ['ri:dʒənəl] 15/1
regular ['regjʊlə] 4/2, 17/2, 19/3, 22/1
regularly ['regjʊləlɪ] 17/2
rehashed ['ri:hæʃt] 18/2
reimbursement [ri:ɪm'bɜ:s mənt] 16/3
reject [rɪ'dʒekt] 24/3
relations [rɪ'leɪʃnz] 14/3
relax [rɪ'læks] 5/3
relaxation [ri:læk'seɪʃn] 19/3
release [rɪ'li:s] 17/1
relevant ['reləvənt] 5/3
relief [rɪ'li:f] 2/3
religion [rɪ'lɪdʒən] 24/1
religious [rɪ'lɪdʒəs] 24/1, 24/3
remain [rɪ'meɪn] 2/1
remark [rɪ'mɑ:k] 15/1
remember [rɪ'membə] 25/1
remind [rɪ'maɪnd] 3/1
remote-control [rɪməʊt-kən'trəʊl] 10/1
remove [rɪ'mu:v] 12/1
renew [rɪ'nju:] 17/2
rent [rent] 13/2
repair [rɪ'peə] 8/2, 13/1
replace [rɪ'pleɪs] 13/1, 13/3
replenish [rɪ'plenɪʃ] 2/3
reply [rɪ'plaɪ] 20/1
report [rɪ'pɔ:t] 23/2
represent [reprɪ'zent] 9/1, 24/1
republic [rɪ'pʌblɪk] 8/2
reputation [repjʊ'teɪʃn] 8/1
require [rɪ'kwaɪə] 17/2
rescue ['reskju:] 12/3

GATEWAY
CENTER